Mastering the Art of Balance

A Practical Guide for Living Authentically

Based on the International Bestseller *The Celestial Bar*

by Tom Youngholm, M.A.

CREATIVE INFORMATION CONCEPTS

Author: Tom Youngholm
Cover Design: Colborn Creative
Editing: Deanne Sheldon-Collins, Paula Ellery

Library of Congress Control Number: 2015900590

ISBN   978-0-9642488-2-3

Also by Tom Youngholm

Books

The Celestial Bar:
A Spiritual Journey
20th Anniversary Edition

International Bestseller

In the Shadow of the Sphere:
A Journey of Heart and Spirit

Whispers of Wonder:
A Journey of Beauty & Balance
Kathy and Kamryn Clarke with Tom Youngholm
Spring 2016

A Fractal Life:
My Life as an Adventurer, Seeker, Sports Enthusiast, Thespian,
Psychic, Author, Musician…
Working title—Winter 2016

Audio

Balancing Meditation Tapes
Winter 2015

An impassioned photographer and rock balancer, Kathy lives with her husband in San Luis Obispo County, California.

"Photography allows me the means to share beauty and joy, while rock balancing is a quiet practice of creativity, balance, patience, and 'letting go.' Experiencing some of nature's exceptional places allows me to blend these two passions."

Also view
Whispers of Wonder:
A Journey of Beauty & Balance

A collaborative work between Tom Youngholm, Kamryn Clarke, and Kathy Clarke

Visit the website clarkeandyoungholm.com

Acknowledgments

I wish to thank Nancy Boyd for "dragging" me to New England. Her beautiful heart provided me the needed support, love and patience, while her sharp mind provided me the technical back-up I sorely needed. I could have never finished this project without her.

Gratitude as always to Lianne Downey for her guidance. Appreciation for their talented editing to the "Aussies from Down Under" Deanne Sheldon-Collins and Paula Ellery. Much thanks to Josie Hanlon, Kevin Killion, Matt Hadden, Joie Pacini, Roberto Benzi, Diana Journy, Valentina Peraro, and many others who have helped me align this material. In case I missed anyone, my heartfelt apologies and thanks for your help.

To Dad

I learned the most valuable life lessons at 13, when I began working with my father at the factory. He was a living, breathing example of treating people of every race, religion, and color with respect, patience, and kindness. For that I will be eternally grateful.

Tell Mom and everyone at *The Celestial Bar* I said hello.

The Quest

I Hang in the Balance
    Not Aware that I Created It

I Am the Balance
    Afraid to Fall into the Unknown

I Am the Unknown
    Not Aware that I Know

I Am the Creating

        the Falling

            the Knowing

So I Let Myself Fall

    And in Knowing Be Creative

So Here I Am Hanging in the Balance

        AGAIN

From the original *The Celestial Bar*

Table of Contents

Author's Note

"The way a book is read, which is to say, the qualities a reader brings to a book can have as much to do with its worth as anything the author puts into it."
Norman Cousins

Mastering the Art of Balance describes the innate practical and soulful need to consciously move towards balance. This dynamic state holds the very aspects that most of us are looking for in life: love, peace, happiness, and fulfillment. This practical guide explains the four aspects of oneself, which are the Physical, Intellectual, Emotional, and Spiritual (PIES). The latter half of this book will describe the natural workings of the cosmos, the Universal Principles, which will illuminate simple ways to live more fully with ease and grace. I explained all of this briefly in my first book, *The Celestial Bar*. (It's not necessary to read, but if you like your insights cooked with some basic truths, simmered over a little adventure, with a dash of intrigue, you might want to try it out.)

Everything moves towards balance, whether it is our bodies, the cosmos, nature, or even our social systems such as businesses, governments, and religions. Know that balance is not a static state but rather a dynamic range that is different for everyone and every system. Our unconscious, busy lives move us away from equilibrium. The uncomfortable reality is that, the longer we stay out of balance, the more stress we physically feel and the more pain we intellectually, emotionally, and spiritually experience. We all desire less stress and more love and happiness, all of which is brought about by *Mastering the Art of Balance.*

There is an art to this process of balance. The major challenge is that most of us have not been taught the information nor have the required skills. The results of this lack appear in the increasing number of people who are stressed, unhappy, and unfulfilled. Evident within our society is a general movement of people who are searching for something different, something more. The truth is that, on a human and soulful level, the talent and the ability to be in balance are innately within us. We just need to be awakened in order to remember that which we already know.

When I use the term "mastering," I do not mean conquering or controlling, but rather grasping, learning, knowing, and practicing. Mastering anything is an ongoing process that never ends. Mastering doesn't mean you can sit back and relax, doesn't mean there won't be any more work or there won't be any more challenges. Once you master a sport, skill, subject, or discipline, you can't just wipe your hands clean and say, "That's that." One still has to be vigilant, conscious, and continually practicing one's art, while balancing other aspects of one's life. Tiger Woods is certainly one of the masters of golf. His pains, surgeries, and personal life have undoubtedly added other challenges. Can he just sit back and not practice anymore? Bruce Lee was mastering his own art of Jeet Kune Do and yet he had to overcome severe criticism from his peers along with a crippling back injury. Thomas Edison, the master inventor, had to overcome thousands of failures along with his wife's death, as well as his plant burning down. Jesus and Siddhartha, the Buddha, were each mastering a spiritual life and yet they were constantly challenged by the beliefs, prejudices, and fears of their times.

Mastering the Art of Balance doesn't mean there won't be struggle, only less struggle; won't be pain, only less pain; won't be challenges, only less challenges; won't be stress, but certainly less stress. Mastering balance *does* mean there'll be more peace, more happiness, and more love in your life. Is that something you're willing to put energy towards?

There are many perceptions about life but, for me, two stand out. First, challenges will always appear in your life—or, simply put, "Shi# happens." A beautiful reframe of that statement can be seen on some bumper stickers: "Shift happens!" The landscape of being human on this planet contains a full gamut of experiences and emotions. Some of these are disasters—disease, pain, and heartache—while others are successes—health, pleasure, and love. Most importantly, though, life is what you make it—or, what will be the mantra of this book: **Your focus is your reality**. No matter what the situation, it's your thoughts, emotions, and actions that will create your life.

Remember the Weeble™ toys when growing up—the ones that, when you knocked them over, always bounced back to an upright balanced position? What enables them to do that is having a strong base. Your base comes from a centeredness that stems from a healthy self-concept. This is driven by being authentic— being your *true-self*. Living authentically requires you to think, speak, and act your truth.

If one was to look for wisdom about how to truly live, wouldn't one want to ask someone who is dying? The nearness of death brings the opportunity to cut through to our core. Studies have asked the dying, "What would you have done differently?" Over the decades the answers have remained pretty much the same. One response with many variations was consistently at the top: "I would have followed my passion. I would have taken the road less traveled. I would have followed my heart. I would have been true to myself." All of these responses are about being authentic.

Many of us are unconsciously driven to partially or totally live lives that have been dictated to us by our parents, schools, religions, and governments. To live authentically demands we take responsibility for our lives, shake off conditioning from others, discover our essences, come from heart, and courageously be ourselves. This process is one of letting go rather than adding on. Every expectation from outside the self is like a veil that eventually needs to be shed. Remember, unless you're in PIES balance, the version of your truth will not be in alignment with your true-self.

Your measurement of success is not in what type or amount of challenges you overcome, but rather by what you think, feel, and do that allows you to get back up. This process of balance builds your character—taking two steps forward and one back, diverting to the left and then the right, falling down and getting back up. Continually regaining your balance from challenges instills strength, skills, and experience that enable you to go beyond: beyond your expectations, beyond your fears, beyond your pain of childhood, beyond whom you think you are, beyond your hurts in relationships, and beyond your hopes and dreams.

My purpose for writing this non-fiction book was twofold. Firstly: Writer, Heal Thyself! The process of writing helped me clarify and put into practice all I've written and spoken about for almost thirty years. My trials and tribulations, over the last six years, provided me with a firsthand opportunity to practice and use my knowledge, skills, and experiences to navigate through the toughest chapter of my life. Secondly, my intent was to present this information trusting you, the reader, might glean or remember something useful for your life.

The following material is by no means a definitive study on any of its topics, nor is it intended to be. This book is testament to the positive results many who have followed its premises have received over the years. I'll provide a different lens through which to look at your relationships with yourself, others, and the planet, so that you may live a more authentic life. Your understanding of what I'll present might be a little different depending on your upbringing, culture, religion, and life experiences. Yet, at a deeper level, this process of balance is eternal and common within all races, creeds, colors, and time periods.

Books are linear—you read page 5 before you read page 71. One of the challenges in this self-help book is that sometimes, to better understand your PIES, you also need to understand some of the future components of the Universal Principles. I ask the reader to allow yourself to temporarily "not be in the knowing" as the concepts develop.

Examining some of these ideas requires observing them from different perspectives. Imagine yourself viewing a multi-faceted gem; enjoy being curious about not only seeing a new aspect but also seeing a familiar one from a different angle. This seeming repetition can be helpful for the newcomer and reinforcement for the more experienced.

To further enhance your experience, there will be questions, affirmations, and techniques to assist you in practicing and living these concepts at your own speed. Use the simple tools provided or be creative and come up with your own. Know that any changes in your behavior will need to be constantly practiced until they become positive habits. All we need in *Mastering the Art of Balance* is a little guidance, some tools, and plenty of experience, which only comes through practice.

I'm not perfect by any means and obviously haven't followed my own advice 100% of the time, so I've also included some reflections and corrections that I experienced through my ordeals. I hope this will illustrate that, no matter if you're wise or lacking wisdom, enlightened or an initiate, author or reader, we all have to maneuver through the various challenges of life.

Just a reminder: my being the author does not imply that I'm the teacher and you're the student, inferring a hierarchy of status or that you're going to learn something new, something you don't already know. We are all teaching and learning in the same moment, helping ourselves and each other in our own ways. I believe all of us, especially those of you who are reading this now, are on the same journey. If you're like me, to truly appreciate the fullness of life you need to experience it in many different ways, so that the richness of the moment sinks deeper. Each layer of learning removes veils of illusions, misconceptions, and faulty beliefs, revealing a clearer sense of your *authentic-self* and a recognition that all the answers you've been searching for, you already knew.

Tom

February 15, 2015

My Story

"Our past is a story existing only in our minds. Look, analyze, understand, and forgive. Then, as quickly as possible, chuck it."
Marianne Williamson

January 2009

I smothered a shout, forgetting that my wife was not sleeping in the adjoining room. I'd just inflicted another paper cut as I tried to open the 150th carton of peanut butter crackers, or maybe it was the 200th—I'd lost count. I pressed pause on the remote, freezing the characters on *CSI: Las Vegas* as they hovered like vultures over a decaying body.

As I rose sluggishly from the recliner, my breath cut short, followed by several quick inhalations. Sitting back down, I released all the air in my lungs and then consciously took a deep full breath. At the height of my intake, I knew that I couldn't hold back anymore.

Tears slowly leaked out of my eyes, as the first sign of water seeps through the cracks of a dam—a few noticeable drops, then quickly a trickle, a tiny stream, and then eventually a gush as the dam breaks. Uncontrolled waves of sobbing rumbled through my very being. I was not in control, not in control of any of it. The reality is that it is impossible to control a breach in the dam. The bawling continued as sounds poured from my mouth that came from somewhere else, somewhere deep inside me. The sounds soon formed words and then conjugated into pleas—pleas to God, pleas to my conscious self, pleas to unseen friends, family, and acquaintances, pleas to anyone who would listen.

"How did I get here? How did things get so bad?" ...another quivering inhalation... "I have what it takes. I have a good heart, I really care about people." ...another breath as my ego wanted to chime in on this onslaught... "I'm not stupid. I have an international bestseller. I have educational degrees. I'm physically able. Women like me."

My sobbing, ranting, and gnashing of the teeth ended a couple of minutes later. The outcries had filled the emptiness of my living room, seeped out the opened windows into the San Diego night, and quickly evaporated into the ethers of the darkened heavens. As rapidly as a tornado strikes and then hastily moves on, the mini-outburst was over. My buried thoughts and emotions now lay scattered in every room of my consciousness.

Stunned by the sudden emotional onslaught, I sat there silently. My recent past had certainly knocked me down but I needed to find a way to bounce back up, better than ever. Another few breaths and I knew what I had to do…I had to get another cold beer.

Wiping away the lingering tears on my cheeks, I surveyed the debris strewn among the stacked, unopened cartons of crackers, health bars, and cookies. With a slight limp, I made my way to the darkened kitchen on the opposite side of the two-story house.

Even though it had been over two months, my recovery from ankle surgery hadn't gone as well as hoped. The doctor had removed bone chips from an earlier ankle break, ground down two bone spurs, drilled a hole in my cartilage to spur new growth, and cleaned up the scar tissue of over a half-dozen ankle sports injuries. I was just shy of sixty, and the surgery had interrupted my weekly routine and immense pleasure of playing softball and volleyball. The lack of physical activity made me feel lethargic, sluggish, and cranky. My present situation felt like a punishment— okay, I'm a recovering Catholic, so everything feels like punishment.

It was just after midnight, so I carefully removed a beer from the refrigerator, not wanting to wake my landlord/roommate/good friend whose bedroom was at the top of the stairs. (Yeah, like my outburst wouldn't wake him but the sound of a refrigerator opening would.) He had graciously offered my wife and me a portion of his first floor to live in until we got back on our feet. (I'd spent all my savings on a down payment for a beautiful downtown condo. But after the mortgage crisis hit, we were in the process of foreclosure.)

Gingerly moving back through the darkened first floor, I placed the cold beer on my paper cuts, hoping to anesthetize my pain. (If only there was a beer big enough and cold enough to sedate my thoughts and feelings!) With a deep sigh, I sat back down in my recliner and took a long sip. As I released the pause button on the remote and placed the beer in the recliner holder, I absentmindedly watched the CSI forensic pathologist picking away at the remains of a mangled body. (Okay, forget about the anesthetizing cold beer. Could I just permanently pause my life before everyone picked away at my remains?) I grabbed the scissors again and continued cutting open the never-ending packages.

As I emptied the crumbling peanut butter crackers into a large plastic bag, my thoughts returned to my predicament. I'd lost my job a year and a half ago, though my boss said that I had actually quit. Technically he might have been correct, but let me ask you: if your boss walked up to your cubicle and told you he'd hired another salesman and oh, by the way, he was giving him half of all your leads, which translated into a pay cut of 50%, and when you expressed your displeasure he flippantly said all you had to do was get 50% more jobs, and you then told him you were out of there, would you feel that you were laid off or that you voluntarily quit? (Soon afterwards, I discovered they sold the business, anticipating the financial crisis, and were trying to bump the sales in order to get a better selling price. They must have figured that two hungry salesmen would bring in more revenues than one satisfied one.)

It was the only sales job I'd ever had but I'd made good money while it lasted. Actually, it had been my sixth career job, all of which had lasted around four years: family counselor, restaurant owner, training specialist, consultant, author, painting company owner, and salesman for retractable awnings. Then there had been a slew of over fifteen side jobs between those careers, including factory worker, various waiter jobs, transport driver for the elderly, DJ for a radio station, fishing mate, landscaper, vet assistant, recreational therapist at a psych hospital, truck driver, umpire, wedding officiate, tour bus driver, transport driver for the county jail, and now a recall food worker.

This present part-time job required me to identify, list, and remove recalled products from stores' shelves, bring them home, remove them from their cartons, cut open each package, empty the insides into a plastic bag, water soak the contents, drag each of the seventy-pound bags into my car, and dispose of them at the county landfill. If I worked a day or two a week I was lucky. This was my third straight day working this assignment. Yahoo!

After my hand cramped up again, I placed the scissors down and took another long sip of my beer. I then let out a long barking belch. There was no one to wake up, at least on my lonely side of the first floor.

My wife and I had had another argument and she'd left to get some breathing room. We'd tried a couple of relationship counselors but nothing was working. We were on the brink of divorce. I'd waited thirty years between my first and second marriage. I'd thought I could do it this time. I'd thought I'd be a better husband. I'd thought I was much older and wiser...I'd thought too much and obviously erroneously.

I grabbed the scissors again, reminding myself that I should be grateful for the several-hours-a-week, $15-an-hour job. Besides, every employment provides some kind of service to humankind. Maybe I was eradicating the spread of some unknown bacteria. Yeah, that's it. I was saving people from the possibility of a painful, writhing, prolonged agony of botulism or some unknown parasite, or maybe even preventing a flesh-eating disease from devastating the body of some unsuspecting peanut butter-craving teenager. The company would never tell you what the recall was about, so...Maybe the reason was just poor packaging.

Okay, focus on the positive, Tom. I should be happy. I was alive. I was breathing. I still had my mental capacities, though some would argue that point. I had lots of friends. My only family—brother, sister-in-law, nieces, and nephew—lived close by. Everyone was in good health. I lived in San Diego with the best climate in the world. I was healthy—okay, somewhat, but I played as much softball and volleyball as I could. I had a million-dollar view of Mission Bay, the Pacific Ocean, and yet...

Still looking at the scissors, I realized this instrument, like anything else in life, could be used for many purposes. It was all my choice. I could use these scissors to trim paper dolls, clip out coupons, trim the raggedy bottoms of my jeans, plunge them, samurai style, deeply into my viscera, or...I could continue slicing open packages of peanut butter crackers.

In that moment I made a huge, life-changing decision. I slowly got up, picked up the box cutter that lay next to me, walked over to the window, which revealed the twinkling lights of the San Diego skyline, slowly pushed my thumb forward, ejecting the sharp blade, then with the precision of a surgeon I swiftly and precisely...slashed open a different carton, not one filled with sticky peanut butter crackers, but one filled with health bars. Every decision, every choice, leads to one's present moment.

The Foundation

1

Who Am I?

We need to stay conscious and answer that question by going within and discovering our own inner knowingness.

Let's begin with the basic foundation of you. One of the keys to life is not so much having the right answers but asking the right questions. "Who am I?" is a profound and yet very basic inquiry. To conceive that question verifies the fact that you are aware, conscious. The ability to ask that question is what makes us unique and separates us from the mineral, insect, plant, and animal worlds. This question directly relates to your search for authenticity. Your answer, or lack of one, also has lifelong consequences. The question needs to be explored in order for you not only to fully realize who you are in this moment, but also to realize your potential. Realize this very basic question can never be fully answered because, as your consciousness increases, so does your ability to perceive yourself more deeply.

The Answer Affects Your Daily Decisions

An understanding of the question "Who am I?" plus your answer provides the basic building blocks of your daily decision-making. The consequences of years of daily decisions create the world you now live in. Your daily interactions, emotions, and relationships will be very different if you believe you are a Darwinian creature who adapts to a dog-eat-dog world, as opposed to believing, like a Buddhist monk, that we all need to be of service to others.

"Not to decide is to decide."
Harvey Cox

The challenge for most of us is that we tend to be unconscious; not being aware of who we are, not making conscious decisions, not knowing what we truly want or who we truly want to be. Much of our unconsciousness is filled with thoughts, feelings, and concepts from others: parents, religions, governments, teachers, media, etc. As this conditioning seeps into our unconsciousness, we sleepily believe it is *our* stuff. We need to stay conscious and answer the question "Who am I?" by going within and discovering our own inner knowingness.

Remove Labels

It's easy to get lost in the everyday world of just working, eating, and taking care of the kids. You have little time for yourself—time to go within and actually get a sense of who you are. A hurried life allows our society to deftly catch us in its web. This is accomplished unconsciously through our language, which attaches pre-described meanings and labels to people, things, and situations. This labeling of "I am a...[fill in the blank: father, wife, student, kid, employee, artist, banker, singer, Catholic, Hindu, American, Chinese, consumer, citizen, Republican, terrorist, pacifist...]" is very common.

My outcry that night of opening crackers was agonizing, because I was focused on my identity of being an employee, a husband, and a homeowner. I felt a loss—a loss of identity, which then led to a loss of meaning. This occurred because I identified who I was by what I did, or a role I played, or a category that was placed on me. All of those names and labels do not address the underlying essence of who I am. I was no longer an employee. I was no longer a husband. I was no longer a homeowner. Each of those names and labels carries emotions and expectations. If I consciously or unconsciously believe I am a husband, a homeowner, a salesman and those roles are taken from me, I'm certainly going to feel pain and anguish. The more strongly I believe those identities define me, the more I will try to hold on to them, and the more pain I will feel when they are diminished or cease to exist.

"It is not the question, what am I going to be when I grow up; you should ask the question, who am I going to be when I grow up."
Goldie Hawn

This detachment is painful because it links to the very core of your believed existence. If you're no longer a wife or a breadwinner, what are you? Now, you're not only dealing with the consequences of your specific situation, but also with the loss of your identity. Remember, the stronger your tie is to any of those labels, the more pain you'll feel when those labels are threatened or taken away. Conversely, the less you identify with those labels, the less pain you'll feel. We need to be vigilant about being conscious, about being focused on our true essences, and with continually examining all of our assumptions in life.

A hint about that vital question of "Who am I?": the more your answer has to do with aspects that can't be taken away from you, the closer you'll be to truly understanding who you are. Think about it for a moment! If something can be taken away from you, that part can't be the essence of you. If you lost your arm, would you still be you? If you lost your job, would you still be you? If you lost your partner, would you still be you? Of course! Maybe a little battered, or in pain, or sad, but you would still be you. So who you are has to transcend the physical, emotional, and—with some kicking and screaming—the intellectual.

Okay, here is a reality check on this concept, with happiness being the indicator. Look at people in your life or on the news who have lost a leg, or a job, or a home. The ones who continue to strongly attach their identities to the lost parts are the ones who feel a greater depth of agony, pain, and despair than needed. The ones who eventually see their predicaments as an opportunity, albeit a painful one, sense that they are much more than their body part, job, or possession. These people are always happier in the long run. Know that your happiness is in direct relationship to your degree of knowing who you truly are. And it all begins with answering the question "Who am I?"

If you were to start a business, how much time, research, and effort would you be willing to put into it? To be successful, you'd have to know the essence of your business. You'd have to be conscious of your business plan. You'd need to know in detail your product or service: how it works, what needs it fulfills, its potential and limits, how all of its interchangeable parts work. If you don't know your business essence, you'll certainly encounter a myriad of challenges. If you went into such a venture without that knowledge, your peers, friends, and family would call you naïve. And they'd be right! Because of your faulty and unconscious premises and unexamined beliefs, you'd probably lose money, pride, and time. But when your business failed, you could walk away and begin anew.

> *"What a liberation to realize
> that the 'voice in my head' is not who I am.
> 'Who am I then?' The one who sees that."*
> Eckhart Tolle

In a matter of speaking, you are your own product, but the difference is that you *can't* walk away from yourself. You're stuck with yourself for the whole ride. So you'd better get a handle on *who* you are. Your very happiness depends on how you realize your true essence, your authentic-self. Wouldn't you say it is of vital importance to put the energy into defining that product— YOU—no matter what the cost, time, and frustrations? Let's explore another model of the human experience, PIES, and see if it helps you answer that question.

Main Points

- Your answer to the question "Who am I?" affects your daily decisions.
- Your destiny depends on your answer.
- You are more than a role, label, or category.
- Spend time and energy answering that question. You're worth it!

Questions

- How have you defined yourself? Were you accurate?
- How have you defined others? Were you accurate?
- How have others defined you? Were they accurate?

***

Reflections and Corrections

In this section of every chapter, I'll briefly share the events and reflections of my past. In conjunction with perspectives and steps I introduce within these chapters, I'll also explain concepts, exercises, evaluations, and practices that I used to correct the imbalances that arose from those past challenges.

***

Obviously my life became difficult as I was in the midst of massive changes. My thoughts and feelings were varied and seemed to focus on the negative. That focus created fears about my survival—not only physical survival but also intellectual, emotional, and spiritual survival. The core of this angst was a sense of loss on an extremely deep level.

The truth is I'd had several losses in the past that have helped me deal with my present predicament. One weekend in Chicago, after going through a divorce two weeks earlier, I nearly lost my life twice—once by a bomb and the next day by a gun pointed at my head. These events rocked my foundation. I began to question my life, my purpose, and my future.

Before that happened, I felt an unexplainable anxiety, a feeling that I should be somewhere else, doing something different. Those unseen boundaries of conformity, normalcy, and adherence restrained me. I shuddered just thinking about losing a marriage, leaving a decent paying job, and extracting myself from the familiar surroundings of my childhood and adulthood. But after that weekend, I felt I was given a sign from the Universe. Six weeks later I left Chicago for an unknown destination, creating the possibility of a whole different life. As difficult as it was to find a new job, new place to live, new friends, and new routines, in the end the fear in my mind was much greater than the real-time obstacles of accomplishing all those things. Ending up in Key

West, I learned that I was much more than a friend, son, brother, family counselor, and Chicagoan. I learned something about who I was and what I was capable of.

Six years later, my double-decker houseboat restaurant sank to the bottom of the Gulf of Mexico. Again I had to deal with confusion, loss of identity, and financial hardships. I could have crumbled and developed beliefs about the world being cruel, ruthless, uncaring, negative, bad, or oppressive. The truth is I did have difficulty with those issues, but I quickly rallied my previous insights and strengths from leaving the Midwest.

After picking up and moving to San Diego, I created a new environment for myself—again. This time, though, I did something different. I began asking those most important questions, "Who am I? What is the purpose of my life? What does it all mean?" To follow that line of inquiry required me to do what seemed an impossible task, like trying to steer the Titanic in a U-turn. I had to change the direction of my focus from outward to inward. A realization struck me hard: "I know I am more than I was taught, than I was told, than I was led to believe." I eventually saw these supposed tragedies as a gift, spiraling me to the core of my self-concept, my soul, my authentic-self.

So when my latest challenges hit me, though I was shattered, it wasn't as painful or devastating or heart-breaking as it had been in the past. I was a veteran who'd had practice in dealing with identity issues and who had built some self-concept muscles.

My advice is not to wait, like me, until the Universe drags you kicking and screaming. Don't wait until you've been catapulted into the unknown. Try to answer that question "Who am I?" now, while you have support, while you're not in the midst of survival mode. Push yourself and dive deep into yourself, *NOW*. (Ahhh, but the conundrum is that many of us need those challenges to provide the motivation for that inward journey.)

Remember, the awareness to even ask that question is the key to authenticity. You need courage to unveil your true-self and allow full expression of your soul—your authentic-self. The released empowered-self will provide you with all the strength that you need.

2

PIES

Until we truly know our self through the prism of PIES, we can never accurately answer the question of 'Who am I?

The range of human experience contains the Physical, Intellectual, Emotional, and Spiritual (PIES), which represents our true essence. Imagine having four unique but intrinsically connected bodies in one; all are necessary to having a meaningful existence. When we operate from a highly conscious awareness of PIES, we have an opportunity to love, heal, and experience life in a fully expanded way. When we come from a balanced PIES, we are living authentically. Before we go into depth about each of these aspects, let's take a look at PIES as a whole, looking at examples to further our understanding of this concept.

Balance Within and Between PIES

PIES is a system that needs balance to function. We need to remember that this balance is not stationary but rather dynamic, changing, and twofold. Each aspect needs to be in balance both in itself and in relation to the other aspects. This is true for any system, whether it be technological, biological, sociological, or psychological.

The same is true for the systems of an automobile. The drive train, steering, braking, and electrical (to name a few) are all needed in order to have a functional car. The steering system needs to have all the components that will make it work, such as a tie rod, pitman arm, track rod, and recirculating ball gearbox. Each of those components needs to be constructed and assembled properly in order to be in balance with the other components. The steering system as a whole needs to be in balance with the drive train, braking, and electrical systems. When balance is achieved within each system and between the other systems, one can have a safer, more enjoyable, and happier journey.

PIES operates the same way. We need to identify what factors will achieve Physical balance. If we are not conscious, or don't even know about the necessary components, then our lives will be, at least physically, bumpy rides. Once we identify the components as a healthy diet, adequate rest, and exercise, we can then attune each one, which will bring balance to our Physical.

Remember, just because our Physical is in balance doesn't ensure us a smooth ride through life. We also need to be in balance with our Intellect, Emotions, and Spirit. This total balance between PIES, or lack of it, directly affects every aspect of our lives, from our jobs, hobbies, aspirations, and vacations to the complex relationships with family, lovers, co-workers, and friends. Are we focused too much on the Physical and not enough on the Emotional or the Spiritual? This week, we might need to pay more attention to our Physical because we are sick, but next week we need to put more attention on our Emotional or Spiritual because of a death in the family. We need to be constantly conscious of our present state of balance.

"Beauty is only skin deep. I think what really is important is finding a balance of mind, body, and spirit."
Jennifer Lopez

Several factors affect this balance, such as biology, culture, and the present status of our own personal developmental stages. This is a bit of a generalization, but let's use an example of a 22-year-old male, in a Western culture, and in a relationship. The tendency of this person, being influenced by the above factors, is that he might put more focus on the physicality of the relationship than on the emotions. This situation has caused many heartaches, miscommunications, and woes for both sexes. If you're a man who is aware of the need for balance, you can act on that awareness by trying different ways other than focusing on the Physical. You could elevate your Intellectual, Emotional, and Spiritual aspects;

for instance, educate yourself on how women might think differently from men and communicate your feelings and thoughts.

"The best and safest thing is to keep balance in your life,
acknowledge the great powers around us and in us.
If you can do that, and live that way, you are really a wise man."
Euripides

This system of PIES can also manifest in social systems. On a cultural level, we can see that American and Western society tend to place more focus on the Intellect, while a Buddhist society places more focus on the Spiritual. These different focuses influence how each of these cultures behaves and interacts with other cultures. One can argue ad nauseum about which is better or worse, but I strongly believe the more each culture is out of balance in one of its aspects of PIES, the greater the chance for conflict within itself and between its neighbors. The opposite is also true: each culture, while still maintaining its own uniqueness, can achieve better harmony within and without by increasing a deficient aspect of PIES.

Dynamic Balance

This dynamic balance of PIES is in a constant state of change as we move through our own developmental stages. When we are younger, our Physical is more dominant, quickly followed by our Emotional, then our Intellect needs to be highlighted. Though our Spiritual is always present, it might not be emphasized until we are much older, if at all. Every person needs to find their own balance in their own unique way. Our task is to be observant about our ever-changing aspects of PIES and then act in such a way as to bring our *self* to balance.

So does the balance we are seeking need to be an equal 25% of those four aspects? Nothing in life is equal all the time—love shared between two people, tasks shared within a household, or love between siblings. Were we in the same state of balance this morning as tonight, or this week as we were last week, or when we are adults as opposed to when we were teenagers? Rarely is balance ever equal, because life is not static and is always changing.

Being a blend of writer and musician, I can hear similarities in the structure of balance between PIES and classical orchestral compositions, such as Mozart's Symphony in C Major, Tchaikovsky's Symphony No. 4, or Debussy's *La Mer*. As in all orchestral pieces, there are four different sections playing: Percussion, Brass, Woodwind, and String. Let's call them PBWS. Throughout the length and life of the musical performance, each section has a different and varied level of presence within several intermingling themes. These various themes and journeys rise and fall in frequency and intensity, from dominant to *diminuendo* and everything in between. Each of the instruments within those sections, and all of the themes within the piece, need to be present for the music to be full, rich, and satisfying. If you were to diminish or remove any one of the sections of PBWS, the orchestral piece of music would sound flat and unsatisfying, and you'd feel as if something were missing. So it is in your own life. If you were to diminish or remove any of the aspects of PIES, your life would feel flat and unsatisfying, and eventually you'd feel as if something were missing.

> *"The key to success is to keep growing in all areas of life—*
> *mental, emotional, spiritual, as well as physical."*
> Julius Erving

The consequences of the myriad decisions and actions in each day make up the threads of our lives; most occur unconsciously. As we become more conscious, our decisions and actions can appear to be very complex. Until we can truly know our *self* through the prism of PIES, we can never accurately answer the question of "Who am I?" And until you can answer that question, how can you truly live an authentic life?

Within the framework of PIES, balance occurs when your body experiences health; your mind is conscious and open to all possibilities, your emotions express in real time, and your spirit connects with love to all things.

When any of your individual aspects of PIES are in balance, other aspects also move towards balance. This relates to the Universal Principle of *Energy is Interconnected*. The more you experience love and connection, the healthier you'll be and the more you'll experience the higher frequencies of emotions, which will then enable you to intellectually accept others more easily. The opposite is also true. If you are close-minded, you'll be more stressed and feel the negative frequencies of emotions, which will affect your health and block you from feeling love and connection to others. Start with any state of balance, or lack of, and it will permeate every other aspect of your PIES.

When one is "in the zone," one is in a high state of balance. I remember seeing Michael Jordan and Tiger Woods exhibit a level of phenomenal play, elevated above even their usual high degree of performance. Seeing Michael's movements on the court and Tiger's precision of shots was like seeing a flawless dance; it was beautiful to watch. Other "zone" situations or periods could be Gandhi's focus on non-violence during one of his hunger strikes, Mother Teresa's love as she worked with the poor and hungry, the Dalai Lama's peacefulness even when China took over Tibet, or maybe a time when you were in nature and felt totally enveloped by your surroundings. Hopefully you have experienced or will experience it sometime in your life. There is no thinking or doing, just *being*—*being* in a balance between all aspects of yourself and allowing everything to flow effortlessly. I'm so ready for that to happen again sometime soon...Come on, Universe!

Practice PIES

How can you be in balance with your PIES? As in everything else, it takes practice. I'll provide a basic exercise to assist you with looking at yourself and others through this perspective of PIES. If we are in equal balance between all four aspects, our acronym might be fully capitalized to look like this: PIES. Describing a person who works out four times a week, is open-minded, but is emotionally and spiritually nonexistent might look like PIes. A person who eats healthily, rarely uses their intelligence to work through life's challenges, is emotionally available, and feels connected to all things might look like PiES. The individual who takes care of their body, shares their thoughts and emotions freely, but is totally against anything to do with the "airy-fairy stuff" of spirituality might look like PIes. I know several people who are spiritually, emotionally, and intellectually right on track, but are not grounded in the everyday existence of this physical world—pIES.

Here are examples from my life:

➤ 5 years old—getting my physical needs met but not aware of anything else—Pies.

➤ 15 years old—having several health and family issues—peis.

➤ 21 years old—graduating from college and realizing I could put my brains to work—PeIs.

➤ 28 years old—after dealing with personal and family-related emotional issues—PIEs.

➤ 38 years old—had my visit to the Celestial Bar—PIES.

➤ 59 years old—opening up cracker packages in the middle of the night after losing my marriage, home, job and having ankle surgery—pies.

➤ 63 years old—healthy again, still feeling emotionally vulnerable, writing this book, and most definitely getting back to my spirituality—PIeS.

If you'd like to practice this perspective, watch or read about your favorite TV/film/book characters and write their PIES acronym for any given moment. What actions did they take, or not take, that moved them further away or closer to being stress-free, happy, loving? (You'll notice the drama, conflict, and sometimes humor of those individuals is always caused by one or more PIES aspects being out of balance.)

Main Points

- Our essence is composed of PIES.
- Balance needs to be within and between all four aspects of PIES.
- The balance we seek is ever-changing.
- Balance can be influenced by gender, culture, and stages of development.

Questions

- Does looking at yourself composed of PIES help you get a clearer picture of yourself? If so, explain.
- What aspects of PIES will bring you more into balance?
- After understanding PIES, try to answer the question "Who am I?"

Challenges

- List three to five challenges you're facing in your life. They might be present-day challenges or, most probably, past challenges that keep reappearing in a different form. Include one to two minor ones, one to two major ones, and the rest medium. Be sure to work on the minor ones, since they might be easier to overcome. Building some level of success will encourage you to work on the harder ones. Be as clear as you can in describing your present understanding of each challenge. Keep your challenges in mind; better yet, write them down and have them handy as you read each chapter. Acknowledge that you might have to continually redefine them. Allow yourself to have an open mind about doing something different to overcome your challenge.
- Figure out how your aspects balance by determining your PIES acronym for each challenge?

***

Reflections and Corrections

The devastated landscape of my life felt like it had no foundation. I was forced to deal with the absence of those familiar signs that most of us use to navigate through life: if I own a home, I'm on the right path; if I'm married, I'm doing the right thing; if I have a job, I'm a useful person; if I have money, I'm successful. These perceived misfortunes created a vibration, as if something was knocking on my psyche and my heart. Those unwanted but internally created intruders were various degrees of fear, confusion, loss, hopelessness, and depression. They clouded my sight just as if I was in the middle of a dust storm. I had no idea which way to turn or if this whirlwind of events would ever pass.

I needed to forget about all the details of my situation. Not that I didn't need to deal with those specifics, but rather, more importantly, I needed to realign my focus to answering "Who Am I?" and remember that PIES was at my core. I knew that I'd Emotionally and Intellectually drown if I continued to focus on "outside stuff" such as foreclosure paperwork, attorneys, real estate agents, government offices, and banks; filing divorce papers, separating property; redoing resumes, signing up with Monster.com and Sales Ladder, applying for jobs. To be authentic, I needed to first go within and balance myself.

One tool that I used to give me direction while being in that dust storm was the Balance Survey, which provided me with a sense of where I was and where I needed to be. This survey acted and acts as a guideline to help me focus and realign myself with clarity and vision. It was a beginning!

Take this test periodically throughout life. Notice any changes to the overall total or the individual points. There are no wrong or right answers, but know that the higher the number the more happy, loving, authentic and less stressful your life will generally be. The opposite also tends to be true; the lower the number the more unhappy, frustrated, stressed, and unauthentic you'll feel.

Balance Survey

1	2	3	4	5	6	7
Never	Rarely	Sometimes	50/50	Usually	Often	Always

Physical

_____ Eat healthy

_____ Get proper rest

_____ Exercise regularly

Intellectual

_____ Conscious of your thoughts, feelings, and actions

_____ Influenced by higher-self not ego

_____ Open-minded to different perspectives and beliefs

_____ Focused on the present

_____ Accepting of others

Emotional

_____ Express emotions in real time

_____ Aware of my emotions

_____ Moderate my emotions

Spiritual

_____ Express love in thoughts, feelings, and actions

_____ Have a knowingness of the Universal Principles

_____ Feel connected to myself, others, and the planet

_____ TOTAL

3

Physical

The Physical is wondrous,
as long as we are present in the moment to appreciate it.

The Physical is the most obvious aspect of our PIES. Much of our lives tend to gravitate towards satisfying our desires and repelling pain. We need to explore our physicality in a new light, bringing a fresh and more accurate assessment of this wondrous aspect of ourselves. In order to achieve that goal we'll discuss the importance of listening and acting on our body intelligence, the over-emphasis on the Physical, the difference between our false and true Physical, and the need to balance our Physical.

Sense the Planet

Our body is a a vehicle in which to experience life. This planet gratefully provides an incredible smorgasbord of physical experiences, including nourishment, medicine, shelter, and enjoyment. Being in nature, or even being on a couch viewing High Definition programs like National Geographic, exposes us to the exquisite detail of the beauty of our planet. Culinary diversifications of our merging cultures are now present in every city, to the delight of our palates and olfactory senses. Technology transmits a cacophony of sounds and rhythms from every sector of our society. In our everyday world, you can experience the mundane yet powerful sensations of touch—whether through the icy kiss of a fallen snowflake on your cheek, the painful throbbing of a stubbed toe, or the soft bristly tickle of a caterpillar undulating on your finger. The physical is wondrous, as long as we are present in the moment to appreciate it.

Body Intelligence

The body—with all of its various organs, muscles, bones, senses, nerves, blood vessels, etc.—has its own intelligence and voice. On a cellular basis, your body knows how to maintain, defend, and replace itself. Your lungs breathe, heart pumps, and digestive system operates 24/7 throughout your entire life without you consciously doing anything—that's intelligence.

This intelligence also has a voice, a feedback system, which alerts your consciousness to your body's present state. This voice talks loudly at times through sensations of hot and cold, pain and pleasure, hunger and satiation. The voice is always talking, but many of its messages are quiet and can only be heard when we listen astutely. "Push away from your desk and stretch your back." "Put down the book, close your eyes, and go to sleep." "No, no, no, I really do prefer broccoli over fries."

Many of us don't really listen to that intelligence until the situation reaches a dramatic point that we can't ignore: the stomach pain that turns into an ulcer, or the slight cough that turns into pneumonia, or the red swelling that turns into an abscess. The body is always talking; it's better to listen and act now when the voice is subtle than to pay the price later when the voice is pain.

When you start your car, you can feel its vibration. After you've owned it for a while, you can tell when it's running well and when there's something wrong. As I will discuss later, the body has its own Vibrational Frequency (VF). In general, the higher the frequency the more you'll feel lighter and a sense of comfort, which are signs of balance. When the frequency is lower, a feeling of heaviness and pain becomes a warning sign of imbalance. These are easily identifiable indicators of your state of balance. Unconsciously you can feel the VF of your car. Most of us can feel when a cylinder is not performing well—not in balance—and can feel a positive difference after a tune-up—in balance. In the same way you notice the frequency of your car, bring your awareness to how your body feels after working out as opposed to sitting on a couch for several hours, eating meats as opposed to vegetables, or sleeping five, eight, or twelve hours. The voice that accompanies the frequency will say, "I feel strong and flexible after doing yoga. I feel heavy after sitting for a long time. I feel light and energetic after having eaten all that nutritious food. I feel lethargic after eating lots of junk food."

My favorite feedback occurs when I experience frisson—a combination of a chill, shudder, and goosebumps. The body is somehow responding to external cues from others or the environment that maybe Intellectual, Emotional, or Spiritual. This voice excitedly tells me, "This is important, so pay attention!" The message could be a warning or a confirmation of a *truth*. Those goosebumps are wonderful examples of body intelligence.

Over-focus on the Physical

Just the fact of having a body places emphasis on the answer to "Who am I?" I'm Physical, of course. Every morning we reaffirm that confirmation through our senses; we hear the alarm and feel our physical body as we roll out of bed, we see ourselves standing in front of a mirror before we smell our coffee and taste our breakfast. Besides our neurology having to deal with two million bits of information bombarding us every second, there are also other factors that reinforce our heavy emphasis on the Physical, such as survival instincts and conditioning.

> *"Physical strength can never permanently withstand the impact of spiritual force."*
> Franklin D. Roosevelt

In the beginning of our civilization, as a species, we paid close attention to our physical selves and surroundings. In order to survive, we met our true needs when we used our muscles—exercised—to provide food and shelter. We also rested when we were tired and didn't stay up late watching TV or worrying about what our bosses would say the next day. An instinct ingrained in our cellular structure was our stress response, the fight-or-flight syndrome, which is mostly an autonomic unconscious response system. If we didn't heavily rely on the physical, we might be killed by a rival tribe or become the meal of a saber-toothed tiger. Though we need it less now, the stress response is still heavily embedded in our DNA.

Our early physical conditioning, during our infancy, contained survival instincts demanding we be sated or suffer dire consequences. The conditioning continued with parents who supplied our physical needs, such as food, water, clothing, and shelter. During that time, we adopted all of their thoughts, fears, and beliefs about the importance of the physical. A little later in life, concerned for our safety, much of the communication we received brought continued attention to our physical attributes. "Did you poop?" "Did you comb your hair? "Did you eat your breakfast?" "Did you brush your teeth?" "Did you wash your hands?" (Hopefully, not in that order.)

As we grew older, during our socialization period, the importance of being accepted by peers was extremely intense. Much of this approval had to do with physical attributes, again hooked up partially to our survival instincts, which included finding a mate. "Am I pretty?" "Am I strong?" "Do I have a nice butt?"

"Beauty is how you feel inside, and it reflects in your eyes. It is not something physical."
Sophia Loren

As humans we have hopefully developed beyond our early ancestral upbringings. Our potential is more than just the physical, more than animals trying to survive in a dog-eat-dog Darwinian world—though it might be hard to tell that fact when looking at the TV news.

Physical Balance

Receiving proper nutrition, exercising, and getting the right amount of rest are the major components of body balance. Does our culture focus on these ingredients? We know the answer, as statistics show the rise in obesity, diabetes, heart disease, and medication over-usage, just to mention a few. On the positive side, in the last ten years, I've seen more institutional policies, programs, and even laws addressing a more positive approach to our health.

Yet there are still many more people who have a skewed sense of the Physical. This slanted perspective is created by the perception of our over-reaching intellect, which creates a false Physical. The focus on this artificial Physical, at times an obsession for many, is mostly concerned with comfort and beauty. Let's explore how we got to this point, so that we can better distinguish between our true and false Physical needs.

> *"Our growing softness, our increasing lack of physical fitness is a menace to our security."*
> John F. Kennedy

False Physical

Most of how we think about our self—our *self-concept*—comes from other people and institutions: parents, schools, peers, religions, media, etc. They constantly send out memes—ideas, behaviors, and messages that quickly spread from person to person. We get a double dose from the media, confirming the importance they place on what I call the false Physical. We see images of beautiful people on magazine covers that are not even real but Photoshopped. We watch TV and see beautiful people in everyday roles such as doctors, coroners, attorneys, and detectives. I know there are beautiful people in those positions, but really! I've worked in both a hospital and a police department and I can guarantee you it is a rarity, as in most other occupations, to see such an abundance of beautiful people.

We have been conditioned to believe there are acceptable and non-acceptable conditions for our Physical. Most advertising preys on our need to be accepted and then displays a false Physical, thereby creating a gap between how we look and what they show us. The only way to close that gap, according to their advertisements, is to buy their products. Advertising goes where the money is and there is a lot more money to be had in the myriad of beauty and comfort products than in healthy nutrition and exercise programs. We hear and read about how all we need is this moisturizer, pill, hair product, or procedure to look and feel better. Let's face it: we're lazy. It's easier to take a pill than to actually take the time and energy to work out and deal with our true physical essences. Oh, shock, it didn't work. Let me try another easy method.

Breathe!
Take three deep breaths and continue.

Bombardments of these messages over time can eventually lead to our accepting this false Physical. These repeated thoughts and actions soon become our beliefs and behaviors; both reside in our unconscious, both form the basis of who we think we are or should be. Once you've hooked your sense of self into the false Physical, you're like a dog that chases its tail. In fact, most of the time, the consequences of those beliefs and behaviors create situations that make things worse. Extreme yet sad examples are Michael Jackson's plastic surgeries or the many women who have disfigured their faces through countless cosmetic surgeries.

Perhaps you're saying, "Hey, I'm conscious. I know what's going on." I believe you. There are many of us who have learned through self-awareness, experience, and education about how not to pay attention to that societal garbage. But with all this bombardment from the outside, it's impossible for it not to affect you, even if you are highly conscious. Living in today's society leads us to focus on the distractions in our daily lives. With that misdirection of busyness, we've unwittingly and unconsciously turned a deaf ear to the quiet voice of our Physical. So, I guarantee you, many of those societal memes and ideas have wormed their way into your unconsciousness, as well as into mine. We have to keep constant vigilance over our thoughts, emotions, and actions to make sure they are in alignment with our true Physical selves.

"Women in particular need to keep an eye on their physical and mental health, because if we're scurrying to and from appointments and errands, we don't have a lot of time to take care of ourselves. We need to do a better job of putting ourselves higher on our own to-do list."
Michelle Obama

Balance your P with your IES

Besides being in balance Physically, our Physical aspect needs to be in balance with our aspects of IES. "Your focus is your reality" is a quote from *The Celestial Bar*. If all you see is the Physical, you'll leave out or limit the other aspects of IES; you'll only know or experience a slice of your total self, a slice of what life has to offer. If you're a parent, you might only concern yourself with putting food on the table and a roof overhead but come up short in providing your children's Intellectual needs. If you're interested in finding a partner, you might focus more on their looks and miss out on the experience of having an Emotionally fulfilling relationship. If you're in nature, you might spend most of your time exploring, hiking, and climbing but never realize the gifts of stillness, where you might discover your Spirituality. This myopic viewpoint will have a one-dimensional perspective, which will only leave you with a superficial knowledge of self, others, and life.

"Spiritual relationship is far more than physical.
Physical relationship divorced from spiritual is body without soul."
Mahatma Gandhi

You experience the Universal Principle *Everything is Interconnected* when you are out of balance Physically, as it throws your IES off kilter. Let's say you're sick; your I and E might be affected by your not thinking straight or feeling agitated. The other side of the spectrum also holds true. When you eat proper foods, exercise, and are rested, your mind is sharper and you'll probably feel happier and think more clearly.

Take Personal Responsibility for Your Health

Another point to remember is that we need to take personal responsibility for everything in our lives, including the Physical. Years ago there was hardly any talk of people taking responsibility for their own health. There was a cultural belief that your doctor was the person who was in control. They were the person you went to when you were sick and it was their responsibility to get you healthy. This has changed within the last twenty years, with more people focusing on what they're eating and also exploring different treatment modalities for their illnesses. The focus of many physicians has been moving away from predominantly prescribing drugs to prevention and embracing the whole person. Let's all jump on the bandwagon, because this is a positive cultural meme that can only bring us closer to Physical and overall balance.

Breathing

Whether we're in a challenging moment or not, we're all looking for happiness, love, and peace in some way, shape, or form. There is a simple and singular Physical key to put us on the path towards those treasured desires. Because the key is so easy, I guarantee you that you won't believe it. Conscious deep breathing!

This process is so simple, yet it will improve the quality of your work, enhance your love-making, increase the effectiveness of your communication, focus the clarity of your mind, deepen the connection to your spirit, and bring you to a greater state of balance. I can't tell you how much being *conscious* of my breath and breathing properly helped me through the tough times and expanded me when life was going well.

"Breath is the bridge which connects life to consciousness, which unites your body to your thoughts."
Thich Nhat Hanh

How can something as uncomplicated as breathing be so powerful? The reason is that breathing connects us to all of the functions within our PIES. Throughout the medical field, it is now widely recognized that deep conscious breathing can improve your health. Deep breathing strengthens the lungs, reduces respiratory problems, improves cellular regeneration, reduces pain, releases toxins, provides more energy, and discharges tension. Increasing oxygen flow strengthens the immune system, makes stronger muscles, improves the nervous system, increases digestion, improves quality of blood, helps to increase muscles, and eases the workload of the heart.

Conscious breathing is an elixir not only for Physical ailments but also for Emotional, Intellectual, and Spiritual imbalances. The more you mindfully breathe, the more your body and brain relax, which stills your mind, brings more positive thoughts, and then tunes you in to the higher emotional Vibrational Frequencies (VFs) of happiness, love, and peace. (This is one of the few circumstances where more is better.) When you consciously breathe, you also bring yourself to the present moment, which momentarily eliminates the stranglehold of past and future thoughts. This state of being in the present unclutters the mind and enables you to hear the voice of your soul. Receiving all of these positive VFs influences our focus, which determines our reality. Can you think of any situation that couldn't be improved by deep breathing? I dare to say there is not one instance that wouldn't be enhanced, improved, or enriched by this simple practice. The best thing is that you can do it anywhere and any time. And it's free!

What also makes deep breathing so powerful is that it replicates the cycle of balance and duplicates our world of duality. You can't have light without darkness, up without down, left without right, or an inhale without an exhale. This rhythm of breath links us to the rhythm of nature and the universe—the Yin and the Yang.

41

"Rather than allowing our response to an event affect our breathing, let our breathing change our relationship to the event."
Cyndi Lee

How can we be so unaware of all the positive benefits of conscious breathing? We look in an outward direction and also make things more complicated than they need to be. Conditioning by society has taught us that our answers lie outside of ourselves. We use binoculars to search beyond instead of a microscope to look inwards. Also, individually and as a species, our unconscious jumbled minds cajole, manipulate, overpower, and strategize on how to obtain our desires and wants. So, in turn, we create complex solutions instead of just noticing the simple and powerful truth of what is before us.

Main Points

- The earth provides a wonderful smorgasbord of physical sensations, so pay attention.
- Listen to your body intelligence and act on its cues.
- Beware of societal memes placing an overwhelming focus on the false Physical of beauty and comfort.
- Our true Physical balance has to do with nutrition, exercise, rest.

Questions

- Where is the majority of your focus—with your true or false Physical?
- Do you focus more on your P than on your IES?
- How does your body talk to you? Do you listen?
- What can you do to be more in Physical balance?

Challenges

- How does any of this material on the Physical pertain to the challenges you came up with in Chapter 2?
- What can you do differently? What can you stop doing? What can you start doing? What can you do to prevent a challenge from recurring or to lessen its impact?

Affirmations

- I am in perfect health.
- I am strong and flexible.
- I am eating healthy.
- I am exercising regularly.
- I feel great!

***

I'll explain and discuss affirmations in the next chapter but
if you choose repeat these lines to yourself for now.

***

Reflections and Corrections

I, along with everyone else, have had times where I had to deal with the false Physical. All of us have become tied, to some degree, into the unhealthy connection with our things—cars, clothes, boats, jewels, homes, savings, and bodies.

My cross to bear as an adolescent was pimples. I was the kid from grammar school through college who had the worst acne. Besides being publicly humiliating, it was extremely painful. Several times my condition was so bad that my face would be totally covered with forty to fifty pimples. I obviously put undue attention on this false Physical, being known as "the kid with the zitty face." Even my parents unknowingly focused undue attention on my Physical, as my facial condition would be the drama topic at family and social gatherings. I was close to obsession about getting rid of that false Physical and followed every doctor's orders to do herbal rinses, facial steam baths, UV treatments, and painful lacerations. In my opinion, I was ugly and undesirable. "How could any girl want to go out with me?" "How will I ever carry on the species?"

> *"A man, who as a physical being, is always*
> *turned toward the outside,*
> *thinking that his happiness lies outside him, finally turns inward*
> *and discovers that the source is within him."*
> Soren Kierkegaard

So I had a choice. I could let that condition, that false Physical, define me and become isolated, withdrawn, and bitter, or I could redefine myself with other aspects of PIES. I'd like to say that I was conscious about PIES and the Universal Principles back then, but hey, I was thirteen and not conscious about anything. I don't remember how, but I eventually became a little more humorous (Intellect), a better communicator (Emotion and Intellect), and a pleaser (which carried its own baggage that I'm still trying to release). The bottom line was that I navigated through this period in my life by focusing more on my positive Intellectual and Emotional attributes and less on the way I looked—the false Physical.

By the way, even looking like I was an infected petri dish, I went to six proms. Bless all the women out there who paid more attention to my humor and communication skills than my looks. You saved me! (Lest you think I was a stud, or a player, believe me when I tell you I never got to second base with any of those girls. Okay, the total count for six proms was three regular kisses, two French kisses, one hickey, three hugs, two handshakes, and one ear nibble. And if you wanted to know the outcome of my pimple condition, the only cure occurred when I was twenty-one and started having sex. Gosh, if I'd only known earlier, I would have been happy to endure the cure when I was younger.)

The second aspect of being in Physical balance, explained in this chapter, concerns the three ingredients of rest, proper nutrition, and exercise. All of these needed to be part of my daily routine in order for me to begin healing and move forward. I needed to be proactive and be aware that the losses of home, marriage, and job would affect my body and then take appropriate action. As far as rest, I know my body needs between eight and nine hours for me to be at my optimum; other people might need less or more. I was able to maintain that without any major effort. I was fortunate, in the case of rest, that I didn't have any children, a high-powered job, or any other pressing matters that would have absorbed my sleep time. Any or all of those circumstances make it more difficult to achieve balance.

Proper nutrition has never been a forte of my daily routines, though I have been getting better. At different points in my life, I was drinking two six-packs of soda a day, I'd eat six fast food meals a week, dinner would be bar appetizers five times a week, and maybe I would drink a glass of water a day. (How am I still alive?) Though I've survived those bad habits, I know they took a toll on my body. Slowly, I began to address those issues more sincerely after my cracker night. I now can report that, in the last two years, I've only eaten at a fast food establishment (not including pizza parlors—I'm not a masochist) three times. I'm down to one or two times a week eating appetizers but have now supplemented salads and fish into my diet. I also now drink five to six glasses of water a day. As far as sodas, I've completely eliminated them except for having a ginger ale with Jack... Daniels that is (Hey, I'm not perfect.)

Exercise is so unbelievably important for one to be in balance. Thankfully for me, I grew up playing sports, which I have continued into my sixties. Because of this continual behavior, it has become a habit, an extremely positive habit. That is why playing volleyball, softball, pickleball, and golf was much easier to continue even when I was suffering through my challenges. While there is not necessarily a ton of cardio going on, there is movement and, of course, a great remedy for any challenge—being outdoors in nature.

Remember, when tough times occur, most of us go back to our old habits, which for many of us is not exercising. But it is the exact thing one needs to regain balance. I understand how, if your body feels "blah," in pain, or sore, the last thing you want to do is exercise. The reality is that, if you don't exercise, a vicious cycle of negativity will most probably create feelings of apathy, powerlessness, and hopelessness. That is why it is so important to provide movement in your life even when you feel lethargic, especially if you feel depressed.

A tougher commitment for me was yoga. Even though I had been doing it off and on for over thirty years, it was still difficult to do in my present crises mode. It would have been much easier to just stay at home, sleep longer, watch TV, or really do anything other than yoga. But I knew of the importance and benefits of doing this practice: improving flexibility, building muscle strength, draining my lymph system, boosting immunity, and increasing blood flow. The biggest motivator, though, is not so much mentally *knowing* something is positive, but rather *feeling* something is positive. No matter how I felt before I went to yoga, I always felt better afterwards. That made it easier to do.

Choose your own activities. It doesn't make a difference what they are but do something, anything that provides movement. Medical studies have proven time and time again that stress compromises immune systems and exercise strengthens them. I know undoubtedly that my efforts in creating Physical balance helped me stay healthy. My confirmation of this fact is that, in the last six years of experiencing extremely stressful events, I only had the flu once.

Something else played a huge role in my Physical wellbeing. Correcting the negative effects of moving through challenges in my life required me to focus on conscious breathing. As a reminder, I've placed the word "breathe" throughout this book. You can dismiss it if you choose, but I challenge you to take three deep breaths then move on to your next sentence; take note of how your reading experience changes—or not. This is a great daily practice to instill in your work day and home life. If you consciously deep breathe throughout your day, it will eventually become an unconscious habit that will positively shape your daily life. There are many different breathing techniques. Most of these methods are derivations of Pranayama, an ancient Hindu tradition, which focuses on the three aspects of our breath: inhalation, retention, and exhalation. Do an internet search and pick the ones you'd like to try, or follow these simple helpful hints to get you started:

- Inhale through your nose, not your mouth. Exhale through slightly parted lips.
- Your inhalation should expand your diaphragm, not so much your chest and definitely not your stomach.
- Fill air into your lower, then middle, and then the seldom-occupied upper lungs.
- Exhale slowly and fully with a slightly parted mouth.
- Breathe regularly and count every inhalation; when you get to seven, start back at one.
- Inhale naturally to a three count and exhale to one long count.

- For a more advanced breathing technique, fill your lower lungs to a two count and hold for one count, then fill your middle lungs to another two count then hold for another one count, and finally fill your upper lungs to a two count and then hold to a one count. Then slowly exhale to an eight count. Go back to regular breathing for several breaths and repeat.

- For best results, do any of your chosen techniques for fifteen to twenty minutes, but less is fine. Remember that conscious breathing, if even for a minute or two, is better than not doing it at all.

> *"I balanced all, brought all to mind,*
> *the years to come seemed waste of time,*
> *a waste of breath the years behind,*
> *in balance with this life, this death."*
> William Butler Yeats

4

Intellectual

Your focus is your reality.

To adequately and efficiently discuss matters of the mind and Intellect in only a few pages is impossible. (I will use the terms "mind" and "Intellect" interchangeably.) My purpose is to just give you a fundamental view of the basics of how your mind and consciousness affect your life. The most important feature is your Intellect being the filter for your reality. One needs to wisely use one's Intellect in order to be authentic. We'll explore *ego-self/higher-self* and *conscious/unconscious*. We'll also examine how our culture over-emphasizes the Intellect, and I'll describe what it takes to get back in balance. Depending on how we use our Intellect, our lives will be filled with stress, frustration, and unhappiness or stress-free with happiness and love. Use your Intellect wisely.

Ego-self and Higher-self

One aspect of our mind is the "ego." From a very basic Freudian perspective, our ego attempts to reconcile both the "id" and the "superego" with our perceived reality. The id dominates in our early years, and it is only concerned with wanting all its needs met. When you were a crying and pooping baby, you didn't care if your parents slept, you wanted your needs met NOW. The id rises up even in our adult lives, as we've all acted, felt, or selfishly said, "What about me?" If we allow our id to dominate our behaviors, we will alienate most other members of our society.

Our superego wants to meet the needs, expectations, and morals of our society. We behave in acceptable ways to get

49

approval from our bosses, communities, children, friends, and parents. If we allow the superego too much leeway, though, we can find ourselves in self-destructive behaviors such as playing the role of the martyr, the victim, or, in my case, the pleaser. There is a fine balance between helping and pleasing others in order to get along in society and still taking care of your individual needs. Being in a healthy balance between our id and superego helps us survive in a world with other people.

As we go through life thinking, feeling, and doing, we use the word "I" to reference our *self.* "I want that." "I perceive this to be bad." "I like that." This word can be confusing in that we actually have two selves—two "I"s. The little *i* describes the ego-self, which is composed of a heavily laden id. If not brought into check, when we're older the little *i* has a narrower mind that gravitates towards the false Physical: "*i* want that dress," "*i* want that person to feel jealous," "*i* am right." The voice of this "*i*" yells, "Me, Me, Me."

The big *I* has to do with the higher-self, the authentic-self, which has a healthy balanced ego and is the voice of our spirit or soul. This conscious state has more of an open mind and is concerned with our true Physical, the acceptance of love, and a deep connection with others. So, to answer that question of "Who am I?" you need to rethink which "I" you intend.

Conscious and Unconscious

There are two parts to our mind: the conscious and the unconscious. The conscious refers to our faculty to conceive, remember, reason, will, desire, judge, and perceive. The unconscious mind is still a mystery with varying degrees of definition, but in general it relates to our intuition, motivations, forgotten memories, habits, repressed feelings, and implicit knowledge. Jung divided our unconscious into two parts: the personal unconscious, which pertains to the sum of our own experiences, and the collective unconscious, which pertains to inherited genetics of information passed on by our species.

Science has gotten to the point of confirming what psychologists have said for a while: most of our decisions are made unconsciously. When I first heard this, I was full of disbelief. "What do you mean? Of course I make conscious decisions! I'm in control of my life." No, it's really all those unconscious beliefs that drive most of your decisions. Brain mapping has shown that, when we are making our decisions, signals from our unconscious are reaching the decision center before the conscious signals arrive. This fact should motivate you to bring to light your unconscious self. Remember, living consciously is living authentically.

"One does not become enlightened by imagining figures of light, but by making the darkness conscious."
Carl Jung

We Create Through Our Thoughts, Emotions, and Actions

How do we create anything, let alone our reality? The process begins with a thought fueled by emotion and manifested by appropriate action. Let's talk about creating some *thing*. The chair or couch you're sitting on had to be created by somebody who first had a thought: a thought about the need for a chair, a thought about what it might look like, a thought about what resources and skills it would take to build one. Look around your world. Everything created had to begin with a thought—trains, buildings, bridges, highways, space stations, furniture, homes, computers, and artificial hearts. I first had to have a thought about creating a book, before you could eventually read this material.

Just having a thought will not make a *thing* materialize. There needs to be a boost of energy to magnify the thought so that it becomes powerful enough to act on. This magnification comes from our emotions, which might range from subtle to passionate; the higher the magnification, the better the chance of creation.

To bring the thought to fruition requires many levels of action, along with appropriate skills and resources. The final product usually occurs after a trial-and-error process; it took Edison over ten thousand tries before he made the lightbulb. (He had to have lots of passion to keep things going.) Writing this book, I went through eighteen edits before I sent it to my editor, who then cruelly made me do another three. Our creative process can be seen as Thoughts + Emotions = Action.

Different Realities Based on Your Focus

An answer to the proverbial question "Is the glass half full or half empty?" could reflect your focus on life. If you're a pessimist, with a focus that says the world is lacking, you might answer half empty. If you're an optimist, with a focus that says the world is abundant, you might answer half full. If you have more of an objective focus, that of no inherent meaning to life, you might say that it is not about the glass but about the water, therefore the water just is. If you're a cynical humorist, like the famous comedian George Carlin, you would quip that they just made the glass too damn small.

This phenomenon of your focus determining simultaneous yet different realities happens all the time. Take a buddy to a sporting event, or read the same book, or see the same film, and you'll easily hear how each of you interprets it differently. Last year I hiked with two friends and observed their reactions to walking on the same trail. One focused on the fear and annoyance of snakes, mosquitos, and ants while the other focused on the exercise, birds, and trees. Depending on their point of view, each one thought and felt differently about their experience; one loved the hike and the other never went hiking again. The 2012 U.S. elections were going on as I wrote this section. I and several friends of different political views listened to one of the presidential debates. After it was over, we all discussed what we thought we'd heard. Everyone in the room had a different perspective of the speech, which just so happened to support their own pre-held political beliefs.

Conditioning

Over time, a repetitive thought becomes a belief and a repetitive action becomes a behavior. We become conditioned when we have the same response to a repeated message or external stimuli. Our thoughts and beliefs around those repeated circumstances will then become unconscious. If we don't change our thoughts and beliefs before we encounter similar circumstances, we'll find ourselves, like Pavlov's dogs, salivating to the same ring of the bell. We see a police car and slow down; we see an ad for weight loss and want to start another diet; we realize it is close to April 15 and do our taxes; we remember it is getting close to holidays and buy presents.

All of those situations contain repeated thoughts, which have become beliefs. The more you're exposed to the same message, the more you're likely to accept it as truth, as reality. You believe that you should obey the law; you believe that you should be slim; you believe that you should be a good citizen; you believe that you have to buy gifts for people at the holidays. All of those thoughts and beliefs come with emotions, whether they are anxiety, guilt, worry, or a smorgasbord of others. When the above situations or similar ones occur, your past conditioning kicks in and those unconscious beliefs create programmed feelings and repeated behavior.

Breathe!

The strongest conditioning comes from our surrounding environment, established by our parents. They usually do this in an unconscious way. What some parents are aware of, or not, is that in every moment they are modeling behavior that their children will probably use to navigate adulthood. We as children were unconsciously observing their behavior and learning about reality through our young and inexperienced minds. Remember, though, our parents were just being themselves and trying to parent the best way possible. As we get older, we need to examine that conditioning to separate out that which is our true intent and that which has been unconsciously given to and adopted by us.

Filtering

Anything that is repetitive, a habit, moves to the unconscious mind. This process is a way for the mind to economize its efforts as two million bits of information bombard it every second. If we allowed all of that information to flow through our conscious brain, we'd explode, or at least go crazy. Our mind's selection process allows approximately 170 bits of information to seep into our unconsciousness and five into our consciousness every moment. To save ourselves from major overload, our unconscious mind filters, selects, accepts, modifies, and perceives mostly that which aligns with our pre-set beliefs and conditioning. This informational exchange occurs without us even knowing about it.

If we don't stay conscious about the type of information we receive, we'll allow it to unconsciously form our beliefs. When we're young and haven't yet formed our own identities, this information we receive from our parents, religions, schools, and media easily seeps into our mind and unconsciously forms our beliefs. As we then continue to process new information, our mind selects the perspectives that support those early conditionings from others. Whether or not this information is positive or negative, the mind filters the information through the lens of our unconscious beliefs and our focus. Over time without any conscious filtering, we then unconsciously believe that those beliefs are our own unique focus—our perspective of the world.

> *"Thoughts are an important part of your inner wisdom and they are powerful. A thought held long enough and repeated becomes a belief. A belief then becomes our biology."*
> Dr. Christiane Northrup

Unexamined Beliefs

If we become too stressed with putting out our daily fires rather than feeding our soul, or if we become so busy that our mind ends up unconsciously assimilating the information coming from advertisers or news programs, we are then nothing but pigeons who mindlessly feed on the scraps of whatever is thrown before us. Before we know it, we're not living an authentic life but one that has been given to us by others. We'll then be truly living within *The Matrix*.

The mind, like a computer, needs to be cleaned up every so often. You need to delete information that no longer serves you, remove malware or viruses—unconscious, dysfunctional beliefs—that have come from other people and are corrupting your internal programs, and rearrange information—balance your PIES—to allow your mind to run more efficiently. The wise action would be to routinely check all the information before it gets entered into your computer/mind.

When a challenge arises and you feel negative emotions, the problem is usually a faulty dysfunctional belief that has infiltrated your mind. Stop that protective response of turning away from the pain, and address the cause of that pain—usually your beliefs. You can then see if your beliefs and behaviors are representing your true intentions. You can then change your thoughts and beliefs to align with your PIES and the Universal Principles.

This process of our repeated beliefs becoming unconscious is not necessarily negative. As we replace our old beliefs with balanced ones and repeat them continually through thoughts, feelings, and actions, they too will then become habit and therefore unconscious. Subsequently, these positive unconscious beliefs will filter all the new information we receive from our daily interactions. This process shapes our focus of the world, therefore creating a different, positive, functional, and balanced reality.

"As a single footstep will not make a path on the earth,
so a single thought will not make a pathway in the mind.
To make a deep physical path, we walk again and again.
To make a deep mental path, we must think over and over the kind
of thoughts we wish to dominate our lives."
Henry David Thoreau

Self-concept and Self-esteem

Your inner, invisible world of thoughts and emotions creates your outer, visible world. Your self-concept is composed of conscious and unconscious beliefs about yourself; it is the answer to the question "Who am I?" Self-concept is the beginning of the equation that determines the quality of your life: Thoughts/Beliefs + Emotions = Actions/Behaviors. Your self-esteem is based on your emotions associated with those beliefs—how you feel about yourself. This is why examining your conditioning, your filtering, and your beliefs are paramount.

Your self-concept is intrinsically and energetically connected to every facet of your life. It is a broad filter that creates a particular vision of the world. Whatever your self-concept and self-esteem, it will affect your job, relationships, vacations, parenting skills, and social life. Remember this fact as you become conscious about your daily interactions.

What do you think and feel about yourself? That the world is against you; that you're ugly, not worthy; that girls shouldn't go into science; that boys should always be tough; that you must be perfect; that everything must be logical and in order? Or do you think and feel about yourself that you're in control of your reactions in life, that you make a difference, that you can become anything you want, that you're human and will make some mistakes, that there is always something to learn from every situation you encounter? Most of us have some mixture of the above beliefs. Remember, whatever you think and feel is a reflection of your self-concept.

Are you still not sure about who you are, or if you have high or low self-concept? Look at the people and situations around you and ask yourself "Are they loving friends, or are they people who take advantage of me? Do I feel energized or drained? Do I feel more negative or positive emotions? What kinds of values do they reflect?" The truthful answers to those questions will provide a better idea of who you think you are and how you feel about yourself. If you don't like some of those reflections or answers, then take a realistic look at your beliefs and change them. Change them to align with not your conditioned beliefs but your authentic-self.

Your Focus is Your Reality

Your conditioning, filtering, beliefs, and self-concept influence your focus. Focus translates to where your conscious—or, usually, unconscious—mind places attention. Where you place your attention is where you will put more energy. More energy relates to action. Action determines what you will create in your life. Your focus then becomes your reality.

Obviously, your focus is of incredible importance and hopefully reflects your authentic-self. Seeing the world through the conscious lens of the Universal Principles and a balanced PIES creates a clear authentic focus that moves inward to matters of heart and spirit.

Sadly, many of us place our focus on *things* outside of ourselves—the false Physical. Cars, homes, beautiful men or women, money, your favorite sport's team winning, status of your job, and other people's acceptance are just some of those *things*. We need to get dirty and be the archeologist of our own mind in order to uncover our focus. Only then can we begin to create a reality that is reflective of our true-self.

> *"Man, alone, has the power to transform his thoughts*
> *into physical reality;*
> *man, alone, can dream and make his dreams come true."*
> Napoleon Hill

Balance Intellect

To operate at its fullest potential, the Intellect needs to be in balance within its seemingly dualistic components of ego-self or higher-self and consciousness or unconsciousness. Adhering to the following advice will help. Temper your ego-self and allow more of your higher-self to emerge. When making decisions, focus on discerning the difference between your *i* and *I*. Operating mostly from ego-self only brings about short-term happiness for you. Operating mostly from the higher-self brings about much deeper feelings of joy, happiness, and connection, not only for you but also for others.

The best thing we can do to bring balance to our mind, our PIES, and yes, even the world, is to become CONSCIOUS. It's about waking up. We all have to wake up! The first step to change is always the same—awareness. Being aware means you are presently conscious of your thoughts, feelings, and actions. Then you can assess your situation and notice if you're in balance or not. If you're thinking about the past or the future, you are missing the only true reality—the present.

Use your consciousness to perceive and create a reality of your choosing. To realize that vision, you need to delve into your unconscious mind, which is usually an arduous and unpleasant task. Examine all your beliefs and only align with those that serve your goals, including your answer to the question "Who am I?" Remember, it's your life and you're worth the effort. All of this is a process and takes constant vigilance.

"The moment you change your perception,
is the moment you rewrite the chemistry of your body."
Dr. Bruce Lipton

Balance I with ES

Now that you know how to create balance within the aspect of your Intellect, you need to have a balance between your I and your PES. We all have a tendency to trust our mind—I—over our PES. We can see this happen when we spend more time with our computers and technology than playing or socializing. Instead of playing outdoors using their bodies, our kids are on technological instruments. Instead of using our mind to focus on reading or meditating, we are watching TV. Instead of socializing, we work harder. Instead of taking time and using some of our focus on our body, emotions, and spirit, we allow our thoughts to run wild.

Take a look at how much alcohol and drugs we consume as a culture to soothe this painful noise. Most of our concerns are rarely about physically surviving but rather relate to a rambling state of mind that we have created by being out of balance with our PIES. These psychological and emotional dysfunctions are consuming our time and energy, leaving a sense of survival—psychological survival. This lack of balance between our I and PES creates our mid-life crises, states of depression, loneliness, career burnouts, stresses, and fears of empty nesting and getting older.

Most of our challenges occur because we use our Intellect as the main component in our choices and decisions. We'd be better off including our PES in the decision-making process—specifically, including our spirit, our authentic needs and wants. Working in a hospice and reading surveys over the years have shown me that, at the end of life, people pretty much have the same concerns: they wish they hadn't lived their lives by others' expectations, wish they hadn't worked so hard, desire the courage to have expressed their feelings (especially love), long to have kept in touch with friends, and desire to have allowed themselves to be happy. We can achieve all of these hopes if we spend time creating a more balanced mind and a better balance with our body and spirit.

A Cultural Over-emphasis on the Intellectual

As a species, we naturally began with an emphasis on our Physical in order to survive. When our brains developed, we easily lifted above the animal kingdom and landed at the top of the food chain. Slowly we have shifted from over-emphasizing our Physical to emphasizing and then over-emphasizing our Intellectual. Culturally, over hundreds of years, the emphasis on the Intellect has risen. Some might say that the focus on the Intellect began with the Greeks, but it really took off in the 16th and 17th centuries. This period of time saw the advent of science and rational thinking through philosophers such as René Descartes: "I think, therefore I am." The major factor that brought intellectualism to the masses was the Gutenberg printing press. Before then, the uneducated populace had a low emphasis on the Intellect. They allowed kings and religions to do their thinking for them. (More precisely, the authorities subjugated the people to that position.)

Breathe! Don't skip this gentle instruction.

This new focus eventually brought incredible advances to our understanding of the body, mind, planet, and universe. Our collective Intellect has formulated our sciences and designed our technology. We can build more unique and efficient shelters, grow more food, and move freely around the planet. Science has stretched our understanding of the universe, from the infinitely small particles within the quantum perspective to the farthest edges of the universe. We live longer because of incredible minds in medicine and advances in food production. We have created everything from the wheel that transported us to the next village, to a spacecraft now exiting our solar system. The list of intellectual achievements is evolving exponentially.

"The mind is everything: what you think, you become."
The Buddha

To be truthful, the unbalanced Intellect, one that is more ego driven and more unconscious, has been given a high precedence in the Western world. This imbalance is fertile ground for greed and power. Collective greed can be seen in corporate practices and ultimate power can be seen in governmental policies of domination over others. This has led to corporations killing, injuring, and diseasing their own consumers by polluting their air, water, and ground. Governments create an immensely stupid overabundance of weapons, which could kill every person on this planet several times over. How can that happen? The answer is simple: the Physical, Emotional, and Spiritual were not major factors in the decision process.

When you incorporate a balanced PIES into your decision process, miracles can happen. People will spend more time volunteering their services to others, spend more energy in working on themselves to effect change, take more responsibility for their thoughts, feelings, and behaviors. You'll then witness more acts like Dr. Jonas Salk's not applying for a patent for the polio vaccine, computer experts using their talent to create communication computers for the disabled, technical and medical experts developing customized prosthetics for war veterans, and many other incredible creations of the mind and spirit that benefit mankind.

I've spent time with some indigenous people in South America, where the emphasis is certainly more on the Spiritual and the connection to the planet rather than the mind. Is their way wrong and ours right? The ego and unconscious Intellect would answer, "Yes, just look at the way they live. They're still living in the dark ages. They don't have any of the mind-created technologies and comfort that we have. Our way is the best way." The soulful and conscious Intellect would say, "That might be true or not. Let me research a little more. Let me possibly try to understand what they experience. Maybe I should meet them or talk with them because a balance of all aspects is generally the best approach."

Many believe this over-emphasis on the Intellect is the way we should all live, their premise being that relying on Intellect is better than living from heart and soul. Living with technology is better than living in a primitive way. One of the reasons we have that perspective is because we've grown up that way and have seen that behavior in most of our surrounding cultures, but that in and of itself does not make it the *right* and only way. From my own personal experience, I've seen happier children running through the dirt roads of Quito than in any schools in America. I've seen more content people in the middle of the Amazon with no running water, toilets, closets, refrigerators, cars, or money than in any cubicles of the Western corporate world.

Life is not about *this* or *that* but rather a melding of many beliefs, actions, and concepts. There is an indigenous South American prophecy that says that, in the beginning of the 21st century, there will be an opportunity for the melding of the Eagle and the Condor—the eagle representing the Western world with its mind and technology and the Condor representing the indigenous cultures with their heart and spirit. Bringing about the balance of PIES in our Western culture will allow us to more easily live stress-free and bring harmony to all on this planet.

Let's expand this process of looking at an individual Intellect balance and a societal Intellect balance. Remember, "A repetitive thought becomes a belief and a repetitive action becomes a behavior." When a significant portion of people share a belief, it will turn to a moral, then law, and eventually, over time, a tradition is socially created. When people repetitively behave in accordance with those morals, you have the beginning of a culture.

In earlier times, and even now, many of our beliefs came from an ego-perspective that was fear based. For our survival, we perceived that anything different or anyone different posed a threat and we must protect ourselves. We progressed from keeping others away, anyone who was not in our clan, to keeping away anyone who was just different from us. We created biases towards people with red hair, people who were left-handed, people who had different faiths, skin colors, shapes of the head, sexual orientations, etc. There is no real physical threat from people who are different from us, only a psychological threat created by our mind. This unbalanced mind supports the ego *i*.

As individual consciousness changes and others adopt similar thinking, our collective consciousness changes—therefore, our culture must also change. When enough people believe that abuse in any form is not acceptable, you'll then have laws that reinforce that belief. When enough people believe that everyone should be able to practice their own religious beliefs, you'll have a society that practices tolerance. When a collective group believes we are all basically equal, a government will form to reflect those beliefs. When enough people believe that slavery is an abomination, they will create laws to change the culture, albeit slowly. When enough people think that we as a species should be promoting love, compassion, gratitude, and forgiveness, you'll see a new spirituality emerge. Even though I've been working on this "stuff" for years, I found that my mind and Intellect wanted to harp on the negative. The action of letting go is not sufficient to stop the negative habits of the mind. I needed to replace each negative thought with a positive one; a thought that reflected the essence of who I am. I constantly worked with affirmations as a way to turn negativity around and frame my life and my expectations in a positive light.

Affirmations

"Affirmations are mental vitamins, providing the supplementary positive thoughts we need to balance the barrage of negative events and thoughts we experience daily."
Tia Walker, The Inspired Caregiver

An affirmation is a great way to use your mind to create a balanced self-concept, a balanced mind, a balanced person. An affirmation is a positive and active statement that reflects the essence and potential of your authentic nature. Our daily life has a tendency to knock us down a notch and influence us to think and feel less than who we truly are. Our mental and spoken affirmations are reminders to our conscious mind of our PIES core and the Universal Principles. Be certain that when your affirmations reflect the workings of the universe and the desires of your soul, they will be more powerful. In the beginning, affirmations are conscious but, when repeated enough times and augmented by similar Vibrational Frequencies of feelings and actions, they become unconscious habits of thinking and eventually behavior. (Finally we've come to an unconscious belief that is positive.)

Say It, Even If You Don't Feel It

Often when we create our affirmations, we're trying to establish a feeling or condition that we may not fully feel in the present moment. This creates a discrepancy between our present thoughts or feelings and our affirmations, which can feel like a lie. Know the reprimanding voice in your head is only your ego not presently believing the essence of your soul. Don't fret! Say the affirmation anyway, because it's true. Believe me, you're not lying. Remember, the reason most of us use affirmations is to change a negative VF in our life to a positive VF. Have faith that, if you can't feel the potential of your affirmation in that moment, you can still acknowledge the essence of what is already deep inside you.

If you affirm the sun is shining when you're under a cloud-covered sky, are you lying? The sun is shining, but because of your present perspective you might not be able to see or feel it. The fact is that photons from the sun are passing through you in that very moment, the sun is shining somewhere in a cloudless sky, and if you were to get high enough above the clouds, the sun would shine every moment. So it's not a lie to say it's sunny when you're not feeling it at that present moment. You're just affirming your knowingness of the constant presence of the sun and of its eventual manifestation in your life.

Envision another situation. Is it a lie for a caterpillar to affirm that it can fly? Even though common sense says differently and every other bug in the tree is a naysayer, the caterpillar knows on a deep level that flying is part of its nature. So for you to affirm that you are loving, forgiving, or strong when you're not feeling it in that moment doesn't make you a liar; it makes you a person who appreciates who you are becoming and who recognizes the true essence of who you are. Affirming those innermost truths will allow you the experience of flying in the light more often.

Another way to deal with the uncomfortableness of saying an unfelt affirmation is to remember layers of knowing. You probably know by now that it takes time to remove all the layers of negativity that have surrounded you. The learning process unravels the truth slowly, so who cares that you might not recognize the full potential of your affirmation in the present? Every layer removed will make it easier and easier to feel and experience the truth of your affirmation.

Act As If

Even if you're still uncomfortable about saying your unfelt affirmation, do it anyway. Act *as if* you're already feeling your affirmation. What are your choices? What are the consequences of continuing to affirm you'll never get what you want or believing that you just don't have enough smarts, will, money, talent, or courage? Will affirming that give you a better or worse chance of attaining your goals? What would be the consequences of affirming, believing, and acting *as if* you're lovable, smart, or worthy, or believing that you have whatever it takes? Will that give you a better chance of opening up new possibilities for your present and future? Your choice!

Main Points

- Know that your reality begins with a thought, which eventually forms beliefs.
- Become less unconscious and more conscious.
- Reduce the ego-self and embrace the higher-self.
- Take responsibility for your thoughts and beliefs—you created them.
- Examine all your beliefs to ensure they are reflections of your authentic-self.
- Your focus is your reality.

Questions

- How can you tell the difference between your ego-self and higher-self?
- How can you become more conscious in your daily life?
- How do your childhood beliefs affect you as an adult?
- What are the factors that influence your focus?

Challenges

- Write down all the beliefs, thoughts, or expectations you associate with your challenges. Examples could be: I expect my wife to act in a certain way. I believe that mothers should always be giving towards their daughters. I believe that I'm a loser because I lost my home. I believe that I'm not good enough. I can do anything. My husband should know what I'm thinking.
- Examine all those beliefs and ascertain the following: are they truly yours or did you adopt them from others? Are they in accordance with the beliefs of your higher-self? Consciously let go of the ones that don't and hold on to the ones that do.

Affirmations

- I am accepting of myself, others, and all things.
- I am conscious in every moment.

***

Reflections and Corrections

Anyone who has been involved in searching for a job knows that it takes a toll on not only your finances and relationships but also your mind, beliefs, and self-worth. I experienced many hurdles with my job search. My eclectic life created a resume that didn't truly reflect my talents, aptitudes, and abilities; I've had several different careers with many jobs in between. Another challenge was the crash of '08, with few employers hiring. The only jobs that appeared were in healthcare, entry positions at retail stores, and customer service, which rendered me over-qualified for many of them. On top of that, I experienced a silent but prevalent discrimination because I was older.

Adding to one of my frustrations was the ordeal of applying online. Putting my resume on such recruitment places as Monster.com, Sales Ladder, and so on was totally discouraging. The online process was similar to the characteristics of a black hole. After sending out dozens and dozens of applications, I never—I mean never—received a reply. I felt at times like I was invisible, that no one cared, that things would never change. What a discouraging and aggravating experience.

When I applied in person the results were the same. A spokesperson for an outdoor travel company—nope. A census taker, one of the worst-rated jobs in America—rejected. Even being a waiter—zip. (My God, I'd owned a restaurant.) Through this time period, though, I did get some part-time jobs, such as working with the "recall" company, driving seniors to appointments, umpiring high school and recreational softball, and some very brief consulting gigs.

I'm a fairly confident guy, but I have to admit not having a full-time job for several years majorly chipped away at my self-concept. Being jobless can feel like having a scarlet L—for loser—written on your chest. I noticed that, once negative thoughts and beliefs found their way into my psyche, my focus began changing to match those negative beliefs of self.

Tom Youngholm

The major way to correct this debilitating reinforcement of negative messages is to follow the advice from the children's movie *Frozen* and just "Let it Go." Over the years, though, I recognized that, after I released a negative thought, a mental void occurred and was usually and immediately filled up with the same negative unconscious belief. I came to the realization that the action of "letting go" was not sufficient to stop the negative habits of the mind. I needed to replace the negative thought with a positive one—a thought that reflected the essence of who I am.

Affirmation Guidelines

*"You must begin to think of yourself
as becoming the person you want to be."*
David Viscott

When you've answered the basic question of "Who am I?" using the criteria of PIES and the Universal Principles, it will be easier for you to create balanced and powerful affirmations. The following tips will assist you.

Begin by using the word *I*. This is not the ego *i*, not the Thomas, Jane, or Sandy *i*, and not the sister, father, wife, employee, consumer, citizen *i*. I'm talking about the big *I*—the *I* that manifests in all the aspects of your PIES, the *I* that transcends all your perceived limits of being human—basically, the *I* that is the essence of your soul, your authentic-self.

Use the present tense, such as *am*. You can use other present-tense statements like "My thoughts are…" or "My body is…" but I've discovered that "I am…" resonates with a higher frequency of truth and feels more powerful. Keep in mind that those words need to be articulated separately: "I am…" is more potent than the contraction "I'm…"

Linguistically and spiritually, the present is powerful because it is in alignment with the truth; there is only the NOW. Past and future language—"I was…I will be…I should be…"—is energetically weaker, because it is not grounded in that reality. The past is gone and will never return. Everything changes. Who you were yesterday is different from who you are today and will be tomorrow. To affirm yourself with the future is to align yourself with something that never happens. My favorite sign is found in bars across the country: "Free Beer Tomorrow." Obviously tomorrow never gets here, so any linguistics based in that future tense will never be as powerful as the present.

Select powerful words that are in alignment with higher VFs and that reflect a state of soulful being. Examples might be: I am loving, I am love, I am strong and flexible, I am abundantly wealthy and healthy, I am accepting, I am happy, I am forgiving.

Emotionally feel your words as you externally or internally repeat them. Your emotions are what fuel your thoughts to bring about actions. The intensity of the emotion will increase the likelihood of its manifestation.

Make it simple and clear. As any good writer, engineer, film editor, or programmer knows, less is better. Creating a concise affirmation actually takes more time, more thought, more clarity, and more focus than creating a longer one. Your effort will be rewarded, as the shorter assertion makes for a stronger impact in your brain and heart. Remember, the keys to life are simple. The Universal Principles are simple. The soul is simple. So keep your affirmations to the point and simple.

Fine-tune your affirmations so that they address the essence of what you truly want and not the form of what you think you want. There is a fundamental difference between the needs of ego and the needs of the authentic-self.

"First say to yourself what you would be;
and then do what you have to do."
Epictetus

5

Emotional

*Emotions are the basis for our passions, creativity, and
inspiration; they are the palate of colors to an artist,
the conflicts of the human condition to a writer,
and the range of lyrical notes to a musician.*

Our Emotional side is unpredictable and seemingly
uncontrollable. Navigating through this aspect of ourselves is like
diving in murky waters or kayaking through dangerous rapids. Yet
grasping this non-linear, non-logical aspect of our self is
paramount to understanding who we are. I will attempt to explain
the following factors pertaining to the bewildering world of
emotions: why their importance has diminished; realizing they are
the zest of life; recognizing they derive from love and must flow;
the need to use our emotional intelligence; and, most importantly,
knowing and acting on the reality that you own them.

To eliminate any confusion, I'd like to mention that some
feelings are not emotions. They are purely chemical reactions
brought on by temporary imbalances within the body. One cause is
the stress response. In my younger years, I played hockey and
occasionally got aggressively slammed into the boards. The first
time it happened, I was surprised. How could I get so angry, so
quickly? The truth is that it wasn't truly anger but only my body's
stress response to a physical situation. My body was ready for fight
or flight. Once my mind realized I wasn't being attacked by an
intruder or a saber-toothed tiger, I continued to play the game
metabolizing and eliminating the hormones—a very healthy
reaction and response. You might feel the same way if you faced
an intruder, were in a car accident, or hung on to a clump of weeds
on a severe slope just six feet away from the edge of a cliff in
Costa Rica. (Okay, I'll save that story for another time.)

Another occurrence is what happens within women's bodies as they experience fluctuating hormones through pre-menstrual stress, menopause, or pregnancy. These mood swings are not necessarily related to their perceptions of the world but are reactions to the hormones being released in their bodies. Men certainly have occurrences relating to their testosterone, which has led to positive and negative outcomes. Other chemical reactions can be caused by numerous events within the body, such as diabetes or psychological disorders.

Just as our physical body can detect pressure, touch, and temperature, we also have an emotional body that can detect love, fear, worry, and joy, regardless of proximity. Have you ever been at a party when all of a sudden your mood changed without anything to do with you, your thoughts, or the person you were talking to? But when you looked around you could identify someone who was emanating that particular emotion. Have you ever felt anger from a spouse before they entered the room, or the love of a friend over the phone? You were just being empathic in that moment, picking up on another's emotions. The emotional body can certainly reach out and touch someone. Putting aside the above examples, the situations I will mainly deal with in this book are the emotions linked to our thoughts, beliefs, and expectations.

Emotions Add Zest to Your Life

Emotions are the basis of our passions, creativity, and inspiration; they are the palate of colors to an artist, the conflicts of the human condition to a writer, and the range of lyrical notes to a musician. The reality is that emotions provide the spark in life. Can you imagine life without feeling the joy of meeting someone new? The disappointment or excitement of watching your favorite sports team play? Even the sadness of losing a loved one, because that also meant you had great feelings of love? Without emotions we'd be like robots. Do we really want to be like Data from *Star Trek*, with no emotions? Life would be incredibly boring.

Think of people you know who might be called emotionally challenged. Their demeanor is plain, their faces rarely show expressions, and their voice intonations are bland. They tend to be dull and lifeless. (Remember, just because that is their behavior, it doesn't mean they don't have emotions; it just means they're holding them back.) There are also people on the opposite side of the spectrum, whose emotions are all over the place. This is an exhausting state, not only for the individual but also for the people around them. Then there are people who show emotions in some situations but not others. I have some guy friends who are very open with their emotions around a football game but not so when they are around their spouses. It's all about the flow and balance.

Most Emotions are Created By the Mind

When we have a thought, belief, or expectation about a person or situation, an emotion will follow. Here are some examples. You have an expectation that your significant other should take out the garbage and, when they don't, you feel disappointment. If you didn't care, you might have felt indifference. The boss reprimands you and you feel unhappy. If you have the prior belief that you might lose your job, you might feel insecure. If you have the thought or opinion that he's just being a jerk, you might feel bitter. Someone overcharges you and your belief in fairness leaves you feeling annoyed. If you have the prior belief that everybody is out to get you, you might feel angry. If you play a game and have an expectation that you should win, you feel upset when you lose. If your belief is that you're out there for fun, you feel joy no matter what the score. The bottom line is that your emotions are closely tied to the type and quality of your thoughts. Change your thought, belief, expectation and you will change your emotion.

Dysfunctional Beliefs About Emotions

"I gave myself permission
to feel and experience all of my emotions.
In order to do that, I had to stop being afraid to feel.
In order to do that, I taught myself to believe no matter
what I felt or what happened when I felt it, I would be okay."
Iyanla Vanzant

False beliefs about the true nature of our emotions come from our culture. In the history of Western, male-dominated societies, emotions were not addressed and even became supressed. Expressing emotion was seen as a negative attribute, a female *thing*, a weakness. This viewpoint has enslaved women in a myriad of ways and has set up unhealthy limitations for men. Our movies, businesses, and relationships also reflect this faulty perspective. Watch some old films and listen to the communication patterns between men and women; it's actually comical to hear it now in retrospect. As a child you might have heard "Stop your crying!" Many women, throughout their lives, have heard "Don't be so emotional." I've consulted in many corporations and the unspoken and sometimes spoken rule was that emotions have no place in business.

The reality is that it's impossible to avoid emotions just because of a business mandate. There are all kinds of positive and negative emotions wafting through the cubicles. Positive emotions occur after someone gives great customer service, helps another employee, shares encouraging news, or completes a project. Negative feelings also permeate the business environment, whether because of employee dissatisfaction with management, faulty communication, fear of layoffs, or gossiping around the water cooler. The real damage occurs, whether for the individual or for a business, when the emotions are blocked.

We also need to be careful about answering the question "How are you feeling?" with "good" or "bad." Those terms are not feelings. This response is a subterfuge, a way of diverting and diminishing your emotional state of being. One point to remember is that there is no such thing as good or bad; therefore, there are no good or bad emotions. (This delves into one of the Universal Principles of *Energy Just Is* which I will discuss later.) *Good* and *bad* are just words created by the mind to describe a judgment about your and others' thoughts, emotions, and actions. Those judgments usually generate from our parents, religions, and governments as a way to control us. Try not to fall into this trap. Our own self-judgments of *good* or *bad* have usually been ingrained in our mind by others.

Breathe!

Other responses to that question of "How do you feel?" might be "Great!" or "So-so" or "Yucky," or simply a shrug of the shoulders. None of these replies are emotions. Since our culture lacks focus on emotions, it lacks awareness of the existing vocabulary to describe them fully. Inuit, who place a high importance on snow, have dozens of words to describe that simple object. Our culture, placing a low importance on emotions, has a limited vocabulary to describe their variant degrees. Subsequently, emotions have not played a healthy role in our relationships which has led to a myriad of dysfunctions.

Besides coming from a faulty cultural belief about emotions, we might have also learned that we should only feel one emotion at a time. The reality is that there are many times we feel several— and sometimes conflicting—emotions, which causes us to be perplexed, bewildered, and confused. Certain situations provoke different and simultaneous perspectives containing diverse thoughts, beliefs, expectations, hopes, and fears. When expecting a baby, one could feel opposing emotions of delight and fear. Starting a new job brings about feelings of enthusiasm yet anxiety. Grieving over the loss of a loved one might dig up sadness, despair, guilt, anger, and possibly relief.

Another facet is that, within our psyche, we have many selves, such as the child, adult, parent, male, female, teenager, employee, and boss. Each self perceives the world a little differently, and, as I mentioned above, have different beliefs, expectations, and desires. So in the case of a woman having a baby, the mother-self is delighted, but her inner child-self is fearful. Sprinkle those selves with unhealed stages such as the abandoned child, the bitter wife, the jilted lover, or the down-trodden worker, and hundreds of permutations add a varied emotional spectrum to any given situation.

You don't need to be confused or uncertain about experiencing simultaneous and different emotions; it is a natural part of your emotional being. The ideal response would be to become aware of your emotion, figure out the belief that preceded it, let it go, and, if you choose, change your thoughts, allowing you to experience a different emotion.

Emotions Need to Flow

"When we direct our thoughts properly,
we can control our emotions."
W. Clement Stone

An emotion, as well as all energy, is meant to flow. Ideally, feel your emotions and then express them in real time. This process is natural but was hindered by our mind as we grew up. We knew how to deal with our emotions when we were younger. Watch a child who has just created a sandcastle on the beach. They jubilantly bounce up and down with joy and then break into sobs when a wave destroys their creation. After a while, they quit crying and then excitedly do something else. Their emotions are moving through them all the time; they feel an emotion and then let it go.

If your child doesn't do their chores or behaves in a multitude of ways that drive you crazy, you might feel disappointed or even angry. You should express your emotion and then work together on a resolution, remembering to allow them to share their emotions—in an appropriate way. If you're stuck in traffic, it's okay to let out a yell, but then focus on your breath. Share your love for your father with words, a hug, or a kiss. Allow yourself to feel grief over losing a pet.

Think of emotions as being like a river. You need to jump in and be swept along. Sure, part of the journey might be bumpy and even scary, but most of the journey is steady and pleasant. Besides, you don't really have a choice; the river is an essential aspect of you. You can try to resist by building mind dams, but if you do, eventually there will be a buildup of energy. When this happens, you'll feel some sense of emotional pressure—pain. The river has to go somewhere, so eventually the river finds a way around the dam or breaks through. If the dam holds back the river, emotions will flow into areas that were not intended. All of us have done this to some degree in our lives. We yell at our kids when we're really mad at our boss. We take it out on our spouse when we're frustrated about something else in our life. This displacement of our emotions has hundreds of different scenarios, but none of them are appropriate.

If the emotions build up over time with no release at all, eventually a situation in your life will occur that causes the dam to break. This energy release usually causes destruction along its path. A personal example is when my father died. I held on to my grief by hardly shedding a tear. I loved my dad dearly but held on to the faulty belief that I had to be the man of the house and be strong. After many months of damming up my feelings, which resulted in my becoming constantly sick, I finally let loose.

I did it again ten years later, when I owned a floating houseboat restaurant. As I mentioned in *The Celestial Bar*, I had certain expectations and lots of bottled-up sadness, frustration, and anger. All these emotions were related to my partner, my suppliers, the long hours, or the sometimes demanding public. It doesn't make a difference what the emotions are, what the details are, or whether your emotions are justified or not. All that matters is that they are blocked and need to be released. My restaurant sank one night, breaking down my dam, and I broke down like never before. Once I started crying, I could hardly breathe before another onslaught of sadness and frustration washed over me. I even lashed out at friends, my partner, and unsuspecting people. When the dam breaks, there will usually be casualties along the way.

Emotions are not meant to be contained by a mind dam. Remember, the river needs to flow. It has to—that is its nature. So feel it, experience it, and then let it go. These days I do just that and feel much better with no real negative consequences. To be truthful, though, there has been one small side effect. I do suffer a temporary bruised ego when friends have teased me about shedding a few tears after watching reruns of *Field of Dreams*, *Somewhere in Time*, *Ghost*, and *Bambi*. (In my defense, I was only ten years old for the latter one.)

Emotional Intelligence (EQ)

> *"Your Intellect may be confused,*
> *but your emotions will never lie to you."*
> Roger Ebert

Similar to the body having intelligence, and the mind having intelligence (measured through one's IQ), we also have emotional intelligence—EQ. This refers to the awareness of your and others' emotions, which then enables you to moderate your own. We need to use this intelligence in order to bring balance to our Emotional aspect.

Emotions act as a mirror for our thoughts and beliefs. The first step in establishing our EQ is to be aware of what we are feeling. Many of us have been conditioned not to feel, so this first phase can be very difficult. Know that the more you become aware and gain an emotional vocabulary, the easier it will become. Constantly check in to see what you are feeling throughout the day. As you sharpen your skills in the identification of this "pesky and ephemeral" aspect, you'll also become better at identifying others' emotions.

As you become more intellectually and emotionally balanced, you'll enable yourself to appropriately moderate your emotions. Remember, our thoughts and beliefs provide accompanying emotions. To moderate them, you'll identify the belief behind the emotion and change it if it is not authentic.

An example might be if your spouse forgot about a dinner engagement and you felt disappointed. Your thought/expectation behind that behavior might have been that they should have remembered. If your thought/belief was that forgetting meant they didn't love you, your feeling might have been despair. If your response was going into a rage, you might discover that your belief actually stemmed from all the other people in your life who had never respected, loved, or cared for you, and this was just one more example.

No matter what your emotion, when your spouse comes through the door, you should express whatever you feel. Both of you can then discuss matters, changing any beliefs that do not support a healthy relationship.

Different Perceptions, Therefore Different Emotions, of the Same Event

"It is the mind, which creates the world around us,
and even though we stand side by side in the same meadow,
my eyes will never see what is beheld by yours, my heart will never
stir to the emotions with which yours is touched."
George Gissing

"Each of us creates our own reality" means there can be different realities within the same moment. Two people go to the same football game; one roots for the home team and the other for the visitors. Each one has a thought or belief and an expectation about their team winning. Let's say the visitors win by a score of 21 to 18. Both spectators watched the same game, at the same time, seeing the same tackles, passes, kicks, punts, and interceptions, yet they experienced very different emotions. The person who was rooting for the visitors might be happy, jubilant, or excited; the home team fan might be disappointed, upset, or unhappy. Both watched the same event, yet each of their thoughts, expectations, and beliefs were different—therefore, their emotions were also different.

We all have attended a family get-together, gathered for a business meeting, or watched the same movie with friends. Did all of your family, team members, or friends interpret and feel the same way about those conversations, presentations, or dialogue? I've been at family gatherings where one comment at the dinner table has brought anger to one person and laughter to another. I've also attended a meeting where layoffs were announced; the person to my right was in tears because she didn't know if she could find another job, while the person to my left was relieved because she wanted to quit, had been afraid of not getting any unemployment benefits, but now could. What about being at a movie theatre where a scary character jumps into the scene and a person behind you screams while someone in front of you laughs.

I'll never forget a great pictorial representation of this concept. My wife and I had gone to the Six Flags amusement park near L.A. I love rollercoasters and believe they're fun, while my wife was not fond of them, but, being a trooper, went with me. I believe one of the rides we went on was the Nitro, where they take a computerized picture of you at one of the scariest points on the ride. After the ride was over, we wobbly-walked over to the photo booth to see our picture. We both laughed out loud. There we were on the same ride, in the same seat, traveling the same speed, and going through the same turns. But the picture caught two different emotional realities; my face was plastered with a grin from ear to ear, and her face depicted utter terror, with eyes popping out of their sockets and her wide-open mouth in the middle of a bloodcurdling scream.

Breathe!
Focus inwards and feel your breath
brushing the walls of your lungs.
Breathe!

There Is Only Love

I would like to propose a very different perspective of our varied emotions: there is only one, ever-present, all-encompassing emotion called love. As with all energy, this unconditional love has a frequency that is constantly present throughout the cosmos. I believe that love is an essential part of our spirit and the basic fiber of the universe. Think of love as being broadcast from an intergalactic radio station, WGOD or WLOV. This frequency is transmitted not only from the cosmic radio tower but from every person and every thing in the universe. The trick is to be able to receive that ever-present frequency without any interference.

There was a time when we didn't block that frequency. From infancy, children exude more of that pure love energy than adults. Infants instinctively smile at parents and also at strangers who are of different religions, beliefs, colors, and status. Even in childhood they carry much of this same innocence. The main reason is that they have received less conditioning from parents, media, and society; therefore, they have less judgments, limiting beliefs, and expectations of others. Children do not have prejudice or hatred in their hearts; it has to be taught to them. They have less blocks and are therefore more receptive to the ever-present frequency of love. One can easily see that the older we get, the more we acquire societal programming, and the result is generally feeling less love.

There have been "Holy Ones" or "Enlightened Ones" who, through years of spiritual practice, have been able to receive a strong love signal by being in PIES balance. They've been able to achieve extended periods of time where they experienced the frequency of bliss. Those of us who have not been so zealous with our efforts might have experienced it a few times, but usually only for brief moments. Yet others have reported experiencing this unconditional love after having near-death experiences. This makes sense in that leaving your body would automatically raise your consciousness, including your frequency, allowing you to more clearly experience that ever-present love.

Personally, I've had three experiences where I felt that frequency of absolute, unconditional love. The first two times it happened, I felt in communion with nature, but they lasted only a few moments. The last time, the connection continued for about five minutes. It was incredible! I wasn't even meditating or in nature. I was putting on a workshop in Sedona, had just taken care of some details, and walked into a room where I had a musician playing for the attendees. The tone of his voice reverberated in every cell in my body. As I sat down to listen to his performance, wham! I was hit hard with an overwhelming feeling of pure, unconditional love. I felt deeply connected, compassionate, and loving to each and every person. There is no way I could fully put into words what I felt, but needless to say I wanted it to continue forever. In that moment, I knew that this was heaven on earth; this was what all of us are yearning for. That was sixteen years ago and

I haven't felt it since, yet the tiniest sense of that feeling lingers within me today.

"The truth is that we can learn to condition our minds, bodies, and emotions to link pain and pleasure to whatever we choose. By changing what we link pain and pleasure to, we will instantly change our behaviors."
Tony Robbins

Own Your Own Emotions

Here is another key factor about emotion that is both powerful, if you are awakened, and disturbing, if you're not aware of all the material in this book. Your emotions are yours and nobody else's. Ultimately you need to own your emotions and take responsibility for what you feel. Once you know, accept, and act on this fact, the ramifications can be life changing. But once you have adopted this fact, you also have to let go of blaming other people for all the negative emotions you've felt in your life. This can be disruptive, disturbing, and scary. Give yourself time to slowly let this concept sink into your consciousness.

You hear these statements all the time: "You made me mad. You make me happy. You made me sad." This is how our communication sounds when we don't own our emotions. These statements are blatantly and emphatically untrue and, sadly, prevalent within our lives. Don't despair; it is such a part of our language that, even if you know better, it still comes out of your mouth. (I've actually heard more than one therapist ask a client, "So how did your partner or child make you feel?" Yikes!) The most damaging part is that those statements are declarations of someone else having power over you. Think about it! If someone can make you feel a particular emotion, then you have no free will and are just a puppet in life, a pawn on someone else's chessboard. What a depressing way to live.

People can certainly influence you in such a way that you might react with sadness or anger or happiness, but they cannot give that emotion to you. We are all capable of having our buttons pushed by a close friend, spouse, family member, or stranger. If someone insults you, of course your knee-jerk reaction is to feel that person made you angry. As much as you'd like to blame them for making you angry, you still have the choice to react to them in any way you choose. The reality is that your self-concept, which is influenced by your thoughts and beliefs about yourself, coupled with your self-esteem and the accompanying feelings, will determine your response. If you're a high-strung person with low self-esteem, you might feel rage, but if you're a Dalai Lama type of person, you might feel delight at the opportunity to let go of the insult and provide the opportunity for the insulter to learn from your response.

If someone can truly make you feel love or happiness, what happens when they go away? Can you still feel love or happiness, or do they take that with them? This belief can be seen in relationships, divorces, and death. What happens to you if your lover moves on to another relationship, or dies, and you still believe or repeatedly say, "They made me happy?" Because they are now gone, are you left alone, in the void, never able to feel happiness again? How can someone else forcibly make you do anything, much less give you an emotion? It's impossible! This kind of thinking, of not having control over your emotions, can easily lead to years of unhappiness and depression. You have the power to allow frequencies of love and happiness to resonate in your own life at any time.

If someone can make you feel angry, that also means you have to rely on them to un-make you angry. If you hold on to that erroneous belief, you'll use your energy to try to get *them* to change their behavior. The outcome of your efforts would be the same as if you tried to get your reflection in a mirror to change without you changing. What a waste of your precious energy! You can certainly ask someone to modify their behavior, but you must still realize that, whatever your emotional reaction happens to be, it is your emotion.

When you take responsibility for owning your own emotions, your communication pattern will sound something like, "When you came home late last night, I was worried and angry." You define the behavior and identify what you felt, rather than saying, "You make me angry when you come home late," which gives someone the power to make you angry. That is a subtle difference, but so powerful. Imagine telling your child, "You made me angry when you didn't pick up your clothes." You've just told them they have power over you. Believe me when I say their minds have unconsciously picked up on that semantic statement, and they will unconsciously test new ways to exercise their acquired power.

Another example is related to a client of mine who had a traumatic breakup with his girlfriend. After she left him, he was extremely upset, with feelings of deep sadness and anger. His thoughts ranged between how could she leave him, there must be something wrong with him, there must be something wrong with her, and if he can't have her, nobody should have her. Each of those thoughts was the basis for his feelings of anger, guilt, hurt, and jealousy. How could his feelings change if she *made* him feel angry, mad, and sad? He was convinced that she was the one who was making him mad, making him sad, making him miserable. The more he focused on not being with her, the more he felt negative emotions. He was miserable—miserable because of the breakup, miserable at work, miserable with his friends, but really miserable about not being in control. It was her; she was doing this to him.

I ask you again, how can someone else forcibly make you do anything, much less give you an emotion? It's ridiculous! After studying this material, he realized that he was the one who was in control of his thoughts and emotions. He needed to stop focusing on negative thoughts about her, about things that he didn't have, and focus more on changing his expectations and desires about himself and her. Only after changing his thoughts and expectations did he experience different, more positive emotions such as contentment, peace, and compassion. By changing his thoughts, he changed his emotions, and he changed his life. Eventually he was even able to feel love for her again. Now they are best friends and experiencing a different relationship with each other on a completely separate level.

What a wonderful concept! You're in control. If this is the only thing you take away from this book, you'll have made a quantum jump to mastering balance.

So own the fact that you are in control of your own emotions; its empowering. Having the power to create your emotions also means you have the power to change them. So instead of using all that futile energy to try to change someone else, use it to change your perceptions. If you don't want to feel angry, then look within and use your emotional intelligence; identify your emotions and then moderate them by changing your thoughts, expectations, and focus.

"Every day we have plenty of opportunities to get angry, stressed, or offended. But what you're doing when you indulge these negative emotions is giving something outside yourself power over your happiness. You can choose to not let little things upset you."
Joel Osteen

Main Points

- Increase your emotional intelligence.
- Become aware of your emotions.
- Allow yourself to feel your emotions and then let them go.
- To change your feelings, change your thoughts.
- There are no good or bad emotions, only positive and negative.
- Love is the main emotion; all others are just lower frequencies that our imbalanced Intellect has filtered out.

Questions

- How has society influenced your beliefs about emotions?
- Have you ever felt someone's emotional energy even though they were not in the same room?
- When have you held back your emotions and what were the consequences?
- What are your fears about letting your emotions flow?
- What do you need to do to be in Emotional balance?

Challenges

- If you'd like to change any of your emotions related to your challenges, then write down a different belief, perspective, or expectation.
- As you fully embrace that new belief, notice what changes occur to your emotions.
- Be patient and loving towards yourself; moving through multiple layers of this process can take time.

Affirmations

- I am allowing myself to experience and then let go of my emotions.
- I am loving and forgiving to myself, others, and all my relations.

***

Reflections and Corrections

Many people, as I mentioned earlier, do not have a high EQ—the ability to identify their emotions and express them in real time. Some people don't know what they're feeling, while others hold tightly to their feelings. The term "emotional reasoning" relates the false belief that what you are feeling is true: I feel sad, therefore I am sad. I feel guilty, therefore I must have done something wrong. If you identify with those negative feelings you're sending unconscious signals to your mind—your self-esteem—that you are a sad person, angry person, or guilty person. Feelings are not a statement about who you are, only a reflection of what you're experiencing in the moment. Tomorrow, later on today, or in the next minute, you most likely will be feeling something else.

Some of us, though, are not even aware of what we're feeling. What has probably happened is that you've been protecting yourself for fear of emotional pain. Each protective moment creates an emotional callous, which eventually numbs you to life.

I thought I was in touch with all my emotions. One of my many beliefs about myself was that I was a happy-go-lucky guy who rarely felt anger. I was partially correct. Indeed, I was open and expressed positive emotions, but I definitely repressed negative emotions of frustration, resentment, and anger. Unknowingly, I needed help, which didn't arrive until I went through several group therapy sessions, a requirement of receiving my Master's degree.

During one session, our task was to express a situation in which we felt anger. I inwardly searched my thoughts, but nothing came to me. Finally, what I thought was a trivial situation came to mind. When it was my turn, I banally stated a conflict I had with my landlord. He was raising my rent but had not done any of the repairs I'd requested. Surprised, I discovered that the more I talked about my situation, the angrier I felt. When I'd finished my little tirade, I felt a bit better. I realized I somehow had kept some emotions inside but felt I was able to release them. Feeling a little

87

proud about my experience, I opened myself up for feedback. I was stunned when my teacher said she didn't believe a word I'd said; all the other students agreed. I was in disbelief. How could no one believe I was angry?

The teacher, a therapist, asked me to go into an empty room next door and repeat, in front of a wall mirror, exactly what I'd just conveyed to the group. Begrudgingly, I sauntered to the next room with a little chip on my shoulder and a bit of a bruised ego, but I did what she asked. That experience has forever changed my life. Within fifteen seconds of expressing myself before the mirror, I instantly knew what my fellow students and teacher had observed. I didn't believe a word that I'd spoken. I didn't believe at all that I was angry. As I'd spoken and emitted what I thought was anger, I'd actually been smiling the whole time.

Many aspects about myself became very clear in the forthcoming weeks. I was fearful of expressing negative emotions. I had been fearful for my entire life. I identified being angry with being like my mother. No one had ever taken me seriously when I told them I was upset. My smile was a dysfunctional, unconscious protection. I was afraid people wouldn't like me if I conveyed anger or frustration. I had been a "pleaser" my whole life. I didn't know when I was actually angry. All of these aspects were preventing me from being authentic.

The beginning point of remedying my situation, of increasing my emotional intelligence, was to become aware of what I was feeling. The following emotional checklist can help you identify your emotions. If you're not sure what you're feeling, copy this checklist and put it by your desk or refrigerator and periodically stop to ask yourself what you're feeling in that moment. I've had clients who have set their phone alarms on different times during the day to act as a reminder. If at first you're unsure, ask yourself if you're feeling any of the headers in the checklist—Happy, Excited, Sad, Mad—and then look below to see if any of the emotions listed are more specific to what you are feeling.

The more aware you are of your own emotions, the easier it will be to identify others' emotions. This consciousness will allow you to have a deeper connection to yourself and others in your life. And, as I will soon discuss, connection is the key to authenticity.

Emotional Checklist

Happy	Excited	Mad	Sad
Joyful	Optimistic	Irritable	Grief
Peaceful	Interested	Annoyed	Suffering
Amused	Hopeful	Agitated	Disappointed
Loving	Playful	Frustrated	Despairing
Fulfilled	Ecstatic	Anxious	Lonely
Liberated	Cheerful	Angry	Regretful
Confident	Eager	Disgusted	Hopeless
Blissful	Exhilarated	Hostile	Guilty
Serene	Enthusiastic	Resentful	Envious
Compassionate	Content	Hate-filled	
Pleased	Enthralled	Panicked	
Affectionate	Inspired	Fearful	
Interested	Hopeful	Grumpy	
Powerful			
Amused			

6

Spiritual

I visualize my soul as a scented bubble
rising from the depths of my unconscious.
There is no work in making it manifest;
there's just allowing it to effortlessly float upwards.
Once it connects with the surface of my consciousness,
the bubble pops, sharing the depth of its knowingness and the
fragrance of its love.

I start this discussion with a disclaimer. To accurately conceptualize and then verbalize the multi-faceted nature of a soul is a difficult task. Despite the varied definitions given by religions, individuals, cultures, and philosophies, a soul's very nature is beyond the Physical, Intellectual, and Emotional, and therefore our language. So to describe its essence, purpose, and nuances is a daunting task. It's difficult enough to truly portray some common earthly experiences. Can a book about the Grand Canyon unfold one's incredible experience within its majestic walls? Can an article about childbirth demonstrate the depth of love and connection a woman feels as she gives physical life to a soul? I'm an author and am limited by my Intellect and the tools of my trade. My explanations of the soul will barely describe a faint shadow of the actual truth, but let's delve in…

Our daily conversations usually entail discussions about our PIE. Physically, we speak of our aches, pains, foods, pleasures, and desires. Intellectually, we share our thoughts, beliefs, opinions, judgments, and ideas. Emotionally, we express our frustration, anger, happiness, and contentment. Rarely do most of us discuss our Spirituality; our passions, our learnings, our deepest thoughts, our loves, or our connections to people and the Divine. Yet those very discussions could help us get to the core of the question "Who am I?" I will attempt to define the spirit—how it manifests, its purpose, and how to allow more of it to show up in your daily life.

Our spirit—or soul, which I will use interchangeably—is about connection, knowingness, and love. Everyone has a soul, not because they deserve it or are blessed, but because it is the essence of every human. Some feel that our soul is a gift from our Creator. Others say the soul is a reflection, a holographic clone, of a larger essence that goes by dozens of different "God" names. Those who are not religious might see the soul as being connected to a Source, the Universe, Humanity, or, to quote *Star Wars*, the Force. Most say that our soul is what survives our life on this planet. Others don't feel we have one at all. Given our limited use of our minds, I feel it would be fair to say that, no matter what our definition of the soul might happen to be, that it's more than we can imagine.

I believe our soul is an entity, an energy package, that temporarily physically inhabits a body composed of the meta-physical aspects of heart/love and intellect/knowingness. This package comprises the essence of the Universe, love—a love that is aware and that has a knowingness of our intrinsic connection to all things.

Connection, Love, Knowingness

Our Spirituality is about knowing our loving connection to the Universe. Your body is a vehicle allowing your soul to experience—connect with—the Universe and all of its mani-festations: persons, places, things, and situations. I'm not just talking about any kind of connection; I mean a deep connection that allows you to feel the essence of things you perceive as outside of yourself.

You can feel this connection in several ways. You may feel an awareness of a deep physical connection, as in feeling the earth, wind, and sky while sitting on a mountaintop, or a sense of unconditional love similar to what I experienced at my Sedona seminar. This connection can also be a sense of knowingness—not an understanding of a situation or person, but rather a conscious sense of peace and calm, usually described as a *knowing* that everything is perfectly fine in this moment and everything will turn out okay. These deep and sometimes subtle, sometimes intense, connections of love and knowingness are what everyone is searching for.

Whether you believe in a God or not, we all have a spirit that is rooted in our humanity—a humanity that is enmeshed within this Universe. There is scientific proof that every one of us is composed from the makings of the Big Bang. Science is constantly confirming our deep physical connection to the Universe. Astrophysicists have proven, at least in physical terms, that we humans have communal atoms left over from the Big Bang. This tells us that each of us is intrinsically connected to the planet, moon, stars, and galaxies. We're also connected to every other human molecularly. Geneticists have exposed the fact that not only has our present human DNA been shared throughout every generation but it is also found within other organisms. Quantum physics has shown that there is no real boundary between our body, the chair we sit on, the trees that shade us, or the earth we walk on. Studies on the effect of consciousness on our bodies are beginning to prove what many of us already intuitively knew—that our deep connection also has to do with our thoughts and emotions.

This connection can sometimes be felt within our minds. Being a species that is sentient, aware of itself, gives us opportunities the plants and rocks don't have. Beyond the physical, we have an ability to retrieve information through our unconsciousness—what Jung called the *collective unconscious*. Since energy can neither be created nor destroyed, the information, memories, and knowledge that have occurred throughout our human existence are present somewhere, in some form; maybe in a metaphysical warehouse, maybe as a frequency we can consciously experience. Joseph Campbell in his *The Power of Myth* explains that our present lives are somehow connected with the archetype lives of humanities past.

Another facet of this profound, complex, and innate connection can be explained by the adage "The sum is greater than its parts." Those who are more conscious may feel there is something more—something greater than us. There are no words to explain that sense of *more*. One can experience this realization when one listens to an orchestra performing music, where the result is much grander than the individual instruments and musicians. A team working together is superior to its individual members. An artisan's product is greater than just their talents, skills, and knowledge. The will of a nation is greater than all of its factions. The bond between a mother and her unborn child is greater than the two individuals. Extrapolate that connection to the mind-boggling concept that, on every level, we are made of the same materials as the stars, planets, and other humans. The magnitude and depth is impossible for our limited minds to fully grasp.

Cosmologically, our minds are still comparatively immature— "young" might be a better way to state it. Even after all these centuries, as a species we still mostly operate from our egos. As this fake sense of self believes in separation, it conjures up a separate, grander entity to fill the void of not understanding that sense of connection.

This sense of something bigger than us could be a recognition of our physical connection to all things, but it could also explain a God, or not, or maybe something grander than we could ever conceive. But I believe that, whatever it is, it is something more than we could imagine.

> *"You have to be able to center yourself,*
> *to let all of your emotions go.*
> *Don't ever forget that you play with your soul,*
> *as well as your body."*
> Kareem Abdul-Jabbar

Something is Missing

The process of discovering your spirit begins with your ego's realization that "something is missing." Your ego believes in a world of parts, which means you can be separated from *things* outside of yourself; therefore, you can be missing *things*. The truth is that your ego-self is merely experiencing amnesia about the presence of your soul. Even if you're aware of having a soul, your human consciousness is probably not at its fullest potential and feels disconnected from the quality, depth, and full potential of your spirit.

Breathe!
Don't just skip this. Do it and see if it makes a difference.

The reason so many people are feeling this angst and searching for meaning is that their spirit wants to bust out of its human unconsciousness. Their soul wants to experience the wonders of this planet through the Physical, a sense of knowingness through the Intellect, and a varied level of love through the Emotions. The higher-self *I* knows you and *I* are actually *we*, because ultimately *we* come from the same Physical and Universal Source. As your soul seeps more into your consciousness, it knows that realization is not about some *thing*, nor is any *thing* missing. Your spirit knows that the Universe is intrinsically, lovingly connected, so there is nothing to find, but rather something that needs to unfold within you. Like a flower in the sun, the world desperately needs the fragrance of our collective souls revealed.

How Do We Know of the Presence of the Spirit?

Looking at our history, it would be easy to be cynical about the presence of the spirit on the planet; but I believe it does exist. The difficulty in recognizing the spirit is that our mind is like a child in a toy store; it is busy reacting to everything it senses. The soul is subtle, and therefore the least recognized part of our self. Because of that lack of attention and awareness, we've not been taught how to recognize, nurture, and express this quiet yet essential aspect of ourselves. Because the soul is invisible rather than seen, it is experienced rather than recognized, and internally known rather than intellectually understood.

You can feel the existence of the spirit when you interact with certain people, places, and situations. The proof of spirit has been seen in the lives of Enlightened Ones such as Jesus, Lao-Tse, St. Francis, and the Buddha and, in recent times, in Gandhi, Mother

Teresa, and certainly the Dalai Lama. Accounts of their presences on this planet are filled with stories of love, compassion, knowingness, and their amazing connections with people, animals, and the earth. When meeting with these beings, most people have experienced *something* that transcends the physical. In their presences, people have felt a connection, a feeling of unconditional love, and a sense of peace that comes from knowingness.

Being around enlightened people is not the only way to sense the soul. Many ordinary people experience their souls in simple private moments away from the media, TV screens, and tabloids. Spirit can manifest when a baby's tiny hand grabs your finger, a whale's eye stares back at you in the Sea of Cortez, or you view the sunrise over the ruins of Machu Picchu. You feel that you're not only a witness to the magical moment but are actually deeply connected to it.

On the seemingly negative side, tragedy is a situation that allows the spirit to audaciously jump front and center. We constantly hear stories of how people risk their own lives to help another person or animals. We call them heroes: barely knowing how to swim, a person jumps in icy waters to help rescue passengers of a crashed plane; a black man saves a white bigoted neighbor from a house fire; a soldier goes against every survival instinct and jumps onto a grenade to save his fellow buddies. After a tornado in my hometown, which was actually called Hometown, I personally witnessed people with no concern for their own lives, searching for survivors in crumbled homes with gas leaks.

If there is no soul and we're just humans composed of animalistic tendencies, how can you explain those people who went against their prejudices, their fears, and even their most primal survival instincts? From my reasoning, you can't, unless there is something within us that is stronger than our own egos, stronger than our minds, stronger than our most basic drive to survive. In the presence of tragedy, the soul-self can trump the ego-self and connect with others by providing service with love and compassion. Even in the horrible tragedy of 9/11, there were hundreds if not thousands of people instantaneously unfolding their souls. In fact, most of the world connected over thousands of miles, disregarding their differences of governments, religions, races, and genders to support one another; that is the very definition of Spirit.

Soul Inside or Outside

"It is not the end of the physical body that should worry us. Rather, our concern must be to live while we're still alive—to release our inner selves from the spiritual death that comes with living behind a façade designed to conform to external definitions of who and what we are."
Elisabeth Kubler-Ross

How can you allow your soul to show up more in your daily life? The answer to that question depends on your answer to "Who am I?" Do you believe Spirit is at your core or are you just a Physical being along for a short, one-way ticket ride? If you believe that this world is all that there is, you'll create a reality based on that belief. A French philosopher and priest, Pierre Teilhard de Chardin, stated that instead of our being a physical body trying to have a spiritual experience, we are a spiritual being having a physical experience. If you believe the former, you'll most likely search outside of yourself to unfold your soul. This quest is more likely to fail because your spirit is inside you. If you believe you're a spiritual being having a physical experience, you will be more inclined to go inward for your answers and probably struggle less in life.

You can look outside for help in living a soulful life, such as with religion, but eventually your journey has to go within. Spirituality and religion are not necessarily mutually exclusive or inclusive. As I mentioned earlier, you can be spiritual and not religious; you can be religious and not spiritual; or you can be spiritual and religious. Most religions have set themselves up as intermediaries and have created their own unique guidelines for what you can do to align with your soul. Some people choose other types of guidelines, and some people make up their own. Please follow whatever rules, rites, or rituals that bring you inward to your soul.

Purpose of the Soul

The purpose of your soul, the meaning of your life, is yours to discover. Believe me, often I'd love to be told my purpose so I could get on with my life. But if I think about it just a little, what kind of life would that be? If I knew everything in advance, all the mysteries, all the details, I'd be bored. I'd also be a puppet, a robot, a player within the Matrix with machines, gods, or others dictating my life. Where's the fun in that?

Breathe!

The best advice to help you grasp your soul's purpose is to focus more on the *how* and less on the Ws; who, where, when, or what. We all tend to focus on the following: who you should be in life—a doctor, an accountant, a city worker, a mechanic; where you should be—in a city, by the ocean, in the mountains, in this country or Italy; when you should be—today, tomorrow, in your 20s, your 50s; or what you should have—X amount of money, sex, and fame. All the Ws above are things, labels, places, and situations that are outside of you—costumes, venues, and props. You can have all the Ws that you ever dreamt of in life and still not be truly happy; look at Elvis Presley, Marilyn Monroe, and Janis Joplin. Your and their unhappiness occurs when you think you should be fulfilling the Ws and your ego's needs rather than the how and your soul's needs.

Finding purpose in your life is more about *how* you are living. The *how* relates to the intent behind your action. The *how* is about a way of living. The *how* is about fully embracing the components of your soul: connection, knowingness, and love. The *how* is about being compassionate, grateful, forgiving, and loving. Living this way enables you to be that way to others. *How* are you of service to others, and therefore yourself? *How* are you *being* in every moment? To be "in purpose" with your soul means you are "in spirit"—inspired—and consciously, lovingly connecting with everyone and everything. It doesn't make any difference who you're with, what you're doing, or when and where you're doing it; just focus on *how* you are doing it. Just do any *thing*, any action, lovingly and I guarantee you'll be following your soul's purpose.

"The spirit of man is more important than mere physical strength, and the spiritual fiber of a nation than its wealth."
Dwight D. Eisenhower

Reveal Your Soul

I visualize my soul as a scented bubble rising from the depths of my unconscious. There is no work in making it manifest; there's just allowing it to effortlessly float upwards. Once it connects with the surface of my consciousness, the bubble pops, sharing the depth of its knowingness, the fragrance of its love.

Here is another way to look at how our consciousness perceives the soul, our authentic-self. Imagine your spirit as a ball of light. Your body is like a fine, sheer, gossamer fabric that encapsulates this pure light, subduing some of the warm and loving light. Each soulless conditioning of parents, family, community, institutions, religions, and media is another cloth covering your soul. As you develop within your culture, you eventually become conditioned by so many different outside influences that you and others barely recognize your soul's light.

Your struggle to be authentic is to consciously examine each of those pieces of fabric, removing those that no longer serve your soul. Each time you accomplish that task, you'll experience more connection and knowingness within yourself; you'll feel more love, compassion, gratefulness, and forgiveness radiating from your essence. Each time you throw off another unbalanced conditioning, your light shines through a little stronger and the world within you and around you becomes slightly more illuminated. This is a lifetime project. There are many layers of cloth that surround you, so just enjoy the light show as you slowly unfold your soul.

Meditation

"What have you gained from meditation?"
The Buddha replied, "Nothing!"
"However," the Buddha said, "let me tell you what I have lost:
Anger. Anxiety. Depression. Insecurity.
Fear of old age and death."

To have our spirit show up in daily life requires us to listen to the voice of our soul. This soul voice is very soft, because it emerges from deep within our unconscious. We really have to become quiet to gets its messages. That's why meditation has been used throughout the ages and is found within all religions. It is one of the few keys that allow happiness and peace in your life. Through the objectivity of being in a meditative state, you can move into your unconscious and begin to discern the difference between the ramblings of the ego-self and the messages of the soul. Being in that meditative state naturally raises your frequency, thus allowing you to experience more connection, forgiveness, empathy, gratefulness, and compassion.

Adhering to the principle that *Energy Must Flow* allows you to fully experience meditation with the flow of breath through your physical body, the flow of feelings through your emotional body, the flow of thoughts through your mind, and the flow of love through your connection to self and Source. The very act of meditation unfolds your soul, by creating a state of non-resistance and acceptance, and therefore a state of love.

Working out and meditation have a lot in common. Both activities relax your physical body, release emotional energy, focus your mind, and create a connection with your self. We dread doing both activities in the beginning, but quickly feel the positive effects and eventually attain the desire to do them rather than not. The effects of following through with a workout routine are beneficial not only while you're doing the activity but also afterwards. Similarly, the effects of developing a meditation practice not only help in that peaceful moment but also enable you to more easily reduce stress, make clearer decisions, let go of thoughts and feelings, be in the moment, and handle difficult situations. Getting into shape builds your Physical muscles while meditation builds your Spiritual muscles. When challenging times occur, and they always do, we need to be in shape—PIES shape.

"Meditation is painful in the beginning but
it bestows immortal Bliss and supreme joy in the end."
Swami Sivananda

Thoughts are Always Present

Meditation is the process of non-attachment, allowing energy to flow. Meditation isn't a matter of not having mind; it's just a matter of using your mind differently. Use your mind to notice your thoughts and then let them go. Training your mind to become more focused and less erratic is a beginning. Guide your mind to focus on something like a candle flame or your breath. Giving your mind a seemingly meaningless task allows you some reprieve from the barrage of your scattered thoughts. This momentary peace will allow the voice of your intuition and your soul to become louder. Think of your kids screaming around your house as thoughts bouncing around in your mind. If they were quiet or, better yet, napping, you'd have alone time for regeneration, some brief precious moments of quietness, and a sense of calm to ascertain your inner needs.

Know that everyone complains about having thoughts run through their mind while meditating. Meditation is *not* about having an empty mind and creating a stagnant state of nothingness. What if a swimmer told you that they got upset about too much water being in their way? You'd react with disbelief and dismay about their frustration. They obviously need the water to swim. The tension between the water's resistance and the swimmer's continued practice builds strength for their becoming physically strong. So why should we be upset about our mind being present during meditation? We need our mind to effectively meditate. The tension between the mind's resistance and our continued practice of letting go builds the strength to make us emotionally, mentally, and spiritually strong.

101

Know that your mind will *always* be busy. Expecting anything else brings about self-judgment about not being good enough. That erroneous belief will play into your avoidance of meditation, because no one wants to do an activity that creates disappointment. So give yourself permission to have your thoughts, and hopefully you can then relieve yourself of any guilt and false expectations.

> *"At the end of the day, I can end up just totally wacky,*
> *because I've made mountains out of molehills.*
> *With meditatioin, I can keep them as molehills."*
> Ringo Starr

A Way of Being, Not Doing

> *"Meditation is all about the pursuit of nothingness.*
> *It's better than the best sleep you've ever had.*
> *It's a quieting of the mind.*
> *It sharpens everything,*
> *especially your appreciation of your surroundings.*
> *It keeps life fresh."*
> Hugh Jackman

Deep, conscious breathing within meditation is a key to our innermost desires for peace and happiness. So why do we shy away from this practice? The major reason is our societal conditioning, which has taught us the exact opposite. We've been taught "to do" rather than "to be." "Idle hands are the devil's workshop" is an old, puritanical idiom that has permeated American and Western society. This belief has transmuted into "We must keep busy!" If you're just sitting there, you aren't accomplishing anything, you're not doing anything, you must be lazy.

The lack of clarity surrounding the answer to the question "Who am I?" is another reason why we don't introduce meditation into our daily lives. Not addressing this query can lead us to being unconscious and remaining in a state of vagueness about the essences of our lives. This fogginess allows society to supplant "Who am I?" with its question "What should I be doing?"

This perspective and lack of clarity leads us to live our lives on the surface and not at the core. At the end of each day, we're vaguely aware that our frantic lives are filled with chores, errands, work, driving, doing, and more doing. Even though we might not be doing the *right* things or be soulfully satisfied, we can say, "Look I'm busy, I'm working, I'm doing something, therefore I'm important." This unconscious perspective allows minimal satisfaction to our egos. The consequence of this mindless behavior is that it doesn't allow us to get in touch with our self, our core, including our true desires and wants. This nonsensical, rote behavior is fertile ground for us to stay within the status quo, being mindless consumers and hapless followers of institutional urgings. Our collective individual behaviors then manifest in the masses and create a Matrix culture.

Meditation allows us to just *be* in the moment. *Being* indicates that you are in the present moment, you are aware, and you are connecting with your self. Within that time of just *being*, that silence, the shrouds of your mind will fall away, allowing you to discover your spirit. Give yourself permission to take time out of your busy life and create silence. There is value in that behavior. Balance is the key to all of your endeavors, so incorporate *being* into your daily life of *doing*.

Main Points

- Knowingness, connection, and love are the key components of your soul.
- The soul is experienced and known rather than recognized and understood.
- Allow your soul to surface through silence and meditation.

Questions

- How have you experienced your soul?
- How have you felt the spirit in other people, places, and situations?

- What do you believe is your soul's purpose?
- How can you allow more of your spirit to show up in your daily life?

Challenges

- Within your challenges, where is your spirit shining and where is it not?
- What steps can you take to be more authentic, more soulful?

Affirmations

- I am of spirit.
- Spirit manifests through me in all that I do.
- I am consciously connected to the Divine.

***

Reflections and Corrections

Taking time for yourself is the most difficult thing to do when life's unending demands constantly grab for your attention. For most of us, our mind and Intellect are like a hyped-up child on sugar. The hardest thing to do is to slow down and allow yourself to relax, but it is also what you need the most. Meditation, like breathing, is one of the few keys to achieving our desires. Ask anyone who has ever meditated, and I'll bet you they never say it's horrible or makes matters worse. Sure, they may say it's difficult, different, or maybe uncomfortable. But anyone who has made it their practice says it is an integral part of keeping their life in balance. How else are you going to know your authentic soulful-self if you don't create a space to allow that part of yourself to surface?

I came to meditation through a different doorway. To say I was an active child would be a bit of an understatement. When I was a child, if I sat down for just a minute, I'd unconsciously begin an annoying habit. While keeping the ball of my foot on the floor, I'd nervously bounce my leg up and down. Another nervous habit that drove my parents crazy was pacing back and forth at the back of the room while I watched TV. I was full of energy. I'm not just talking about my own observations. The nickname given to me was "Tilt." (Even the kids, now adults, of my ol' buds from Chicago call me that name.) To this day, I'm still not sure how I got that nickname, but I believe it described me to a tee; I was like a pinball bouncing back and forth and eventually causing the machine to light up "Tilt."

During high school and college, I'd always be busy doing something, rarely sitting back and taking life easy. Even through my adulthood, after work I'd fill my time with playing sports, being in community theater, and hanging out with my buddies. It was a rarity for me to be home at night more than once a week. (That behavior was also one of my faults that led to the end of my first marriage.) The peak of my "busy" was when I owned a floating houseboat restaurant in Key West. The stress level is always high in any restaurant business but, because I and my partner had to be there at 6am and close up around 11pm seven days a week, it was insanely high.

After the boat sank and I moved to San Diego, I consciously decided I wanted to do things differently. So when a friend told me about how yoga could improve my ability to play sports into my old age, I had to try it. My first session was a challenge. I had to consciously breathe, slow down, and keep my focus on the present, all the opposites of how I'd been living my life. After shivasana, a final relaxation posture, I literally felt transformed. I never knew how tight my body and mind were until I felt how relaxed I could become. My yoga experience made it easier for me to transition into meditation. It was the beginning of the end of "Tilt." Yoga, breathing, and meditation play a humongous role in creating balance in your life, in stripping away the layers, in revealing your authentic-self. If you're beginning your journey, let me get you started with the basics of meditation.

"Remember what people used to say about meditation?
Now everyone is doing it."
Shirley MacLaine

Meditation

There are many diverse methods of meditation, so to get you started I'll briefly mention some basic types. Remember, it doesn't make a difference which one you choose; just use the one that suits you for the present moment.

Mantra Meditation is repeating a saying or chant, such as "Om Shanti, I am that I am, I am that, I am…" or even one of your own affirmations, such as "I am loving, I am forgiving, I am resilient." Focus your mind on the intention of each word.

Sound Meditation is vocalizing a sound, such as "Om," and, if you choose, raising or decreasing the pitch. I usually start low and then move up one note at a time to an octave; notice where these notes resonate in your body. You don't have to be on pitch but, in my workshops, I use a mini-xylophone to help.

Guided Meditation is accomplished by following the suggestions and guidance of a person or CD. (I will soon release a "Balance" meditation CD to assist you.)

Spiritual Meditation is communication with the Source, God, Divine, or whatever that might be for you. Examples might be saying prayers during times of Lent, Shabbat, or Salat, or using prayer beads.

Focused Meditation places the attention of the mind on an object, place, sound, or process. Examples might be a candle flame, tree, rock, lake, chants, or your breathing.

Movement Meditation is accomplished by moving slowly as you focus on your body or surroundings. Saunter in a Zen garden or labyrinth. Walk slowly from one end of your backyard to the other, noticing everything that falls in your sight; take two to five seconds for each step, feeling the movement, balance, and tension of your feet, legs, and breaths. Try a modified form of this when you are hiking and notice how it changes your experience. Children do this all the time as they run in nature and focus on a butterfly, then an ant, then a blade of grass, and then their little finger. You can also practice Tai Chi, or just close your eyes as you move your hands or arms slowly in a repetitive movement.

"Everyday I try and do breathing exercises, meditation, and yoga.
These things sound awfully cliché,
but they help me slow down and try to point to a truth."
David Duchovny

Body Meditation—Sit in a comfortable and upright position for ten minutes. Take your shoes off and close your eyes. Make a mental note of your tension or state of relaxation, of different parts of your body.

Breathe deeply, filling your upper chest, and then slowly exhale. Don't force your breath; just find your own natural rhythm. Imagine a warm, comforting relaxation starting from the top of your head and then slowly melting down your face. Relax the back of your head and forehead, then eyebrows, eyelids, and eyes. Relax the bridge of your nose, cheeks, lips, chin, and jaw. Relax your ears, neck and shoulders. Feel a warm sensation easing through all of your back muscles to your lower back.

Then place your awareness on relaxing your throat, and let that warm blanket of relaxation slowly move through all of your viscera. Relax your pelvic area and hips, then gradually move the relaxation down your thighs, knees, calves, ankles, feet, and eventually toes.

When you're done, take three deep breaths, then make another mental note of how different you feel from when you started.

Practice this procedure as many times as you want during the week. You can't overdose on this prescription for balance.

Research the many different types of meditation and tools to use. Experiment with them and use the ones that are more comfortable for you.

Here is my advice whether you are a newbie or a seasoned pro. When you try to meditate, if your mind is very busy, loud, and running all over the place, know that is the time when you most need to meditate. Instead of backing off, please try a meditation method that grabs your busy mind, such as a guided meditation, a repeated mantra, or a sound meditation.

Keep in mind that open-eyed meditation keeps your focus on the outside and assists you in connecting with the object of your gaze, and closed-eyed meditation keeps your focus inward and assists you in connecting with your heart and soul. I can't stress enough the importance of meditating, even if it is only for five to ten minutes a day. Remember, meditation is not about *not* having thoughts and feelings. No matter how Spiritual you are, everyone's mind is chatty at times.

Workings of the Universe

7

The Universal Principles

*These guidelines, which are not written down and are
therefore invisible, have not been created by others or by ourselves
but are a reflection of what is found deep within the workings of
our lives and the Universe.*

There is a cosmic order to the Universe. If we can just sit back
and observe its beautiful, intricate, and simple workings, we can
align ourselves with its rhythm. The Universal Principles (UPs) are
guidelines for our journey through life. They can be seen, to some
extent, as generalized physical laws of the Universe and as laws of
spirituality. These principles apply to many things, seen and
unseen, but especially to our PIES—our Physical, Intellectual,
Emotional, and Spiritual aspects.

Everything is Energy.

Energy is Interconnected.

Energy Just Is.

Energy Moves Towards Balance.

Energy Must Flow.

Energy Has A Vibrational Frequency.

Energy Attracts Like Energy.

Energy Designs Form.

Energy is Limitless and Powerful.

These UPs are what I've gleaned from quiet moments in meditation, reading books, observing nature, coaching clients, and counseling families—basically, my experience of living life. Primarily, though, I'd like to think of them as just common sense that anyone could gather by simply and objectively observing our personal and collective journeys. Whether or not you've been conscious of these UPs, I believe they've always been in place and apply to much of our physical world as well as the metaphysical world.

For the Skeptics

When I talk about energy, many of my techie and scientific friends have stated that I'm not really talking about the same energy as physicists. My answer has always been "Yes, I am!" though neither I nor present science can prove all of it just yet. My purpose in using the UPs is not to have any scientific discussions or prove any physical laws, but rather to provide a context that makes it easier to navigate through the unseen world of thoughts and emotions. So I ask you to see these UPs not as literal or definitive but as broad concepts that may help you grasp your internal interactions with yourself and the world around you.

I've been involved in many discussions about science and metaphysics: does ESP exist, can *things* exist in the metaphysical world, is there an afterlife, what is consciousness, what is a soul, and what determines reality. I like asking the question "Can something still be real if, at the present, it can't be fully proven scientifically?" I then retort to those friends and students with a question: "What is or has been the most important *thing* in your life?" After listening to hundreds of people, I've found the general responses, when boiled down, are usually the same—love. Even if love isn't in their top ranking, most people believe that love does exist. So if love is present in your life and might be the most important thing in your life, prove it. You can use all your science, all your technology, all your logic, and all your rationalization, but there is no way you can prove the existence of the most meaningful thing in life—LOVE. But it does exist, so there must be ways beside left-brain analysis and scientific methods to *know* the existence of matters just outside of our mind's reach.

> *"The greatest thing you'll ever learn*
> *is just to love and be loved in return."*
> eden ahbez

Many teachings, experiences, and references of the mystics, yogis, and "Enlightened Ones" might one day be explained by science. Quantum physics is just at the starting gate of explaining such things as bi-location, particles travelling backwards and forwards in time, and the presence of multiple dimensions.

So I ask a favor from those of you who might be skeptical or more factually oriented. Temporarily place some of your rational and logical inquiries on a shelf when reading this book. Allow a little more of your right side of the brain—the intuitive, holistic, and subjective—to absorb the material. As when learning golf or tennis, there is a time to analyze the parts of the game, the mechanics, and the logical side of the sport. There is also a time when you just have to exercise the feel of the game without using your brain. It's about balance, so just allow your higher-self to feel the validity of the UPs and then go back and pick up from the shelf your logical side.

> *"The day science begins to study non-physical phenomena, it will*
> *make more progress in one decade than in all the previous*
> *centuries of its existence."*
> Nikola Tesla

Happiness Follows the Universal Principles

Think of each of these principles as having a scale from one to ten—one being you never live your life in accordance with this principle, and ten being you always live your life in accordance with this principle. If you're close to a ten, you're probably a reincarnation of Jesus, the Buddha, or Lao Tse and certainly don't need to be reading this book, unless of course you enjoy reviewing a different perspective of how to be in balance.

Remember, no matter where you might place yourself on that scale, you're never stationary. You might be at a four and move to a six, then drop down to a five before going up to a seven. At any given period in your life, or even during your day, you're moving towards either one or ten. Just as in the stock market, the daily fluctuations don't really matter but the overall trend certainly does.

I've seen and experienced that the closer you are to one, the more you feel unhappiness, depression, a lack of purpose, pain, and no realization of your potential. The closer you are to ten, the more you feel happiness, engagement with the world, a sense of purpose, peace, and a realization of your potential. I've been teaching these principles for over twenty-five years and have witnessed this truth 100% of the time; I have never seen an exception yet.

Choose Your Pain

Using the UPs promotes growth, which requires change. This process always brings some form of discomfort or pain. Don't let your fear of change dissuade you from applying these principles. Realize there is a difference between ego-pain and soul-pain. There is the pain of letting go of your ego, in order to serve your soul. This pain is like the prick of a pin; it is immediate but tends to be short-lived. Then there is the pain of moving away from your soul to satisfy your ego. Soul-pain tends to be more cancerous; in the beginning, there is a faint awareness of something amiss, but if not dealt with over time it becomes deep and disabling. Pain is a necessary part of life. Choose your pain wisely.

Signs to Follow

Two factors come into play as we drive through life: what signs we notice and who is driving. As we literally drive, we use several types of signs—such as information, marker, warning, and regulatory—to keep us on our path and arrive safely. Informational signs tell us what path to take in order to arrive at a certain destination, such as a hospital, library, or convention center. Marker signs tell us what road we are on, such as I805 or Highway 60. Warning signs alert us to dangers that are ahead, such as street closures, railroad tracks, and curves. Mostly, there are signs that tell us what to do—or not do—on our journey: Stop, Speed, Wrong Way, No Parking, Yield, Pass with Care, One Way, Do Not Enter, and Do Not Pass.

As we figuratively drive through life, there are similar signs that are supposed to make navigating trouble-free. The easiest signs and guidelines to identify are the ones others create, which are written down for all to see. One example might be if your destination was to be a proper citizen. Informational signs—such as constitutions, citizenship guidelines, ordinances, and laws—would assist you on your journey. You could then easily follow the regulatory signs (Pay Taxes, Obey Laws, Stop) to keep from going against the main traffic, and Do Not Enter to avoid certain places. If you didn't want to cause or be in any trouble, you could heed the warning signs—Go Directly to Jail, Pay Fines, or Tax Audit Ahead.

Breathe!

Another example might be signs placed by your religion, if your destination was to get to heaven. Informational signs, which guide you to be in God's graces, could be the New Testament, the Bible, the Ten Commandments, or the Qur'an. Some regulatory signs on how to get to heaven might look like this: Go to Church, Do Not Die (with a mortal sin on your soul), No U Turns Allowed (there is no reincarnation), Do Not Drive On The Other Side of the Road (homosexuality is discouraged) Do Not Follow (signs of other gods or religions), Do Not Enter (into premarital sex), etc. You will certainly see the warning signs of Go Directly to Hell or Excommunication.

Many of those written signs can be confusing and conflicting. Our uncertainty while driving through life heightens because many of our guidelines are invisible. Some of them are the unwritten taboos, customs, traditions, and mores of varied cultures: shake with your left hand, not your right; bow your head when greeting another; no dancing allowed; no direct eye contact; only speak when spoken to. There are many other invisible signs about how you relate to women, men, your God, and foreigners. Go against those unwritten signs and you could be in trouble, from getting a fine to getting killed.

Other invisible signs we create for ourselves depend on our life experiences. When a woman says "no" it might mean "yes," when my father calls me it means I'm in trouble, if someone yells at me I need to be acquiescent, when I lose my job it means I'm a loser. This list goes on and on. These signs are created from our minds, and we learn them through the conditioning we've received from parents, the media, and society.

"Let the mind be enlarged...to the grandeur of the mysteries, and not the mysteries contracted to the narrowness of the mind."
Francis Bacon

Who is Driving Your Life?

Addressing the issue of who is driving your life means considering each role you play. Each of us is composed of many different selves—such as parent, husband, sister, employee, citizen, and consumer—which all have their own sets of signs to follow. Our ego-self and soul-self also follow very different rules, along with our varied gender roles. You could be an American, consumer, Latino, Christian, sister, wife who comes more from the ego-self. You could be a Persian, employer, Muslim, widower, uncle who comes more from the soul-self. The combination and varied degrees are infinite. Each of those people will pay attention to a different set of signs that relate to each of those selves, some of which are written down, invisible, created by others, or created by the person's own life experiences. Considering all of the above, there will certainly be conflict between some of those roles.

So how do we get anywhere? How do we prevent ourselves from driving in circles? Well, just like when you drive a car, you can only have one driver but that driver needs to take into consideration the other people in the car, such as their spouse or children. That driver is determined by the part of your self, or role you are playing, that is dominant at that particular moment, whether it is conscious or unconscious. Many times, the driver is determined by the self that is in the most pain, and their goal is usually to drive to a destination that gives them pleasure or at least lessens the pain.

Is the child driving or the adult, the ego or the soul, the father or the wife, the poor man or the rich woman? For the same reason that each driver will notice and use different signs to arrive at a destination, each driver will drive differently depending on their skills and experience. Just like the drivers on our highways, they could be cautious or reckless, slow or fast, conscious or unconscious.

In life, there are hundreds of decisions to make: should I have fish or meat, stay at work or pick up the kids later, turn right or left, sleep or go out partying, stop or go, do this or do that. All those different aspects of you that are present in the car will be fighting for control. Hence, you will be stressed and probably have several accidents along the way, accompanied by some discomfort and pain.

Besides our different selves, we also have our PIES. In order for your PIES to move towards balance, it needs to follow a different set of signs—the Universal Principles, the guidelines of the Universe. These procedures, which are not written down and are therefore invisible, have not been created by others or by ourselves but are a reflection of what exists deep within the workings of our lives and the Universe. By paying more attention to those guidelines, you can ferret out the signs that do not allow for living authentically. The UPs are reminders of how the Universe operates, which actually simplifies your journey. No matter what road you take, what role you're playing, what relationship or business you're in, or what country or culture you live in, these principles are helpful. If you pay attention to them, you can make real-time adjustments while driving through life.

My advice is to have only your PIES drive your car. If you want your journey to be enjoyable, you'll need each of your PIES, your drivers, to collaborate. Your decisions will have far better consequences if they are made in a way that considers the input from all four.

These UPs are nothing new. You can see bits and pieces of them in books, religions, science, films, workshops, and teachings. You can experience them by being aware of the consequences of your thoughts, feelings, and actions. Hopefully the UPs will become another reference or map that is available to you in your internal library. Incorporating them into your PIES will provide a safer and smoother drive through life.

Main Points

- The Universal Principles are the primary set of signs and guidelines for your life.

Questions

- What signs have you followed in your life?
- Where did they lead you?
- What types of signs do you follow now?

Challenges

- What signs have you followed that have led you to your listed challenges?

Affirmations

- I am consciously living my life through the Universal Principles.
- The Universal Principles presently flow through my thoughts, feelings, and actions.

***

Reflections and Corrections

Over the years, as I've worked through seemingly similar challenges, I've made judgments about my lack of progress. Being jobless—after my restaurant sank and then, years later, when I was laid off from General Dynamics. Being divorced—after four years of marriage and then, thirty years later, getting married again only to divorce again after four years. Being moneyless—after creating several successful businesses only to find myself in financial crises again. Many of us run away from problems—women, men, or certain situations—only to find ourselves once again facing them in a different situation, a different time, a different manifestation. At times, I certainly felt like I was going backwards. The biggest example for me was seeing myself as a "teacher of this balance stuff" for over twenty years and yet experiencing my triple-whammy challenge. I'd chastise myself for being in a supposedly similar situation and then experiencing bouts of negativity, guilt, and self-criticism.

My self-judgments were mostly based on an erroneous expectation that, once I became aware of the lesson, once I understood, once I *knew*, I wouldn't have to learn it anymore. The mental belief system was that I got it: I see. I'm done. Phew...I won't have to deal with that issue again. (For those who are old enough to have watched the TV series *Kung Fu*...I was such a *grasshopper*.)

Learning rarely occurs like turning on a light. Wisdom is more like playing a video game; as we continually make mistakes, we hopefully learn from them. When we repeat our challenges and find ourselves at the same point in the game, we need to remember what happened last time. Before, when I tried to go through the dragon gate, I got burned by the warlords. This time, I'm going to do something different; I'm going to jump to the right instead of just standing there.

The Learning Process and Layers of Knowing

"Many men go fishing all of their lives without knowing that it is not fish they are after."
Henry David Thoreau

You could be from Italy or America, take the high road or the low road, already know about all of this personal growth "stuff," or have been to the school of hard knocks, but any of those paths will have provided opportunities to learn along the way. Most of us are at least aware of the necessity of learning from our adventures, but rarely do we think or get taught about the process of learning. Every step of your learning processes requires awareness, courage, and action. Every step involves removing a layer of misinformation, a layer of conditioned thoughts, a layer of untruthfulness. Your knowledge of this process can help you grasp the difference between understanding and knowing, and assist you in uncovering the core issues in your life. You can then eliminate unneeded frustration, disappointment, and self-criticism in your journey and replace it with acceptance, satisfaction, and compassion.

Difference Between Understanding and Knowing

The definitions of understanding and knowing are typically defined from the perspective of the brain and mind. Understanding is an intellectual process requiring one to think and use concepts in dealing with people, situations, or things. Knowing can be experienced on two levels, the basic and the soulful. On the basic, humanistic level, knowing is a sense and skill acquired through information and experience. On the soulful level, it is about a deep awareness of the essence of the Universe through love and connection. Think of understanding and basic knowing as adding layers of information and perceptions, which enable you to gain a better perspective of this world. I consider a deeper level of *knowing* not as adding anything but rather removing layers of conditioning, revealing the soul to the Divine in all things.

I can know, through my mind, that the sun rises in the same general direction every day, but I might not understand, through my brain, why that happens. After gaining—adding—new information about how the earth moves within our solar system, I can then understand more completely. Even with or without that understanding, I can still *know,* through my soul, the intrinsic beauty and connection between the sun and myself. Our soulful journeys are more about this type of *knowing.*

> *"When you cease to strive to understand, you will then know*
> *without understanding."*
> Chinese proverb

Living in this dualistic world, we have a tendency to think of our journey in terms of this/that, either/or, I understand/I don't, you know/you don't. The reality of our learning process is that we rarely ever just open a door and instantly "get it." Believing that your learning process is about zeroes/ones, off/on, sets up false expectations. That kind of understanding can happen at the basic level, such as getting the concept of 9-5=4, but life is more complex; we are more complex. Because you understand the simple answer through subtraction doesn't mean you know mathematics, calculus, or fully comprehend string theory. Because you understand how babies are made doesn't mean you know the dynamics of sex, challenges of motherhood, or the complexities of relationships. As you move up the scale of complexity, your level of knowing comes in many layers. The deeper knowing requires awareness, courage, and action.

Awareness is the First Step

The beginning of your learning process starts with being conscious. You can't know anything unless you are aware of your conscous mind. When we are unconscious, we tend to become numb and inert. Staying unconscious leads us to repeat behaviors while expecting different results; Einstein stated that this was the definition of insanity. Our puppy-like focus on the constantly changing distractions of the media, other people's problems, news-created fears, and the busyness of life all move us away from our true-self. When we're aware of our thoughts, beliefs, feelings, and actions, we have the opportunity to change them if they do not serve our true intentions. We need vigilance to keep us on our soul path.

Courage is the Fuel

> *"I have learned over the years that when one's mind is made up,*
> *this diminishes fear;*
> *knowing what must be done does away with fear."*
> Rosa Parks

Awakening to our authentic-self requires us to examine our beliefs with an honest self-appraisal. There is a reason we rarely go through this process: it's painful. We've been taught to run away from pain and move towards pleasure, or at least to a place of less pain. Usually, the only reason anybody stops running and faces their demons is that the present pain of not dealing with them is greater than the perceived pain of facing them. The consequences of not dealing with those demons can lead to experiencing a slow, unconscious, mental or emotional death. Looking inwards, and taking personal responsibility for how we have created our lives, takes courage. This internal act of bravery is needed every time we face our ego-perceived shortcomings. Talk to anyone who has successfully gone through this process and they will tell you that they needed courage to move through their challenges.

Action Completes the Process

> *"I have been impressed with the urgency of doing.*

Knowing is not enough we must apply.
Being willing is not enough, we must do."
Leonardo da Vinci

This learning process is active, not passive, and requires action on your part through your Physical, Intellectual, Emotional, and Spiritual aspects. You can't be lazy, submissive, stationary, or idle during this process. *Energy Must Flow*, whether through crying, changing a belief, or helping to build a fence. I know this action phase is not always easy, but there is no other way around it, especially if you feel stuck or depressed. Your lack of action is probably what got you into your messes. Do whatever it takes to provide movement in your life.

Knowing Through PIES

Our authentic-self knows what is true or a lie, what is positive or negative, what moves us towards balance or away from it, what is ego and what is soulful. Physically, we *know* through our senses when we touch, feel, see, hear, smell, and taste our world. Our Western society has put a higher, if not exclusive, value on Intellectual *knowing*, especially through understanding. This usually involves left-brain thinking with reasoning, logic, and analysis. We need to remember that this is not the only way of knowing our world. Emotionally, we *know* ourselves, others, and the planet through our feelings. Even though this kind of Emotional knowing has mostly been discounted by the male species, it is still a valid way of experiencing our world.

Spiritually, we *know* through what many call a Divine Knowing. This occurs through our insights, intuition, or sixth sense. It is the recognition and acknowledgment of Vibrational Frequencies that are beyond the parameters of our usual PIE way of knowing. This way has been neither taught to us nor modeled in our schools, families, or businesses. Therefore our knowledge, skill, and awareness levels are extremely limited. Yet all of us have experienced, to some degree, this unexplainable sense of *knowing*. Whether or not we have followed its wisdom is another story.

After you move from basic knowing, to understanding, to deeper soulful *knowing*, there comes a realization that you already knew. This remembering is a major step on your spiritual path. Your task is to then remove the blinders that have blocked your memory of "knowing that you know." Your focus will move inwards. Your efforts in seeking answers will transmute, from gaining more information, money, and power to eliminating all conditioned thoughts and beliefs about changing the outside world.

> *"We cannot teach people anything; we can only help them discover it within themselves."*
> Galileo Galilei

When you realize that your soul-self already *knows*, you feel empowered and your journey becomes much simpler, more focused, more loving, more enriched, and more successful. All of my explanations, musings, and sharing of my concepts, beliefs, and experiences are really just ways to assist you in remembering that you already *know* this stuff. So, to reiterate, learning is not a process of learning anything new, but more of uncovering what you already soulfully know.

Level of Knowingness

> *"Nothing that can be taught is worth knowing."*
> *Oscar Wilde*

Some levels of knowingness are hierarchical and requires you to know one thing before you can know another. You need to know addition before you learn calculus. You need to crawl before you walk. You need to love yourself before you can truly love someone else. According to Maslow's Hierarchy of Needs, you need to satisfy survival needs before becoming a team player, before becoming self-actualized.

124

When it comes to our inner soulful journey, *knowingness* is an ongoing process that usually happens in layers, taking a circuitous route through our psyche. This multitude of layers ranges across Totally Unconscious, Mostly Unconscious/Somewhat Conscious, Conscious/Unconscious, Mostly Conscious/Somewhat Unconscious, and Totally Conscious.

The different aspects of our PIES and the different selves that reside within us may be at different stages of consciousness. I could be Physically conscious but Emotionally unconscious. My hurt little boy self might be unconscious but my writer-self is very conscious. I will use my own son/mother issue as an example of this learning process. Up to fifteen years of age, I was totally unconscious about the effect my mother had on me. I only became conscious when some of my physical effects of stomach problems, acne, colon disorders, and other stress-related symptoms were seemingly related to my relationship with her. Yet I still went through my teenage years staying mostly in the Unconscious and Slightly Conscious stages.

As I became older, I wanted to truly know the baggage of my childhood so that I could make better choices in my life. My journey was arduous and sometimes intense. I moved away from being Totally Unconscious after taking college classes in Communication and Psychology, which helped me understand human behavior. I continued my schooling with a Master's program in Human Relations and became a social worker. My hope was to do a better job at helping people, but I soon realized that I was really trying to help myself. Working with dysfunctional families greatly improved my knowingness of my own family dynamics and moved me to being more Conscious than Unconscious. This reflective process helped me deal with many different personal issues, such as being a pleaser, not being assertive, and shying away from powerful people. After exploring and understanding a few layers, I thought I'd completed the learning process. Believing you're totally conscious about anything leaves you with the illusion you'll never have to deal with it again. I certainly did. I felt I "got it" and didn't need to do anything more.

We All Have Core Issues

You have to know that, with complex issues like relationships, there is always more to reveal than you think. I believe we all come in to this world with what I call core issues. These are major issues that carry the same theme throughout your life and will repeat themselves in different manifestations. Many of them are embedded within our family dynamics, such as issues of patience, control, lack of love, abandonment, forgiveness, egocentricity, or being a martyr. Because of the depth of these issues, we never completely work them out, never being totally conscious of how they are disguised within many of our behavioral traits. Like eating an artichoke, the more we taste and experience and then digest each individual petal, and not in any particular order, the closer we get to the heart. There are many petals—many layers, so to speak—to experience before arriving at the true center of our being.

"The only true wisdom is in knowing you know nothing."
Socrates

You never really know it all. So remember, when you think you've completely solved a core issue, it will probably raise its head again. When it does, you might say to yourself, "Boy, what *good* is any effort I put into releasing this crap when it's going to come back and bite me?" You'll probably become self-critical, frustrated, mad, and think less of yourself. This self-recrimination occurs because you believe that the learning process is like turning on a light—that, once you've "got it," your learning process is over. Your ego-self also sets up false expectations, believing that, once you understand something, know the reasons, there is no further need to explore or examine. We forget that each learning involves many facets of the same person or situation and entwines with many other aspects of our psyche. Though I was conscious about many issues concerning my mother, I was still unconscious about others. There was still more work to be done, more layers to be unveiled. My responsibility to my soul is to work and dance through this stuff and let go of all the layers, becoming lighter and brighter in the process.

My Core Issue

"Knowing others is wisdom, knowing yourself is Enlightenment."
Lao Tse

In my relationships with women, beginning with my mother, my significant others would raise their voices when frustrated with me. (I know it's hard to believe anyone could be upset with me.) I didn't realize until I was nineteen that I'd shut down emotionally when my mother yelled at me. I moved out of my house when I was eighteen. It wasn't until four years later that I became aware that women yelling at me equated with my mother yelling at me. There are layers to go through as one becomes aware, then "gets it," and then actively and heartfully deals with all the different manifestations. Eventually, the time between the actual event and my awareness of my reaction quickened over the course of other female relationships, from weeks to days. I eventually got to the point where I immediately heard, in my mind, a loud metal door slamming shut every time my mother's or significant others' voices reached a very particular decibel level. If I had a decibel meter, I'm sure it would have been around 78db. Anything up to that point I was fine with, but, as soon as it reached that particular level, I'd shut down. This immediate awareness gave me the opportunity to deal with it in real time, which I did.

The learning process, though, does not stop with my awareness. During all those Unconscious and Conscious stages, I needed to have the courage to deal with whatever I had unearthed. This step involved taking responsibility for whatever my role was within my dysfunctional relationship. That's a big step. I had to face my fear of rejection, my fear of standing up for myself, my fear of not being liked, my fear that something was wrong with me, my fear of being a *bad* little Tommy, and my fear of being in my own power.

The next measure was to take action by changing my thoughts, feelings, and behavior towards the loud voice. When that steel door slammed, I needed to find an immediate way to open it up. I painfully learned that being closed off to someone brings you one step closer to emotional death in the relationship. Once I knew and felt that I was still okay, even if someone yelled at me, I felt strong enough to confront my mother. When I finally got the courage, which didn't happen till I was in my mid-thirties, I calmly asked questions about why she was so upset with me and what it was that that she really wanted. I told her how I felt, and that I shut down when she yelled at me, ensuring she wouldn't get whatever she wanted. Okay, I was on the right track, saying the right things, and truly kept heart-centered during the process. Lo and behold, my mother responded with...total denial. While denying ever raising her voice to me and denying being upset with me, she was yelling at me...at a level well above the 78db. Are you kidding me?!

Okay, another lesson learned. No matter how somebody responds to your genuine attempt at better communication, if they're not ready, nothing will change. I had a plethora of choices; I could continue my avoidance behavior, never talk to my mother again, never deal with the issue again, or only date mute women. But the truth of this, or of any of my situations, is that it is all about me and my life and how I choose to live it. In the end, I chose different issues to engage my mother on, and had some modicum of success. To my credit, though, I did continue to deal with the raised-voice issue with other women—and, by the way, with incredible success. No one has yelled at me for years.

Another Layer, Another Tear

The daunting learning process doesn't always stay such a struggle. Each subsequent time of experiencing a different bud of that artichoke becomes a little less of a battle and more of a dance. So after a couple of decades of going through this process, I felt I was done with my mother issues. (Again, what a grasshopper.) When writing my second book, *In the Shadow of the Sphere*, I felt my protagonist, Digger, didn't have a big enough internal obstacle to overcome. So, being a *good* author, I dove deeper into myself, my unconscious, and discovered there were still some painful gems hiding in the darkness—gems that I could use in my writing to help Digger. (Even though my mother had died three years before my first book was published, there were still things that bothered me about our relationship. Yeah, sad to say, relationships are never over, even if the person is dead or what I call being at *The Celestial Bar*. That's because it's always about you; it's your reality, not theirs. Deal with it now, so it doesn't haunt you for years to come.)

I became conscious that, when I talked about my dead mother, I'd get a little more animated with my voice and hand gestures. I felt heavy and drained after talking about her. If you still get a charge when you think, feel, or talk about someone or something, know that is a sure sign there is still work to be done. Checking in on my feelings, I discovered I felt some repressed anger. So I went to work on any scraps that were left in my unconscious mind. The process was like a deep cleaning, where there were still stains of parental conditioning that stunk of unworthiness and resentment. I soon realized that, for Digger (Okay. For me!), that forgiveness was our salvation.

There are layers and layers of the knowingness of any truth. These truths are present in many forms, and we need to realize them from many different perspectives to fully appreciate and truly know them. My journey began with one simple awareness, what I thought was going to be one lesson—that of my displeasure at my mother's yelling. But this basic insight transgressed through every aspect of my life. My journey was truly a self-journey, as I crisscrossed between dealing with her anger, her vocal outbursts, her embarrassing ways with my friends, her lack of respect for my concerns, to confronting my issues of withheld anger towards her, not feeling loved, not establishing boundaries, giving away my power, and playing the victim.

This learning process uncovered the fact that my mother did the best she could. Most of us give that core truth a passing sleight of hand and lightly say, "We all just do our best." But to really accept that fact about someone you feel resentful towards is extremely difficult. I'm not excusing her behavior or anyone else's, but, given all that she learned from her parents and all of her conditioning, she lived her life the best she could, albeit fairly unconscious. I realized that I can't judge other people on what I

129

think they should have done; I can only control my life by the way I think, feel, and act.

My process was distressing and painful, but also filled with relief and love, as I moved from being unconsciousness about the effects of my mother's yelling to consciously feeling a deep level of forgiveness. After four years of writing, Digger and I were thankful it was over.

As we all move through these layers of knowing, we can become frustrated. We need to have patience with ourselves and look for different ways to measure our success. One way of looking at progress is to observe the time it used to take you to recognize and then deal with your dysfunction compared to now. Remember, it took me twenty-some years before I became aware that I emotionally shut down when someone yelled at me. Over time, my awareness shortened from several weeks to days, to hours, and eventually to the moment. That's success.

Within each of our learning processes, there are also adjustments. As much as everyone would like our journeys to always move ahead and never backwards, the reality is that they never have and never will. Energy doesn't work that way, therefore life can't work that way. The way up to the top of the mountain is never an unending straight line. Your path might be flat, rocky, steep, clear, or bushy; you might move up and to the right, then down and to the left. You have a choice at every given moment to move in any direction. The way to measure your progress is not in each and every forward, sideward, or backward step but in the overall movement of your life.

So when you go through the layers of your learning process and experience self-induced frustration, disappointment, and self-criticism, replace it with peacefulness, satisfaction, and compassion for yourself, *knowing* that, as you act on the Universal Principles and become more conscious, your life is progressing in a soulful and loving way.

8

Everything is Energy

"We are whirling through endless space
with an inconceivable speed.
All around us everything is spinning, everything is moving,
everywhere is energy."
Nikola Tesla

Briefly exploring this first Universal Principle, one can easily drown in all the theories, definitions, and speculations. Perceiving the day-to-day world we live in as energy provides us a common denominator to perceive our seemingly crazy lives. Again, I am not trying to prove any physics laws; instead, I am providing broad strokes and concepts that can help us grasp how the outward, visible Physical can be affected by the inward, invisible aspects of Intellect, Emotions, and Spirit.

For now astrophysicists state that matter comprises about 4% of the universe, dark matter about 23%, and dark energy 73%. We have just begun to barely understand our tiny 4% of the universe and now recognize the possibility of the other 96%. Depending on whose interpretation, simply put, $E=Mc^2$ tells us that matter and mass are interchangeable, identical, equal, and different forms of the same thing. In the pseudo-spiritual-scientific community, the principle that *Everything is Energy* is widely used. I'm presenting this concept as a context to make the material I present here easier to comprehend.

Another part of this discussion involves our focus on *things* that are visible rather than invisible. The solidity of our universe includes galaxies, planets, animals, cars, rockets, insects, mountains, rivers, you, and me. We all have a tendency to define our world by what we can see and touch, and because of that focus many of us believe our universe is composed of *things*. This focus on *things* has placed a higher importance on matter, such as bodies, homes, food, cars, pools, and clothes.

Yet the overwhelming composite of our universe, of our lives, is space. When we look up into the heavens, there is mostly space, and if we study the sub-atomic quantum world, the same is true. Science has proven that atoms, which we thought were the building blocks—matter—of the universe, are only made up of .00001% matter; that leaves 99.99999% of space. This space within and between matter was and still is a confusing nothingness. Because we do not see or touch this invisible world, our mind does not gravitate towards it. Much of our lives, though, are affected by the properties that inhabit this ethereal realm. Our thoughts, emotions, and spirit not only play, create, and dance in this domain but also play a major role in the quality of our lives.

"The more you lose yourself in something bigger than yourself, the more energy you will have."
Norman Vincent Peale

We Are Energetic Beings

Your body and all of its functions are just energy. Your thoughts, perceptions, beliefs, likes, wants, needs, and desires are all just energy. Your happiness, love, hurts, and frustrations, along with your other emotions, are just energy. Your spirit is just energy. We are energetic beings. Seeing the universe as a whole composed of energies that interact, share, and create offers us the opportunity to re-think how we choose to perceive ourselves, others, the Universe, and then re-act differently—if we choose.

Perceiving yourself as an energetic being is different from perceiving yourself as a Tom, husband, writer, ballplayer, or musician. Knowing you are an energetic being requires a new roadmap for your life. The Universal Principles, along with an understanding of PIES, help navigate this energetic journey.

*"Enthusiasm is the energy and force
that builds literal momentum of the human soul and mind."*
Bryant McGill

Characteristics of Energy

Energy's major characteristics and functions are found within the UPs: *interconnection,* having *no meaning, moving towards balance.* We'll begin to discuss these in the next several chapters. To help you understand those major characteristics, I will briefly discuss the following aspects of energy: *having a frequency, needing to flow,* and *attracting similar energies,* along with axioms of *designing form* and *being limitless and powerful.*

While the principle *Energy Has A Vibrational Frequency* might not hold up to all the scientific criteria, it is a helpful tool to conceptualize energy's invisible characteristics. The concept of energy is not only cerebral but also visceral, much like feeling the vibrations of instruments within our body when listening to a live musical performance. Imagining this can help us to grasp the invisible reality that our thoughts, feelings, and actions have a vibrational energy that plucks at our PIES. Whether or not we have the present capability to actually *feel* those energies, we can still *know* they have an effect on our lives, then act accordingly.

Energy Must Flow is an obvious and integral aspect of the Universe. This principle underlines the fact that our world is in a constant state of change. Most of us place a lot of energy in attempting to keep life normal, controlled, or within the status quo. We need to remember that resistance to change is usually more painful than the actual consequences of change. The effects of living your life by restricting energy are obvious. When you hold on to Physical energy, parts of your body begin to malfunction. When you hold on to thoughts (your Intellect), you become obsessed, biased, and limited. When you hold on to Emotions, you become unforgiving, frustrated, and depressed. Your goal is to allow energy to flow in every aspect of your life. This principle is key to living life authentically, with passion and as little pain as possible.

133

If you expand your thinking to a larger scale, you can see that institutions, which are merely a mass of individuals, are subject to the same UPs. A major example is the historical attempt of governments and rulers to limit the flow of creative freedom and self-expression for their citizens. The consequences are that despots and dictators arise and revolutions, civil wars, and death soon follow.

Breathe…ah, ah, don't just go on to the next paragraph. Breathe!

Energy Attracts Like Energy is similar to the Law of Attraction. Presently this principle is the most widely talked-about concept. At its core is that your reality starts with, and will be a reflection of, your thoughts. Your energetic body—PIES—has a particular Vibrational Frequency, which will attract similar frequencies. Obviously, you need to do more than just think or believe something to make it happen. You also need to feel and then act on the thought in order to manifest your intentions. But what can't be overstated is the importance of knowing that your thoughts and beliefs are really the basis of what you experience in life. You are in control—not of others' experiences or situations, but most assuredly of how you think. And what you think will manifest in your life. Be conscious of your thoughts and feelings, then modify them to be in alignment with your soul desires.

A couple of axioms of the UPs begin with *Energy Designs Form*, which is different from energy creating form. Everything has already been created; it's just a matter of rearranging, altering, shaping, igniting, combining, and modifying what the Universe has already given us. There is not a lack of anything. Everything we need to live our lives is before us in every moment. We are like a cook who is in the ultimate kitchen, with every ingredient and tool present. All we need is our imagination and a willingness to act.

Energy is Limitless and Powerful counters the belief that we live in a world with scarce resources and power. On a Physical level, we often align ourselves with the belief that there is not enough—not enough jobs, money, women, men, food—or that we don't have enough skills, strength, knowledge, or looks to get ahead in life. The reality is that we have it all, albeit on different levels, to design what we want in life. As in being the cook, we just have to decide what it is we want and then use the appropriate tools and ingredients to make it happen.

Again, let's extrapolate this to larger issues, such as solving world hunger. How can people still go to bed hungry when there is enough food in the world to feed everyone? It's not a problem of quantity, of not having enough, but rather multiple problems of allocation, economics, geo-political issues, environmental concerns, and belief systems. Our energy crisis is not a problem of not having enough power. Look at how much power is released from splitting a few atoms. Some of the problems, including the ones I just mentioned, are lack of imagination, status quo thinking, present technology, and limited belief systems. Like a frightened child, when we perceive this world as having limited resources and power, we fight for, grab, and control as much of the resources as possible. Our world has reflected that fearful belief for thousands of years and we can see the consequences. To add an often-repeated comment from Dr. Phil, "How's that working out for you?"

"Sit down before facts like a child, and be prepared to give up every preconceived notion, follow humbly wherever and to whatever abysses nature leads, or you shall learn nothing."
T. H. Huxley

Main Points

- Everything is Energy.
- Energy is Interconnected.
- Energy Just Is.
- Energy Moves Towards Balance.
- Energy Has A Vibrational Frequency.
- Energy Must Flow.
- Energy Attracts Like Energy.
- Energy Designs Form.
- Energy is Limitless and Powerful.

Questions

- How does seeing yourself as an energetic being affect your thoughts, feelings, and actions? How does it affect the way you look at others?

Challenges

- Look at the characteristics of energy and note how understanding them might re-define any of your challenges.

Affirmation

- I am an *energetic* being.

***

Reflections and Corrections

My night of momentary anguish while slicing open cracker packages coalesced an array of thoughts and emotions. I was overcome with thoughts of negativity and self-recrimination, along with feeling overwhelmed, sad, frustrated, out of control, and hopeless. I'm sure many of you, at some time, have felt that way to some degree. No matter who you are, when your world seemingly falls apart from every angle, it's difficult to get your bearings. Everything is confusing and you don't know where to begin. I write, believe, and live this stuff and was still overwhelmed. I can't imagine trying to move through it without knowing this information in some shape or form.

Believing in this first UP, *Everything is Energy*, establishes a common denominator within the chaos of life, allowing you to address your challenges energetically. This process of working with the UPs doesn't happen overnight; it took days, weeks, months, and years. I'm still working on everything I've mentioned, even as I write the final touches of this book.

So what was I going to do with the mess in my life? I wrote down all the things that had recently happened to me—the loss of job, marriage, and home, along with all the accompanying feelings of despair, frustration, anger, and confusion.

Now that I had written it down, I felt worse. All the details, the various pieces, of my debacle stared back at me. What could I do with this avalanche of circumstances, thoughts, and emotions? Okay, I've got it! Throw it all together in the same pot, stir it vigorously, and bring it to a boil. Now take a big gulp of self-pity and then feel like I was the only one who was going through all of this stuff...ahhh...it's such a wonderful feeling...for at least a few seconds.

I stayed on the "dark side" for a moment and contemplated about driving my car to the Coronado Bridge and jumping off, two hundred feet into the San Diego Bay. With my luck, though, I'd probably be one of the rare survivors and have to swim, bruised and battered, to Seaport Village, where I'd have to traverse slippery sharp rocks till I found land. And, because I didn't have a job and had lost most of my savings, I wouldn't have any money for a taxi, so I'd then have to walk soaked through the crowded Gaslamp District of San Diego's downtown streets and watch as people gave me pity stares. Disheveled, cold, and broken, I'd continue uphill for five more miles before I reached the top of Bay Park, stumble into the house, and then crawl into my bed—alone. (Oh, I can be a drama queen at times—or is it just being a good writer…or maybe both.)

Or I could tell myself, as I actually did, that enough is enough, no more drama, no more feeling sorry for myself, no more feeling downtrodden, and no more feeling overwhelmed. All of my negative feelings stemmed from not following the guidelines of our society: stay in your marriage even though it might not be the best for you; stay in a job, any job, even if it goes against your core; do whatever it takes to have a home, because that is a sign of success. My circumstances were deemed negative by those signs in society. I was a failure, a loser, someone to be pitied.

I eventually remembered that, to get through this chaos, I had to abide by other guidelines: the Universal Principles. I knew that the common denominator between everything is…*energy*! I needed to see *Everything as Energy*; even all the unpleasant events, people, and situations. I needed to remember that my situation was somehow assisting me to *Move Towards Balance*. I needed to remember that *Energy is Interconnected*. I needed to remember that *Energy Just Is*, including my thoughts, feelings, and actions, which have no meanings other than the ones I create. I saw it all as energy, knew it to be energy, and followed the guidelines of the UPs as they applied to my PIES.

"There is no constellation or nebula, no sun or planet, in all the depths of limitless space, no passing wanderer of the starry heavens that does not exercise some control over its destiny—not in the vague and delusive sense of astrology, but in the rigid and positive meaning of physical science."
Nikola Tesla

This change of focus helped to simplify, for my mind and heart, my overwhelming situation. By remembering the characteristics of energy, I could formulate different questions and perspectives about my predicament. I couldn't continue to feel like there weren't enough jobs or money in the marketplace. I couldn't play the victim. I needed to discover where energy was not moving in my life and free it. I needed to perceive my thoughts as being energetic and change them so that I attracted positive moments.

A couple of questions that provided a change of direction were these: What kind of energy kept me from positive movements, from joy, from love? What kept me in those moments of fear, of stagnation, of unauthenticity? The answer was simple—the fear of pain.

Most steps along the way of mastering balance incorporate, to some degree, resistance. Instead of fleeing, I needed to explore and correct any false beliefs I had about pain. I needed to "boldly go where no man has (wanted to go)." I needed to face, accept, work through, and let go of pain.

> *"Your pain is the breaking of the shell*
> *that encloses your understanding."*
> Khalil Gibran

Pain

Pain is a natural condition of existence. Even though we know it is part of life, the very thought of pain makes us tense, anxious, worried, or stressed. Our reluctance to experience pain on a Physical level helps ensure our survival, but our unwillingness to experience it on an Emotional, Intellectual, and Spiritual level inhibits our personal growth. Instead of avoiding it, we need to explore its nature. The more we understand the purpose, positive and negative effects, varieties of and remedies for pain, the easier it will be to use it as an ally rather than avoid it as an enemy.

Negative Beliefs

In order to change anything, including an unexamined belief, we first need to be aware of its existence. Once a belief is brought out into the light of consciousness, we can examine its veracity. Most common beliefs about pain are negative—for example, that it should be avoided or, once felt, should be eliminated. Those beliefs morph into others—that crying is a weakness, men don't show pain, holding back emotions displays strength, I need to mask my pain. Holding on to these negative beliefs goes against the principle *Energy Must Flow*. The stark reality is that, by not allowing energy to flow, you actually create more pain.

> *"Numbing the pain for a while will make it worse*
> *when you finally feel it."*
> J. K. *Rowling,* Harry Potter and The Goblet of Fire

Positive Beliefs

The very act of changing your negative perception of pain can reduce pain. Uncovering the necessity and benefits of pain will uncover positive beliefs—for example, that pain is an integral part of life, has a message, brings us into the moment, and shows us our present limit. You can transform your beliefs about pain into these: it's to be expected, it's a warning, and, once felt, it should be dealt with. Once we've faced pain, we can decide to avoid that pain, diminish it, or cautiously proceed so as not to cause any further damage to our body, psyche, or soul.

Fear of Pain

Realize there is a difference between the actual event of pain and the fear of pain. Obviously, you should heed your appropriate survival fears, such as walking out into traffic, sauntering into a dark alley, or jumping off the roof of your house. The fear of pain that stems from these safety concerns is positive, and you should notice and then deal with it in a balanced way. Most of our fears, though, do not consist of survival or physical concerns, but rather are composed of emotional and intellectual matters. Remember, the fear of pain is almost always greater than embracing the fear. Experiencing the fear of pain doesn't necessarily mean you should run away, but rather that you should notice your fear is likely a perceived limit on what you think is possible. These fears of pain are usually associated with our past or future. Not dealing with the fear of changing a belief or behavior will keep us stagnant, inhibiting us from progressing as individuals and as a species. Fear of what might happen—of being in uncharted waters—also limits the potential of our future. Much of our day is consumed by our painful fears of not meeting our ego's needs, which usually stem from our past conditioning—for example, fearing we're not pretty enough, smart enough, rich enough, or thin enough. If we buy into the future possibility of this illusory pain, given to us by other people and advertisers, we spend money, time, and energy to alleviate it. This kind of focus not only leads us to neurosis and psychosis but also deters us from experiencing our soul.

> *"Find a place inside where there's joy,*
> *and the joy will burn out the pain."*
> Joseph Campbell

Pleasure and Pain

Everyone tries to avoid pain and move towards pleasure. Freud introduced this concept, the Pleasure-Pain Principle, as a way to explain the motivation behind our behavior. On a rudimentary Physical level, this can be easily seen and understood: keep your distance from fire, be careful of sharp objects, don't get eaten by predatory animals, put food into your stomach, find shelter, seek companionship, and enjoy sex. In reality, though, we don't always act only for pleasure. If that were the case, on a primal pleasure level, we'd have sex with anyone at any time. There is a dynamic balance constantly playing out between pain and pleasure. As our mind and emotions move through our ego and superego, we might hold off on that pleasure for fear of the pain of guilt for hurting someone else's feelings, or the fear of being ostracized by others, or the fear of being killed by another suitor.

This Pleasure-Pain Principle is a driving force of, and clearly observed through the lens of, our Physical. But as we experience life through our Emotional, Intellectual, and Spiritual lenses, the experiences and meanings of pain and pleasure become hazy. As we evolve from ego-self to soul-self, our perceptions, motivations, and choices change, re-defining pain and pleasure. This murkiness creates different parameters of pain and pleasure. Going through a divorce might bring about the pain of sadness but also the excitement of a new beginning. An adventurous person would anticipate pleasure over an upcoming river-rafting trip, whereas a fearful person might feel the pain of their fear of water. Your task is to use this driving force as a motivation to satisfy the pleasures of your soul.

> *"Illusions commend themselves to us because*
> *they save us pain and allow us to enjoy pleasure instead.*
> *We must therefore accept it without complaint*
> *when they sometimes collide with a bit of reality*
> *against which they are dashed to pieces."*
> Sigmund Freud

Physical Pain

Physical pain is an unpleasant sensory experience we associate with actual or potential tissue damage. We try to avoid pain at all costs and therefore wish for ourselves, and our loved ones, a life with no pain. Be careful about what you wish for. If you've ever known of anyone who has the physical condition CIPA, Congenital Insensitivity to Pain with Anhidrosis, you would soon realize the dire consequences of not feeling pain. You could injure or mutilate yourself without ever knowing to get medical attention, which could lead to a life-threatening situation. Remember, pain is a warning sign that brings you into the present moment and has a message. When you feel physical pain, you immediately stop what you are doing and attend to your injury. Your body yells at you, "Stop! Fix me!" which is a very positive yet unwelcomed response.

"Without pain, there would be no suffering,
without suffering we would never learn from our mistakes.
To make it right, pain and suffering is the key to all windows,
without it, there is no way of life."
Angelina Jolie

Non-physical Pain

Many of us are not aware of what is happening to our Emotions, Intellect, or Spirit during the course of the day, let alone our pain associated with those aspects. We seldom pay attention to those pains when they first occur, because there is rarely the same unpleasant initial intensity as with Physical pain. Not attending to these pains, we only notice them after they've brewed and intensified, eventually developing into a painful boil on our mind, heart, or soul. We're usually just doing, living, surviving— medicating ourselves into an unconscious state with our busyness, ignorance, drugs, and alcohol. Staying in our self-inflicted stupor for any period of time prevents us from realizing the depth of our pain. In that numbness, we tend to think everything is normal.

The process of eventually realizing this pain is similar to being in a minor car accident. Immediately after the event, you might hurt a little but still continue with your daily activities. Only afterwards, after the adrenaline or dopamine has subsided, do you realize the extent to which you're hurt. This pain from our minor Intellectual and Emotional car wrecks are masked by the adrenaline coming from our busy lives and our focus on our outside possessions, TV, and electronic devices.

All of these IES pains are caused by not adhering to the principle *Energy Must Flow*. Intellectual pain is caused by an unconscious and rigid mind lacking flexibility in beliefs, opinions, and perspectives. Emotional pain follows this rigidity and occurs because of the lower emotional Vibrational Frequencies attached to these limiting thoughts. Emotional pain is also caused by not expressing emotions. Spiritual pain is caused by the unconscious imprisonment of the soul, evidenced by a lack of connection and love in thoughts, feelings, and actions. Let's briefly look at these non-Physical pains.

Intellectual and Emotional Pain

Intellectual and Emotional pain are intrinsically connected, making it difficult to ascertain their origin and cause. The source of Intellectual pain stems from an unbalanced mind being unconscious, rigid, or ego-based. The actual pain, though, is from the ensuing Emotions brought on by those unbalanced thoughts and beliefs. Observe people who are exclusive, uncooperative, negative, or who portray a limited belief system of right/wrong, left/right, or "My way or the highway." This portion of their Intellectual process is judgmental, biased, racist, or sexist. Their corresponding Emotions will probably range from exasperation to frustration to anger to rage.

Breathe!
Feel as if your lungs are located where you feel the pain.
Do this for several minutes,
feeling the pain leave you with every exhale.

An ego-based mind is more closed than open and has limited beliefs and unrealistic expectations. Ego-pain can be easily induced by others' beliefs, opinions, or attitudes. The more you have a struggling, immature, or unhealthy ego, the larger and more sensitive it becomes. Envision walking down a busy city street with your overgrown and hyper-sensitive ego as a physical extension of your body. You'd feel lots of pain as you bumped into hordes of other people. Emotionally, this Intellectually based pain can be triggered by an apathetic comment from a loved one, a discouraging remark from your boss, a flipped finger from an irate driver, or the misbehavior of your child.

A balanced mind is conscious, reflective, and based on the higher-self. This open mind is more flexible, and therefore more accepting of others' beliefs. A general rule of thumb is that the more your mind is conscious and open, the less emotional pain you'll feel. Observe people whose words and behaviors are inclusive, collaborative, cooperative, and positive. You'll sense someone who is more at peace with themselves and exhibits the higher emotional VF of joy, contentment, forgiveness, and love.

> *"There is no coming to consciousness without pain."*
> *Carl Jung*

Spiritual Pain

Spiritual pain is the most powerful and yet the most difficult to identify. This pain can occur after only one incident but also after months or years of not living through the essence of your soul. Like Emotional and Intellectual pain, Spiritual pain is caused by not allowing energy to flow—not allowing your soul-self to blossom. Imagine the internal pain of a growing crab being kept in its shell or of a caterpillar being blocked from becoming a butterfly.

The levels of pain can begin as a growing angst or reach a full-blown, gut-wrenching soul-pain. The first time I noticed a soul-pain was when I became aware that there was something missing in my life. That pain started as a growing feeling of angst, followed by an intuitive *knowing* that I should be living my life differently. I *knew* there had to be more. The ego wants to answer that feeling and knowing with more money, a different job, more pleasure, or a different relationship. The truer answer appears when the search goes inward and the soul responds with insights about needing to think differently, feel differently, live differently, and basically *be* different from what our societies deem right. This intuitive state brings about a sense, which bubbles up from your

145

unconscious, about a dynamic blueprint of your life, which includes being happier, more loving, more loved, and more at peace with all things. I believe many people today are experiencing, to some extent, that angst, those insights, and that sense.

"History, despite its wrenching pain, cannot be unlived,
but if faced with courage, need not be lived again."
Maya Angelou

This soul-pain could arise from cheating on an exam, lying to a friend, or not acting with integrity with a business deal. You generally feel soul-pain when you go against the essence of your authentic-self. You can experience this in many different ways—for example, I once, instead of catching and releasing a big game fish, bludgeoned and killed it because I wanted to hang it on my wall. To this day, I still feel soulful regret for allowing my ego to have a trophy rather than respecting and honoring my connection to all creatures on this planet. A deeper soul-pain could be seen in a narcissistic CEO who, on their deathbed, finally becomes conscious about living a life of total personal gratification without ever caring for others; a prisoner who, after decades, soulfully realizes the devastation they caused killing another human; a father waking up after an alcoholic stupor to discover he caused a crash that killed a child. I believe that some of the psychological pain that many returning armed forces feel is, at its core, a soul-pain incurred by participating in or witnessing the killing of others. These deeper levels of pain would be my definition of a hell—a feeling of loneliness, self-torture, and agony created by the chasm of awareness between how you actually lived your life and your true-self.

"Do you not see how necessary a world of pain and trouble is
to school an intelligence and make it a soul."
John Keats

Blocked IES Pain Moves Into Other Areas

When we don't deal with our invisible IES pain, our VF decreases, thereby moving into our Physical body. All of us have felt, to various degrees, Emotional stress manifesting as Physical discomfort. Our frustrations with our children, bosses, and spouses directly connect to our beliefs and expectations. If we don't change them or express them, we'll experience blockages and pain in our Physical body. Everything from constipation to headaches, infections to insomnia, ulcers to psoriasis, and heart attacks to cancer are, if not created by these IES blockages, certainly exacerbated.

Breathe!

We unconsciously use language to reveal the IES pains manifesting in our bodies: "I can't stomach that thought." "My heart is breaking." "You sicken me." My personal experience of a Physical pain manifesting as a limiting thought happened when I was twenty-one. I didn't deal with the death of my father. My unexamined belief was that I had to be the strong one in the family. I also had a faulty belief that Emotional pain was "bad" and should be avoided. So I tried not to even think about it too much and held back my emotions when they surfaced. The pain was still there; it wasn't going anywhere, just being blocked and stored.

My reaction to my father's death is also an example of how *All Energy is Interconnected*. Since *Energy Needs to Flow*, my dammed river of thoughts and emotions eventually poured into my Physical body. I finally developed an excruciating sore throat; it felt as if I were swallowing razor blades. I went to the emergency room several times because the pain was unbearable. Over the next several weeks, the doctors never found any infection or reason for my illness. One day, I experienced an "aha" moment and made the connection between my father's death, my unconscious belief in needing to be strong, my learned behavior of holding back emotions, and my sore throat. No wonder I had a difficult time swallowing—I couldn't swallow my father's death. That awareness broke down my Emotional dam and a torrent of tears flowed over the following week. I felt better afterwards and my sore throat disappeared.

> *"To truly laugh, you must be able to take your pain, and play with it!"*
> Charlie Chaplin

Dealing with Pain

Your restrictive mind, Emotional blockages, and Spiritual stasis cause most of the pain in your life. As I've discussed, to progress in life you need to deal with your present pain and face the fears of potential pain. There is no better way to move through fire than to move through the fire. Face the pain. Feel the pain. Acknowledge the pain. Discover the root cause of the pain. Forgive yourself for creating the pain. Change and act on your findings. Thank the pain. Let the pain go.

9

Energy is Interconnected

*When you act in accordance with this knowingness,
you are in sync with the rhythm of the Universe.*

As a young kid looking up at the heavens and seeing billions of stars, I was filled with awe but also loneliness. Tens of thousands of light years of space separated me from those magical and mysterious lights. Many years later, I read *Cosmos* by Carl Sagan and learned that everything emanated from the Big Bang; helium atoms were created, then hydrogen, then carbon, until we arrived at all the elements on the periodic table. All of the universe—from furniture to buildings, rivers to forests, plants to people, and clouds to nebulae—were designed from that brilliant, creative instant. Sagan revealed that every cell of my body derived from those distant stars. So I *was* connected to the heavens. Those mystical stars and I were actually a family—a family of light.

At the core of this UP is the Universe's natural state of being. Every part of this world to some degree is connected to, and affected by, every other part. Forms of this interconnection are found within the quantum world, the cosmos, nature, relationships, humankind, and also man-made systems and psycho-social systems, to name just a few. If you see this world as being connected by an intrauniversal highway that allows energy to flow back and forth between all things, you will find it easier to navigate through life. We can witness this interconnection through our bodies and understand it through our minds, but the essence is recognized by our hearts and souls. When you act in accordance with this knowingness, you are in sync with the rhythm of the Universe. If you make an honest assessment of how many people behave and how corporations and governmental agencies establish their policies, you'll see they are not in accordance with this UP. They believe and act as if they are separate—separate from

149

themselves, separate from others, and separate from the future. Their unconscious everyday decisions and actions are in opposition to the way the Universe truly operates. Whether it is in the personal or the international arena, living life as if there is no connection, as if you're separate from others and nature, causes almost every malady on earth.

I'll briefly address the concept of Oneness, discuss the notions of reflection and of energy attracting like energy, and also define interconnection and seperateness and provide examples of their consequences.

Oneness

Quantum physics is beginning to explain what the mystics have known throughout the ages: we are all One. You can see this Oneness in the different aspects of PIES. If you were able to see yourself, in the sub-atomic world, sitting in a chair or hugging a friend, you wouldn't see any separation, just energy fields that are intermingled. Physically and Emotionally, we might experience Oneness with another person while making love or while pregnant. Intellectually, we rarely experience that sense, but certainly there are moments. Einstein and others have certainly tapped into it at times, as well as artisans who have briefly found themselves in moments of inspiration and creativity. Emotionally, the one true emotion is love. When you are truly in love with another person or any aspect of nature, you experience not a lack of separation but a feeling of Oneness.

Spiritually, people from the Buddha to Jesus to the Dalai Lama have spoken about our common heritage of Spirit. If you believe in a monotheistic God that created the universe, then we all have to be products of that creation, such as the Big Bang. If you believe that your soul is a holographic clone of the Divine Source, you might sense that we are all One. This notion is heavily present within Eastern philosophies, and I believe it is at the heart of all religions. At its core, Oneness involves the very definition of Spirit—feeling a loving interconnection to the Source, the Universe, and all energies.

Interconnection

*"You and I are all as much continuous with the physical universe,
as a wave is continuous with the ocean."*
Alan Watts

Even if you can't logically comprehend that we are all One, I feel you can still Intellectually grasp how this world is intrinsically interconnected. This principle is a truth that transcends all Physical and metaphysical disciplines. While science and spirituality have seemingly been at odds over the last several centuries, they are now treading the same waters. Every field of physics, humanities, economics, medicine, and psychology is beginning to realize this principle is in play at all times. The rapid increase of the population, spread of information, and other manifestations of globalization have made interconnection much more apparent. While one can argue the level or degree of the effect of this interconnection, this principle has been present throughout the ages.

Newtonian physics and quantum mechanics have unveiled a relationship, an interconnection, between all different forms of energy. The obvious event that dramatically shows the interconnection between the infinitely small and the infinitely large is the Big Bang. What happened between sub-atomic particles quickly, cosmologically speaking, affected the formation of the galaxies and our world. Subsequently atoms, molecules, bacteria, plankton, and DNA all interconnected to form our world. The planets within our solar system affect the earth with their gravitational pull, which then affects the shape of the earth, which then affects our climate. The activity of the sun affects our earth in many ways, but one is by reducing the ozone layer, which then cools the stratosphere, which causes temperature contrasts, which then causes varying distributions of storms. Weather conditions in the Sahara affect the development of hurricanes heading towards the United States, which then affect the lives, infrastructure, insurance companies, stock market, and so on in the U.S.

Over the last few decades, interdependence—which presupposes interconnection—has been a subject much written about. These papers discuss such topics as the relationships between military use and international policies, thoughts and water molecules, social media and society, computer networks and information structures, consciousness and behavior. You can read any of the hundreds of theories and essays by just doing some quick research on the internet, which itself is an interconnective tool for information that affects our lives in a myriad of ways.

The effects of this interdependence, interconnection, can be felt worldwide, as demonstrated by the 2008 American housing crisis; an African dictator instigating genocide; a hurricane devastating the east coast; the tragedy of 9/11; the Arab Spring arising after Mohamed Bouazizi burned himself in Tunisia; flu epidemics; the spread of AIDS, STIs, and Ebola; the use of pesticides on crops; Russia taking over Crimea; the U.S. sending a man to the moon; ISIL running rampant through the Middle East; the creation of an aerosol can; or Princess Diana's death.

> *"Learn how to see.*
> *Realize that everything connects to everything else."*
> Leonardo Da Vinci

Take a look at this interconnection through the lens of PIES. As Physical human beings, we are connected to every other human and mammal. We share 99% of the same genes as monkeys and 99.9% of the same genes as every person who has ever been born on this planet. Your body is totally interconnected. What happens in your circulatory system affects your nervous system. Your blood chemistry affects your brain function. Your liver affects almost every other organ. Walking with a limp after ankle surgery affects different bones and muscles. Your Physical balance—diet, rest, and exercise—affects how you think. How you think affects your feelings. How you feel affects your body. How you are in alignment—or not—with your soul affects your PIE.

Investigative journalist Lynne McTaggart, in her book *The Field*, reveals that we are a packet of pulsating power constantly interacting with energy and that our consciousness literally shapes our world. Recent research reveals that thoughts, positive or negative, physiologically affect our biology, as Bruce Lipton discusses in *The Biology of Belief*. Many studies have concluded that music directly affects your brain and your emotions, which in turn positively affects your health. Dr. Masaru Emoto has shown how consciousness affects the molecular structure of water. Presently, there are numerous research studies being conducted that address interconnections previously thought not to be possible. There are, obviously, some criticisms about these studies, but what is evident is the increasingly open attitude and mind about the many possibilities of interconnection.

> *"No man is an island entire of itself.*
> *Each is a piece of the continent, a part of the main."*
> John Donne

We do not, and cannot, live in a bubble. We are social beings and require connections to others, not only for our Emotional and Intellectual needs but also for our survival. Who you are as a person affects, to different degrees, your siblings, parents, children, classmates, co-workers, and neighbors. Your neighborhood, being affected by its constituents, manifests many degrees of interconnection—jobs, crime, economy, roads, and resources— with other neighborhoods, which in turn affect other communities. Ripple this out, like a pebble in a pond, from cities to counties, to states, to nations, and eventually the world, and you can see how *Energy is Interconnected*.

Another way to understand an interconnected world, whether through physics or social scenarios, is to see it as comprising systems. Everyone and everything within a system affects, and is affected by, other components of that system. These systems can be man-made or natural, psychological or sociological. Some man-made systems are automobile assembly plants; delivery systems such as FedEx, UPS, or USPS; computers, sewerage and water facilities; and interstate highways. Change one part of the system and everything else is affected.

I saw a special on the Discovery Channel, which crystallized the point about our interconnection on a humanistic and planetary level. Local authorities were trying to discover the reason for the disappearance of a certain rare mammal from the interior of Africa.

Over the years, the population of this particular species greatly diminished and then slowly returned for no apparent reason. One scientist finally widened his research by rifling through decades of old handwritten records, which led him to study ecosystems in coastal areas hundreds of miles away. He discovered that, when these mammals were disappearing in the wild in central Africa, the fish population on the coast had also declined. He checked with other scientists around the world in seemingly unrelated areas of biology, fish populations, and water conditions. After years of dedication, he found the connectivity of various factors that led to the decline of this mammal.

To sum it all up, intermittently, warmer ocean temperatures off West Africa changed water and weather conditions, causing an El Niño, which caused the depletion of plankton, which caused the fish population to decline, which caused a food shortage for the coastal region, which caused people to seek out other food sources, which caused an increase in the poaching of these rare mammals, which nearly caused the extinction of this mammal. This process also affected socio-political systems. Because of the lack of food on the coast, the poachers crossed national borders, which affected the tribes whose lands they transgressed on, which created military and political responses from governments, citizens, humanitarian groups, police, and animal rights activists. So what appears to be an isolated event is really a complex problem involving cause and effect and interconnection, beginning with the tiniest creature on earth—plankton. All of life is interconnected. Can you think of anyone or anything that is not?

The PIES state of the individual interconnects to past, present, and future generations. Looking at family systems, we can see the parent, child, sibling, mother, and father each play a different role. Each of their roles affects the other roles. Throw in alcoholism, abuse, disability,an accident, or an illness to any person, and all others will be affected. Throw in getting a job, overcoming an illness, getting an education, or overcoming any major obstacle, and the reality is the same; others are affected to some degree. How we treat our bodies, our positive or negative beliefs and emotions, and how much of our Spirit shows up in our actions are all part of the conditioning that we consciously and unconsciously received from our past family unit, which in turn affects our present family, which in turn will affect our children's families.

Breathe! Allow yourself to feel the natural rhythm of your inhalation and exhalation.

There are several derivations, axioms, from this UP of *Energy is Interconnected*: *Energy Attracts Like Energy* (the Law of Attraction) and *Energy Reflects*. I will explain each of these briefly, as we will explore them in more detail later. All three of these axioms say the same thing but with a slightly different angle.

"Whatsoever a man soweth, that shall he also reap."
Galatians 6:7

Energy Attracts Like Energy

One of the major reasons energy returns to you is because of the Law of Attraction—or what I call *Energy Attracts Like Energy*. Many different frequencies have a quality of magnetism. This attraction, or sometimes repulsion, occurs in every moment within the Universe. What happens to you occurs because it somehow resonates with energy you emit. An oversimplification of this might be the example of a person who is always negative. Look at their life and you will probably observe that not only do they perceive negativity even in positive circumstances but that actual negative—lower-frequency—events happen to them more often than to a positive person. *The Secret* by Rhonda Byrne delivers dozens of tips on how to exist within the Law of Attraction.

A personal example was a picnic I went on when I was younger. The day was beautiful, along with the spot that we picked to eat. The girlfriend of my buddy was, to my mind, a negative person. When this woman discovered that my friend had packed Coke instead of Pepsi she became very upset. From that point on, the blanket was too scratchy on her skin, the ground was too lumpy, and there wasn't enough fruit. These were all her internal perceptions, but what also happened was that she seemed to externally attract more gnats around her head, more ants clambering on her food, and when we hiked her feet seemed to stumble on more rocks than ours. Basically, her negative energy created more negativity in her surrounding reality. I have seen this occur time and time again, both in the negative and the positive. So I try as hard as I can to be within the positive frequencies. Energy moves in a circular fashion, which means that the energy fields we emit will, in some form of manifestation, return to us. If you're nasty to people, other people will probably be mean to you. If you help people, you'll probably receive help from strangers more than people who don't. If you don't think highly of yourself—having a low self-concept—you'll probably notice people not treating you well. Circular energy isn't necessarily returned in the same manner or from the person who emanated it. It is the frequency of your actions, emotions, and thoughts that will return in some fashion. Whatever range of frequency you emit will return in a form that has the same range of frequency. Kindness has a frequency, but it can be experienced in many different forms. If you act kindly to someone by opening a door for them, later someone might give you a quarter on a bus because you're short of change or a customer service representative might go the extra mile for you.

Karma, a basis of Hinduism, is certainly one of the best representations of *Like Energy Attracting Like Energy*. Classically, karma says every action has a reaction—a consequence. Your *good* deeds will be rewarded and your *bad* deeds will be punished. In the context of this book, according to the UP of *Energy Just Is*, there are no rewards or punishments, just similar energy frequencies created by your actions returning to you. The second basis of Hinduism is reincarnation, which basically states that, over time, energy will eventually return to the soul that created it. Whether you believe in reincarnation or not does not negate the fact that energy returns to you in this lifetime.

Reflection

From the Physical or theological perspective, who we are is part and parcel of the Oneness. Within that context, and also considering that *Energy Attracts Like Energy*, the world around us is a reflection of us—as we are a reflection of the world. Again, remember that your focus is your reality. If we are the creators of our own unique world, we also have the power to change, delete, and modify that world. Imagine looking at yourself in a mirror. You might like some of the things you see but not others. Imagine trying to change the mirrored images of the things you don't like. If you saw a blemish on your reflected face, would you try to remove that blemish by changing the mirrored reflection? You'd be called crazy; you can only change yourself, which changes the mirrored images. When you look into your Spiritual mirror, you see not only yourself but also the people and situations of your life. If you observe that you are surrounded by loving people, that's a reflection of you. If you observe lots of angry people, that's also a reflection of you. When you see attributes you don't like in someone in your life, you might attempt to change the other person. Remember, that person is reflecting something about you or your perceptions, so, instead of wasting your time trying to change them, change yourself, which by definition will change how you perceive others.

"If we could change ourselves, the tendencies in the world would also change. As a man changes his own nature, so does the attitude of the world change towards him. ...We need not wait to see what others do."
Mahatma Gandhi

Separation

If the workings of nature, our souls, and the cosmos are all about interconnection, how did we as individuals and a species get so far off track? How did we condition ourselves with the exact opposite—that we are separate from others and the Universe, disconnected from ourselves and from nature?

Our early developmental process contributed to our sense of separateness. It started with being violently disconnected from our mother at birth and our fear of separation from her teats for our survival. As we got older, our Intellect, filtered through our ego, betrayed us by superimposing our struggle for Physical survival over our Emotional and Intellectual survival. So now, when a boss yells at us, another person doesn't like us, other people don't meet our expectations, or we can't fulfill our false needs, we feel Emotionally and Intellectually attacked. Our body responds with the stress syndrome, just as if we were being Physically threatened. All of this reinforces the Intellect's belief in separation.

Breathe!
When you consciously breathe, can you feel more connected to your body and maybe even to your soul?

From an intra- and inter-personal perspective, the belief in separation stems from an over-active, childlike ego and an under-active consciousness of Spirit. When we psychologically and socially do not transcend our own id, we hold on to a myopic view of the world that focuses more on itself than others. This belief system of separation appears in the proverbial *me* versus *you*. The spoiled child aspect of us wants to have all the toys, even though that means creating a roomful of devoid and crying children. Even when we develop our superego, meeting the needs of others, we can still carry the same fears of separation but just expand our concept of *me* versus *you* to *us* versus *them*.

Holding on to a separate belief system about our world, we use all of our perceptions to reinforce that thought. We then consciously and unconsciously choose bits of information that reinforce that belief. We seek out criteria that seemingly differentiate us from others—skin color, religion, place of birth, or even more mundane things such as beauty, hairstyle, pitch of voice, and displayed attitudes. The criteria you use don't make a difference; if you believe in separateness, you'll perceive separateness in any form.

Many of us feel separate, disconnected, from ourselves and forget that everything begins from within. When we feel disconnected from our self, our conscious mind will not connect to our unconscious actions and our heart will not connect to our mind. We will look for love, because we feel it is outside of our self, which is just another way of saying love is separate. Through habit, we believe that other people are better suited to solve our problems, rather than trusting that the solution is usually within us (though it certainly doesn't hurt to get feedback from others). We search for our soulmate to complete us, when all we really want is the ultimate relationship with our self. Along this lonely journey, we'll feel separate from our authentic-self. We can become sad, hopeless, and even depressed, which in turn creates even more of a gap. Separation is an illusion, an illusion that has created the majority of our challenges on this planet.

Separation Started in the Beginning

Historically, our separation belief began from our theological conditioning, which states we fell from grace in the Garden of Eden. One interpretation is that Adam and Eve—our human species—were thrown out of the consciousness of our intrinsic connection to the Divine Source.

Our past and present societies have delivered similar separation beliefs, creating a societal conditioning that has infused every institution. One way separateness has evolved is from a mechanistic worldview of parts, beginning with Descartes' philosophy. We wanted to know how things worked, so we took them apart to study their intrinsic nature. While this brought about the creation of the sciences, the Industrial Revolution, and a better understanding of the universe, it is not the only way to think. We also need to see the world as holistic, by using our right brain along with our left.

Encouraging this feeling of separateness within our culture have been our governments, our politics, some religions, and the media. They have created an artificial fear of survival that targets our emotions and ego. Control and money are behind this consciously contrived fear mongering. We are told to be afraid of others—the socialists, the other political party, the rich, the minorities, the communists, the devil, and the gays. It is intoned that we should fear old age, looking unattractive, pain, and the list goes on. The people who create this fear are usually the ones making money, through our votes and buying habits. By not examining our unconscious beliefs, we tend to live lives that follow what others have decided is our path.

Examples of feeling and being separate appear in every strata of society: neighborhoods based on ethnicity or money, walls and fences between nations, jails, mental institutions, everyone spying on everyone else, LGBT discussions, laws preventing equal rights, the Middle East drama, right versus wrong, dogmas that state that someone is the chosen one, heaven and hell, inequality between men and women, the Native American genocide, East versus West, I'm better than you, you're better than me, my gang is better than your gang, bullying, any crime against another person such as spousal abuse, murder, theft, rape, robbery, Republicans versus Democrats, left versus right, have versus have not, and the exploitation of our planet. It all stems from believing in separateness.

The negative consequences of not seeing our world as interconnected is ever present through, for example, overly extracted resources from our natural lands, medications put into our livestock, pesticides sprayed on our crops, chemicals put into our soil, genetically modified foods, and pollution in our air. We have treated our planet poorly and killed off most of the people whose philosophies and actions were in harmony with the planet: the indigenous peoples who were connected in every way with nature. Throughout the ages, on a global level, this separate belief system has been an integral part of colonialism, dictatorship, monarchy, and empire building. These actions stem from a belief system that *we* are better than *them*, we are above nature, and we are separate. Whether it is physical abuse in a relationship, corporate abuse of employees, or humans' abuse of the planet, the root cause is a faulty belief system of separateness. And since everything is interconnected, our abuse is coming back to us through global warming, declining species, poor air quality, increased diseases, violence, and greed.

It's a tough lesson that all human beings on this planet are learning right now. We have lived too long with the belief that we are separate from other people and our planet. The consequence of our faulty belief system has manifested in everything from domestic abuse to war, from the class separation of the wealthy and poor, and from the satiated to the hungry. The feeling of separateness is based on fear—fear of not having enough love, money, beauty, possessions, etc. Fear that other people might get more than we have, fear that they might hurt us, fear that they have what we want so we need to take it from them. So we hoard Physically, Emotionally, and Intellectually to ensure we survive, or at least survive with more comfort than others.

The challenge in our world is that people are not realizing the UP of *Energy is Interconnected*. We need to change our thoughts to a knowingness that we are all One, which will change how we interact with others—*them*. The *them* is us and we are all on the same team. Any team uses their differences in talents, skills, and experiences to accomplish shared goals. Any business that wants to be successful, any family that wants to be healthy, and any civilization that wants to survive need to adopt the ever-present reality that we are all interconnected.

Main Points

- We are all One.
- Whatever energy we put out will reflect and come back to us.
- The belief in separateness has caused most of the pain in the world.
- Believing in and acting on interconnection will enable us to move through these difficult times.

Questions

- Describe any moment when you have felt "at one" with nature, God, yourself, or another person. How were you before that moment arrived, and how can you attain that state of being again?

- How do you see the belief in separateness manifesting in your life?

Challenges

- Review your challenges and identify any that are created by your thinking, feeling, or acting from a belief in separation. For your solution, find ways to overcome your challenge by thinking, feeling, and acting as if you're connected. Be creative!

Affirmation

- I act in ways that reflect my interconnection to all things.

***

Reflections and Corrections

As I worked through my challenges, I tended to withdraw, not only Physically but also Intellectually, Emotionally, and Spiritually. This protection is the opposite of interconnection. I needed to find a way to engage rather than disconnect. Any such correction needs a heart that is open and a mind that has no expectations towards its efforts. A major avenue for staying connected to everyone and everything is to be compassionate and grateful. If everyone behaved this way, our world would instantly transform into a utopia. In fact, if only 15% of our population, or whatever number constitutes a critical mass, acted with compassion and gratefulness, our present dysfunctional reality would quickly begin to dissipate and a new reality of cooperation, service to others, prosperity, and love would begin to emerge.

Compassion

Compassion begins with the awareness of another's suffering, which brings about concern and empathy. You exemplify compassion, the essence of an authentic-self, by living the UPs. Having compassion means you resonate with another's condition. But if you are blinded by your own busyness, ego-state, or small-mindedness, it is very difficult to be aware of another's situation, no matter what the circumstances.

Compassion does not necessarily mean taking away another's suffering. Allowing the other person to be in their pain and allowing yourself to be without judgment or desire to control the situation illustrates *Energy Just Is*. Most times, there is really nothing that anyone can do to alleviate the cause of their pain and suffering. Many times, all the other person needs is to be heard, or for someone to silently be there in heart and spirit. At the same time, having compassion doesn't necessarily mean sitting and doing nothing. To be proactive about compassion means to follow the intent of the bumper sticker and make "Random Acts of Kindness" a way of being.

Many years ago, after my mother died in hospice care, I made a promise to myself that if I ever found myself with extra time I would volunteer at a hospice. Well, I had plenty of time now with no relationship or job. I wanted to help others at the most difficult time in their lives, but I would be dishonest if I told you that I always felt so altruistic. I certainly had brief moments of self-absorption: "I have my own problems. I want the world to be compassionate to me. I don't have time to help others. I need time for myself. I don't have the energy to help others."

There is a fine balance between taking care of yourself and using those above-mentioned beliefs as excuses to wallow in your *stuff*. I authentically and soulfully knew better than to continue with those lines of thoughts. Wanting to be of service to others, I also knew whatever positive energy I put out would come back to me—in some shape or form. So, giving some compassion to myself for having those separate and ego thoughts, I volunteered.

The major role of a volunteer is tending to your patients' needs while simultaneously giving the caregiver a needed break. Most volunteers would talk, read to their patients, or just be there while the patients quietly rested. I secretly hoped to have a patient who wanted to explore the ideas of death and come to some form of healing and peace. I had explored, read, discussed, and written about death. Maybe I could be a sounding board for someone, which would help me feel as if I were helping them. (Life rarely goes according to one's expectations.)

To qualify for hospice, one has to have a prognosis of less than six months to live. My patient, who resided at a nursing home, was a tiny Southern belle from Texas who was ninety-seven years old, had dementia, and was dying of old age. Her only family was a cousin hundreds of miles away. She couldn't walk, eat, or go to the bathroom without assistance and had no idea where she was or who I was. Most of the time she was in her own private world—so much for having enlightening conversations. I was at a loss as to how I could help her and, since she was in a nursing home, I wasn't giving any help to a family caretaker. She slept for most of our time together; other times, she was frightened because she thought I was an intruder who wanted to harm her, so I had to leave.

There was a grand piano in the reception area, so I decided that I would wheel her out, sleeping or not, and place her next to me while I played. I had an old music book that had hundreds of songs but mostly ones from the early 20th century that she hopefully would recall. She showed brief moments of recognition towards some of those old songs, but mostly she just slept. Every once in a while, though, she'd attentively listen and, after a song, would feebly extend her shaky hand. She'd then look into my eyes and deposit imaginary coins into my cupped palm, giving me a tip for my services.

"If you want others to be happy, practice compassion.
If you want to be happy, practice compassion."
The Dalai Lama

Gratefulness

One of the beautiful aspects of energy is that you don't really know where or how far your energy, your actions, your love, your gratitude, or your compassion can travel. Many hospice patients die within the first few weeks, but I spent nearly three years playing the piano for her every Wednesday. A by-product of my efforts occurred every week as a small gathering of women in wheelchairs congregated by the piano. They listened to the songs I played for my patient and then asked for their favorite songs, singing what words they could remember. My purpose was to provide my patient's comfort, but, as *Energy Interconnects,* I inadvertently provided comfort for others and myself.

One afternoon, after I'd been feeling a little down about not receiving any benefits or recognition for my efforts at job hunting and writing this book, a lady rolled her wheelchair next to the piano. My patient as usual was sleeping on the other side as I played her favorite song, *Five Foot Two, Eyes of Blue.* When I finished, the unknown lady slowly leaned towards me and said, "Even though she's sleeping, I know that she hears you playing."

I nodded at her. "I think so, too."

"I've heard you for weeks," she added.

"I'm sorry, I don't recognize you," I said, a little embarrassed.

"You wouldn't. This is the first time that I've been able to be in a wheelchair. I've been stuck in my bed for over two months, but every Wednesday I could hear your music echoing down the hallway. I just wanted to say 'thank you.'"

Holding back tears, I whispered into her ear, "No…thank you. You don't know how much I needed to hear that."

Compassion has the ability to morph into gratefulness, which begets more compassion, which begets more gratitude, creating a wonderful vortex of circulating love. Sad to say, I don't feel people share enough gratitude or, for that matter, receive enough gratitude. Know that the best chance of receiving gratitude is to give it, because—as you already know—everything begins with you.

Most of us are wanting, searching for, and desiring more out of life. From an ego perspective, wanting is actually a statement of lack. The ego interprets wanting happiness and love as not having, or not having enough, external superficial things, such as cars, beautiful men or women, or money. If we attach happiness and love to our ego, we'll forever be lost. The id and ego tend to be on an outward journey leading to something outside of our self. Our higher-self is on an inward journey leading us back to our authentic-self, where the real answers always lie. Practicing gratefulness is an internal process that honors what we already have. Since *Everything is Energy*, *All Energy has a VF*, and *All Energy is Interconnected*, all those wants are already present within us.

> *"If you are really thankful, what do you do? You share."*
> W. Clement Stone

Since everything begins with a thought, it helps to have a belief that all you need is present and within you. We need to believe and become aware that we already have happiness, love, and balance. One of the constant themes of my material has been that everything is about you—or rather, if I'm talking about myself, that everything is about me. This book has to do with *being* all those things you're looking for outside of yourself, recognizing that happiness, love, and balance are already vibrating through you.

To avail yourself of those VFs, you must be open to receiving them. If you're too full of your ego, there is no room to receive heart and spirit. If you're too full of your problems, there is no room for solutions. If you're too busy, there is no time for anything. One way to be open to all you desire is to appreciate what is already present in your life. Being grateful for what is already present is a prerequisite to meeting your desires. If you can't do that, how can you attract those things or even be aware when they finally appear?

Focusing on gratitude raises your VF. As you attain higher VFs, you'll be more open to receiving similar VFs from many other aspects of your life. As you develop your skill of gratitude, you'll become more aware of the positivity, wonder, and beauty in otherwise unnoticeable situations. Once you learn to appreciate everything and anything, you might feel the simple joy of seeing a sunset, appreciate more deeply the budding of spring, or be grateful for the smile of a friend. After a while, you'll discover that you're surrounded by more appreciative people and then be thankful for that.

One minute a day of giving thanks is a powerful technique for being stress-free, happy, and loved. There are an infinite number of things to be grateful for. Start with the obvious, whatever that might be for you. Be thankful for having your health. Be grateful for having a roof over your head. Be appreciative of having a loving relationship. Be thankful for having a job you like. Be thankful for having a healthy mind and heart. Be thankful while listening to your favorite music. Be appreciative of having a TV, sound system, a refrigerator, and running water. Be appreciative of good friends. Be appreciative of your miraculous body, of having emotions and a clear mind. Be grateful for being of Spirit and on this wondrous journey you call life.

*"Be thankful for what you have; you'll end up having more.
If you concentrate on what you don't have,
you will never, ever have enough."*
Oprah Winfrey

Move on from there, look outside of yourself, and be thankful for this planet and all of its gifts. Be thankful for the trees in your backyard. Be appreciative of your pets. Be grateful for having a car and paved roads to drive on. Be thankful for grocery stores and their employees. Be grateful for the food you eat. Be grateful for every breath and every moment. Be appreciative of the silence. Think of all the people who have contributed to your play—your life—and be grateful for them.

Think of all the works of creative artisans throughout the centuries. Appreciate their works of beauty; their tireless hours of sculpting, building, writing, singing, film-making, dancing, painting, and quilting. Be appreciative of these words and this book. (Okay, had to get a plug in here somewhere.) Kidding aside, I'm grateful for my pens and paper, computer, editors, distributors, bookstores, research material, graphic designers, internet, and yes, most importantly, you my reader.

Be thankful for any object in your home or office: pencils, phones, lights, computers, calculators, paper, copy machines, cubicles, desks. Be appreciative of the chair you are sitting on and for all the people and resources who have put their effort into its creation and delivery to you: the designer, manufacturer, line workers, furniture store, salesman, delivery woman, the delivery truck and all who built it, the plants distilled into oil to fuel the delivery truck. Delve as deep as you wish. The further you go, the more aware you become of how interconnected everything is in your life. The more conscious you are, the more grateful you become. The more grateful you become, the more you'll receive from the Universe.

Breathe!
Inhale gratefulness and exhale compassion.

If life is tough for you, then be grateful for at least having any job. If your health is not the best, then at least be thankful for the parts of your body that are healthy. Have thanks for being able to see or hear or feel. If you lost your home, then be thankful for having a place to rent, or a friend's place to stay, or a shelter that takes you in, or a blanket that covers you. If you're not in a relationship, be appreciative of still having the capacity to love, or for having had love in the past. Be grateful for all the seemingly negative events in your life, for they have brought you the opportunities to learn, heal, and love in deeper ways. When you can see life as filled with learning lessons, there are always things to be grateful for. Be appreciative of the pain, the heartache, the disappointments, and the tragedies, for they all come into your life bearing gifts—opportunities for you to learn, to grow, to become more aware.

When I had no job, home, marriage, and income, there were times when it was difficult to be grateful. But once I let go of my self-pity, I could begin to see through that self-induced fog. So when I didn't feel like getting up in the morning, I attempted to be thankful for the bed I slept in, the blankets that kept me warm, indoor plumbing, water for drinking and showering, food in the refrigerator, the roof over my head, and the air I breathed. I became thankful for receiving unemployment checks, having a place to stay, having a part-time job, and having something in my account to last me a little longer. When that ran out, I became more appreciative of having friends and family who cared about me, having a (mostly) healthy body to play sports, having the ability to play the piano, having eyes to see the sunset, enjoying living in San Diego, and knowing that life always provides an opportunity to learn.

One of my biggest learning lessons from that night of opening packages of crackers was that I had received a wake-up call from my soul. I was thankful for that. I'd temporarily walked away from my path—my internal, invisible blueprint—of teaching classes and writing. I had to get back on track using my answer to the question "Who am I?" I had to get back in balance. I could have sat there and blamed other people, the economy, the president, or whomever else I chose, but I was the one who needed to change, and gratefulness was a great beginning.

10

Energy Just Is

There is an innocence to this principle that is usually exhibited by children and Enlightened Ones. This is not an innocence born from naiveté but one that is pure and exciting, that originates from being in Spirit.

Energy Just Is states that there is no intrinsic meaning to any form of energy. There is no moral value, no good or bad, no better or worse that can be found in any atom, molecule, animal, person, ocean, or star. Meaning is a relative concept created by our own Intellectual perceptions and observations of ourselves, things, others, and the many situations of our lives. Usually, meaning is conveyed to us through others and then, over time, we unconsciously accept it as our own. Remember, our individual realities depend on our focus; therefore every person's unique view of reality contains a different interpretation of what is meaningful. This chapter will delve into the basic components of explaining how *Energy Just Is*, how most of us live in opposition to this principle through morals and judgments, and what we can do differently.

Search for Meaning

> *"Life is without meaning. You bring the meaning to it.*
> *The meaning of life is whatever you ascribe it to be.*
> *Being alive is the meaning."*
> Joseph Campbell

This by far is the most difficult UP to grasp. If you're new to this concept, try not to become discouraged or even rebellious; just allow yourself to take it in at your own pace. As in all *knowing*, there are layers and layers to uncover before you can fully align yourself with core truths. I've been attempting to fully embody this principle for almost three decades and I still struggle at times.

Don't confuse living a life by the UP *Everything Just Is* with living a life without purpose, love, or fun. I know this principle sounds like a paradox, yet it is still true. Once you allow yourself to flow in accordance with this principle, you'll be accepting of all that life has to offer, which will bring love, knowingness, and connection. Those qualities, inherent in our Universe, are the definition of our Spirit. The meaning of life is more a recognition of those qualities than a meaning superimposed by others from our past and present.

Energy Just Is ultimately reflects a universe of action and consequences—cause and effect—and not one of pre-established meanings. Our culture has labeled many life events with positive or negative meanings: losing a home is a horrible event, getting married is a wonderful event, getting mugged is a terrible happening, becoming a parent is an expected goal for everyone. Many laws, societal norms, morals, and media have labeled our behaviors and traits in accordance with meanings that will serve them. Our challenge is to eliminate meanings that are not authentic to our unique self.

Witnessing the chaotic events that happen around the world, we struggle to make sense of it all. Our mind wants to perceive order in the Universe and searches for meaning to make sense of our lives. While looking at the randomness of the stars in our heavens, our mind attempts to see familiar patterns, such as the constellations of Scorpio, the Big Dipper, or Leo the Lion. We then put meaning, albeit astrological, to the appearance of these patterns. We place meanings behind celestial events, the appearances of animals, and planetary events, along with the cycles of life, such as birth and death, famine and abundance, and droughts and floods. If we can't find meaning, we perceive our gods delivering them to us. And if something is still beyond any sense, fairness, or rationality, we throw up our hands and say, "Only God knows the meaning of…"

In earlier civilizations, we perceived that our gods and religions provided meanings, some of which were positive and some of which were not. Behind every action was a meaning that would either be rewarded or punished. If our mind accepts a theological concept of a controlling God that places meanings on the events of our lives, there can be very confusing consequences. I know people who have all the things we wish for—such as money, fame, and houses—yet are greedy and manipulative. Did God reward them? Is the meaning of Hurricane Katrina to punish the LGBT community? Is the meaning of you catching a touchdown pass a reward from God? If that statement is true, then the opposite must also be true: if you drop the next pass or are injured on the field, you must have been punished. If you're poor or were involved in a natural disaster, you must have deserved the consequences. All of those made-up meanings are rubbish and serve no purpose but self-degradation.

I believed, at one point in my life, that God doled out rewards and punishments. Once I stubbed my toe immediately after I told a lie and was sure that God had punished me. The reality was that, after I told the lie, my mind was focusing on my guilt and not paying attention to where I was walking. I believed the act of masturbation was an evil deed and that was why I had such bad acne. In reality, it was the consequence of being an oily, pubescent teenager who was stressed out because of his mother's hyper-controlling behavior.

"To live is to suffer; to survive is to find meaning in the suffering."
Friedrich Nietzsche

Know that this type of thinking leads to countless forms of unnecessary, agonizing pain. Extrapolating this to more serious matters, I've been with many friends and family who have experienced the death of a loved one. The mental and emotional pain alone is difficult, but when they start putting negative meanings on their actions, the pain becomes intolerable, sometimes lasting for years. Their comments usually sound like this: "If only I'd done this instead of that, so-and-so would still be alive. Auntie Joan died after I left the hospital and went home to get some rest; if only I had stayed. If I'd been a better person, God wouldn't have taken my son." Putting that kind of meaning on a person's death assumes you have control over life's events. This negative guilt frequency provides countless ways to torture yourself.

The bottom line is that people die for many reasons, all of which have to do with the perils of being a human being, not from the pre-ordained acts of a deity or having personal, mysterious powers over life and death. Yet many people whip themselves with guilt, lament, and shame. We have free will to feel the consequences of all of our actions and provide our own meanings to our lives. I have a difficult time believing that the creator of this wondrous universe is a puppeteer of our lives; how boring, how uncreative, how egotistical. If you want to explore this discussion more deeply from a theological and sociological perspective, please read *When Bad Things Happen to Good People* by Harold Kushner.

Breathe!

Living our life with the belief that *Energy Just Is* provides us with the opportunity to be non-judgmental about what is present before us. Every moment can then become a clean canvas on which we can paint our world. Observing our own minds and then acting without pre-conceived notions can help us to not become entangled in others' made-up meanings or drown in those negative emotions. Being objective ensures us a fresh focus, which can provide beauty, awe, inspiration, and maybe even insight.

To be honest, most of us are lazy, which makes it easier for our institutions and others to provide us with meanings. Self-examination of our beliefs, and letting go of others' meanings, takes effort and requires lots of energy and consciousness. Is it worth the effort to do all of this work? Just take a look at our world, and you can see the consequences of being unconscious and not putting in the necessary effort.

"Never let your sense of morals
get in the way of doing what's right."
Isaac Asimov

Feeling Disorientation

Meanings give us benchmarks in this world and bring us some comfort in knowing our place. Our mind—really, our ego—panics if we're left on our own, with no meaning to grab on to. Know that, once you accept this principle, you will feel disorientated. Eliminating meaning temporarily places us in a void where we can feel alone and disconnected: "If there is no meaning, what's the use of living? What's the point to all of it? How will I know what to do?" You might feel like a fish out of water or, as they say in my ol' stomping ground of Jimmy Buffett's Key West, "a parrot-head without a margarita." (Okay, maybe I just said that.) I'm asking you to just allow yourself to feel that uncertainty for a while. Like a sailor in the open sea, you'll have to trust your intuitive navigational skills. Without any markers on your horizon, you'll have to go inwards for your guidance and use the UPs.

Others' Meanings

As you begin this process of letting go of meaning, you'll have to accomplish two simultaneous actions: become aware of unexamined beliefs and their meanings, and take responsibility for creating your own meaning. After the mental dust storm of disorientation passes, you need to free yourself from all meanings, positive and negative, that you accepted from your parents, peers, schools, institutions, and media. This cleansing process requires you to bring into the light of day your unexamined beliefs. Ask yourself if you adopted them from someone else. Be totally honest and check, not with your ego but with your soul, to see if this belief truly resonates with you. "If I can't accomplish xyz, it means I'm stupid." Is that true? Who said that—your teacher, school testing standards, or one of your classmates? "I'm a *bad* wife if I'm a mother and have a career." Whose meaning is that—your husband's, society's, or one that you adopted from your parents? "I'm not a *good* son if I don't want to go over to my mother's house for Thanksgiving." (Oh, did I just say that out loud?) Many of those and other meanings originated from outside of you, such a long time ago that they just seem like they're your own.

Know that these meanings can be delivered in many ways—through, for example, words, thoughts, non-verbal behavior, and emotions. My mother showed me through her words and behavior that traveling was a very positive part of life and that education was paramount. Although it was rare, in her calmer moments, she'd emphasize that I could do and be anything. Even though those were positive meanings, I still needed to reexamine them to make sure they were true for me and not that I believed them just because my mother told me to. Sadly, though, many of us have received negative beliefs and meanings. My mother always told me I was a lover, not a fighter, and that I had to study harder to catch up with my schoolmates. Not horrible beliefs to pass on, yet once accepted by my unconscious, they created a set of challenges in my life. We've heard all of these: "You'll never be pretty or smart." "You have to watch out for men; they only want one thing." "You'll never be strong enough." "Life is hard." "Money is the root of all evil." Yet another list that goes on and on.

Create Your Own Meanings

Believing and acting on the fact that your focus creates your reality is an incredibly empowering feeling. You are unique and should revel in that fact. *You* are in control of how you interpret life and can therefore create an improved, poignant meaning that benefits you, others, and the planet. Living this way dumps the heavy load of personal responsibility square on your shoulders. What relieves that heavy load is knowing that, since you create all your meanings, you can always un-create them. You have the power to delete, add to, or edit others' meanings and your own. When you embrace this concept, you'll begin to drag yourself away from being Intellectually and Emotionally controlled by others and institutions. You'll begin to eliminate all the unnecessary feelings of guilt, shame, and unworthiness associated with living under others' meanings. Instead, you'll begin to feel enriched, alive, and free. Know that you can live a life filled with authenticity that aligns with your uniqueness and soul.

Recognizing this personal responsibility for meanings implies that you can't play the blame game anymore. Know that allowing others to provide you with meaning is a way of abdicating responsibility. "I'm not responsible because my parents told me...or my pastor said...or the law says...or the internet stated..." You can't pass the blame on to others for your thoughts, feelings, and actions when you are the one who ultimately creates or accepts them.

Innocence

Let's look at a different facet of this concept of *Energy Just Is*. There is an innocence to this principle that is usually exhibited by children and Enlightened Ones. This is not an innocence born from naiveté but one that is pure and exciting, that originates from being in Spirit. Infants are not born believing the meaning behind racism, bigotry, hate, and prejudice. Children also do not portray any of those beliefs or meanings, at least not until they have been taught them. The meanings behind all of those faulty traits are not inherent within any person or situation but rather created and then passed on by small, unaware, ignorant, and fearful minds. Watch young children play with each other; they have no prejudice or judgment about nationality, ethnicity, or social status. They have not put meaning on all those factors like adults have. They just have the joy of sharing that moment with another soul. So what would your life look and feel like if you could do that from now on?

Living Counter to this Principle

"No human race is superior; no religious faith is inferior."
Elie Wiesel

Living counter to *Energy Just Is*, as if there were inherent meaning in certain people, places, or things, results in unbalanced morals and judgments. This can lead to intolerance, bias, racism, and bigotry, ranging from having a negative judgment about overweight people to joining the Aryan Brotherhood. This behavior thwarts the progress of our species, along with causing much personal and collective pain. We'll explore some definitions of these morals and judgments, why they are so detrimental, how they might have started, and the consequences of these faulty beliefs.

Morals

"About morals, I know only that what is moral is what you feel good about after and what is immoral is what you feel bad after."
Ernest Hemingway

Morals are *others'* meanings of our thoughts or actions, which have been passed down through the ages. Our morals have to do with rules of conduct that have been imposed by cultures, religions, and governments. These rules are usually written down as dogmas, commandments, or laws. In our past, these societally implanted rules of behavior have been created by theological perspectives and then subsequently through social, legal, and political interests.

In the beginning, we gathered in tribal societies. Establishing a well-organized community that functions efficiently and meets the needs of all, while not treading on individual pursuits, is difficult. When you have people with over-active ids taking care of their needs over others', you'll have stealing, greed, violence, and killing. Morals, customs, and mores needed to be established to create order within the community. The more these primitive societies could control people and nature, the better chance they had for survival. Acceptance within a group increased chances for individual survival, so our superego developed and tried to also fulfill the needs of others. The penalty for not being acceptable in our early societies was to be shunned, and you can still see this penalty today in certain religions, cults, and tribes. This form of punishment led to a harder life and probably earlier death. So a strong desire to conform ties in to our fears for survival.

We are now in a different stage of development, at least within Western society. Our concerns for physical survival in a hostile, Physical environment have been replaced by our concerns for psychological survival in a hostile, Intellectual environment. This Intellectual environment is filled with signs, morals, expectations, and judgments, to keep us away from supposed dangers. Because our minds create our realities and our bodies follow cues from our minds, we have strong survival angst when we stray from society's morals and expectations. We feel in a visceral way that obedience is required to ensure our physical survival.

I'm not saying that we should have anarchy, there shouldn't be consequences, or we should throw out morals and religions. Many of these morals and laws assist in creating a functional, creative framework to live in harmony and protect us from dysfunctional behavior. Many of our morals morphed into religious codes and eventually, over time, into laws and unwritten societal norms. Some of them, though, transitioned into protecting us from anyone who is different, or has unusual traits, or thinks outside the box.

Breathe!

Negative meanings of "bad," "evil," and "unacceptable" have been placed on the unwanted behaviors and traits of being left-handed, having red hair, being a woman, belonging to certain religions, being mentally or physically challenged, or having the "wrong" skin color. Positive meanings of "good," "God-like," and "acceptable" have been placed on the wanted traits and behaviors of those who are law-abiding, God-loving, and follow the status quo. Again, there's nothing necessarily wrong with the latter but it creates a slippery slope.

As you become more conscious, you can see that many of these morals are not about survival for the community but have evolved into a mechanism to keep us under control. Whoever is at the top wants to keep power, control, and money. As these forces align with present-day morals, they attempt to influence our behaviors so that we will stay within the status quo. The less we think for ourselves and the more we accept what has been handed down to us, the easier it is to control us.

Placing negative meanings and labels on the behavior of people who look and act different, who stand up against the status quo, who challenge leadership, and who question authority and longstanding, unexamined laws and morals diminshes creativity. Don't forget that the traits of creativity, being different, and thinking outside the box are needed for a society to evolve and grow.

The truth about the advancement of humankind is that it occurred because of the efforts of people who did not fit into the societal mold. Many of the people we admire today were at the forefront of science, democracy, theology, art, politics, and innovation. Those people—Leonardo da Vinci; Marie Curie; Albert Einstein; Jesus; Martin Luther King, Jr.; Mother Teresa, Nelson Mandela—had to fight their ways through the stifling morals of the masses, many under the threat of death. This is why the healthier path is to see everyone and everything as "just is," rather than as filled with incorrect or untrue meanings.

Judgments

"When you judge another you don't define them,
you define yourself as someone who needs to judge."
Wayne W. Dyer

You create judgments, which are based on thoughts and beliefs, when you form a notion, opinion, or conclusion about someone, something, some situation, or yourself. Expressing and acting on relative concepts of labeling, right/wrong, better/worse, and good/bad are forms of judgments. The meaning you give a judgment is partly your own genuine, unfiltered thinking, but mostly conditioning that you received from others. In and of themselves, judgments are not necessarily a negative thing. Many times, we need to make judgments in order to make decisions: "Should I date that person?" "Is this company the best for me?" "Should I send my child to that school?"

Judgments based on the *relative* concepts of labeling, right/wrong, better/worse, and good/bad are usually subjective and negative. They diminish others and yourself, creating a detrimental effect that ripples through your psyche and society. There is nothing finite, factual, or divine about these relative beliefs, which may or may not be true. So the meanings behind these judgments need constant monitoring to ensure their objectivity.

Your judgments will run counter to the principle of *Energy Just Is* if your ego is not in balance or your self-esteem is low. The id is all about "Me, Me, Me." If unchecked, it will make judgments about people to reinforce that focus. Your ego wants you to be the best, the top dog, the most beautiful, and the strongest. It will find negative, not positive, aspects about other people, in order to create an illusion and attitude of "I am better than them."

Another facet of judgment is judging others in order to control them—and also accepting others' judgments, allowing yourself to be controlled. We do most of this unconsciously. We can witness these judgments in words and thoughts such as *should, must, ought,* and *supposed to.* We also inject them into good/bad and right/wrong. "You should do this." "They should do that." "I'm better than you." "You're better than me." "What you have is better than what I have." "I'm right and you're wrong." "Poor you." "Poor me." "I'm not good enough." "You ought not to do that." "I've been a bad person." "She must do that." "What I've done is wrong."

Those thoughts and judgments are limited, ego driven, and accompanied by feelings such as pity, loathing, jealousy, envy, shame, worry, powerlessness, embarrassment, disgust, anger, hostility, and contempt. Did you notice that those emotions are negative, have a lower frequency, create Emotional pain, and demonstrate a lack of love? They are definitely not in tune with the UPs.

Have you ever felt positive about being negatively judged, being told you are bad or not as good as someone else? Do those comments ever leave you with positive information to change your behavior or to help you make a better decision the next time around? So why would you pass judgment on someone else? For the person who is delivering the statement, their judgment only serves as a faulty ego boost, based on a false belief that they are somehow better than the other person. For the recipient of the judgment, the negative meaning accosts their self-worth. Again, realize there is no inherent good/bad or better/worse in any form of energy; all meanings are made up. Every person and situation *Just Is*.

"*Judge not, that ye be not judged.*"
Matthew 7:1

Societies' and Institutions' Use of Judgment

Our superego needs to fit into society, which, if not checked, makes us susceptible to all of its influences. Everyone's ego wants to be *good* or *better than*. When society's ego takes on these collective judgments, there is fodder for manifestations of intolerance, bigotry, prejudice, and racism. We are born into existing socio-political systems that perpetuate many falsely based morals and judgments. Humankind has been exhibiting these characteristics for centuries: "My skin is a better color." "My gender is better." "My race is better." "My religion is better." Substitute *good* for *better* and you have the same relativistic but ego-satisfying tenet: "It is good to be white, to be male, to be Christian, to be rich," which presupposes "It is bad to be black or brown, to be a woman, to be Jewish or Muslim, to be poor." This kind of thinking initiates human rights violations, world wars, and genocides.

This belief system of *good* and *bad* is so embedded that it is difficult, if not impossible, to not be affected by its false premise. "A good citizen doesn't oppose wars, a good wife would never want to vote, a good husband should be the breadwinner, a good employee would never blow the whistle on her boss. If I go to church, I'm a good person. If I'm good, I'll go to heaven. If I'm bad, I'll go to hell. If I smoke pot, I'm a bad person. If I dance in the streets, I'm a rebel." So the lesson is "If I'm good and follow the rules of society, I'll be accepted and have a better chance to survive, whether it be Physically, Intellectually, Emotionally, or Spiritually."

The institutions of our society have injected their individual messages with that knowledge in order to manipulate us into figuratively and literally buying their product, service, loyalty, patronage, or deity. "If my body gets older and I get wrinkles, people will think I'm not attractive." "If I'm a childless woman in her forties, there must be something wrong with me." "If I don't wear designer jeans, I'm not a part of the 'in' crowd." "If I'm gay, I'm immoral." "Bodies I see on TV and in magazines are better than mine."

These institutions don't want you to use your higher Intellect, because if you did you could easily see through their passive control and manipulation. If we stay unconscious, our ego will buy into this game ad nauseam and justify each level. By placing meaning on what they deem we should do, be, and look like, the controlling factions of our society go against the UP of *Energy Just Is*. If you buy into those meanings, you'll eventually become unhappy, because you're not living authentically; you're not serving your true-self, your soul-self.

As I've pointed out, these judgments and morals are totally relative. They depend on who makes the statement, geo-political influences, social mores of the time, and a million other mitigating factors. Yet, when we are unconscious, we have a tendency to believe that many of these morals and judgments are true. Once we feel consciously or unconsciously that something is the *truth*—a fact—we tend not to further analyze or to seek additional information or perspectives. If we stay unconscious, we think those meanings are actually our own and we will fight long and hard to continue living by those beliefs. So what I'm asking, and it is difficult, is for you to be aware of the UP of *Energy Just Is*; do not fall under the unconscious spell of judgments and morals.

Do Something Different

All the relative meanings of those lower-frequency beliefs carry expectations and demands that require a lot of energy. Examine all that conditioning and only retain what is meaningful to your authentic-self. Change those beliefs and meanings into soul serving, and you'll live an easier life with grace and ease. Accept people and the world as they are in this moment. That way of thinking doesn't mean you need to roll over and be a punching bag, but it does mean you should see the world objectively and then act authentically based on meanings that are genuine and truly reflect you.

Every person's situation needs to be looked at from an objective viewpoint. In order to change the meaning of my situation, I listed my challenges in an objective way, became aware of my thoughts and their accompanying emotions, and then changed my thoughts to create new meanings, a different reality. There will be a big difference in your psyche and emotions if you change the meaning of losing your home from a horrible situation to a challenging situation, losing your job from "being in a bad way" to just needing to use your ingenuity, or being divorced from "being a loser" to seeing a new opportunity for growth. *Basically, you reframe the meaning of your situation.*

There are a million scenarios regarding what I'm addressing here. I know this explanation tends to be very Intellectual and at times esoteric. Remember, I said this might be difficult to digest. All I'm asking you to do is be conscious, be alert, and let go of judgments or morals that don't align with your authentic-self. Feel the innocence of every person. See every moment as a fresh canvas. If you don't and unconsciously assimilate meanings from others, you will end up living in the cookie-cutter community within *The Matrix*. The truth is that, when you truly get that you are the creator of meanings, a sense of power permeates your being, creating a foundation for you to live an authentic life.

Main Points

- There is no inherent meaning in atoms, molecules, people, animals, situations, or any energy form.
- We create our own meanings.
- Seeing the world "as is" allows you a fresh perspective.
- In dealing with morals and judgments, let go of meanings created by others and take responsibility for your own.

Questions

- Which morals and judgments are not in balance with your authentic-self?
- What would your life be like if there were no meaning to anything?

Challenges

- Identify how your relative meanings, beliefs, morals, and judgments have created your challenges.
- If you remove or create different meanings, what will happen to your challenges?

Affirmation

- I am accepting of myself, others, and all things.

***

Reflections and Corrections

Much of the pain I felt going through my challenges I've attributed to my attitudes and judgments about the events that occurred—not seeing my world as *Just Is*. To some degree, I received those judgments from society. Losing a home, letting go of a marriage, and not having a job are difficult enough, but putting negative labels on those situations as *bad, horrible, unfortunate, sad,* or *devastating* made it more difficult. Letting go of those labels and perceiving those situations as potential opportunities creates a different, more positive, and perhaps enlightening scenario. One of my favorite Zen stories says it all.

Once upon a time, there was an old farmer who had worked his crops for many years. One day, his horse ran away. Upon hearing the news, his neighbors came to visit.

"That's awful," they said sympathetically.

"Maybe, maybe not," the farmer replied.

The next morning, the horse returned, bringing with it three other wild horses.

"What good luck!" the neighbors exclaimed.

"Good luck? Bad luck?" replied the old man.

The following day, his son tried to ride one of the untamed horses, was thrown, and broke his leg. The neighbors again came to offer their sympathy.

"That's very unfortunate!" they exclaimed.

"Fortunate? Unfortunate?" shrugged the farmer.

The day after, military officials came to the village to draft young men into the army. Seeing that the son's leg was broken, they passed him by. The neighbors congratulated the farmer. "That's wonderful!"

"Maybe, maybe not," said the farmer.

If the farmer had placed societal meanings on those events and become emotionally wrapped up with every one of those situations, can you imagine how draining that would have been? I can't tell you enough how freeing it is to remove labels, judgments, and expectations about people and situations. When I started to fully live life as *Energy Just Is,* I became aware of how much energy I'd been wasting throughout my life. If we could act as if *Energy Just Is,* we'd save all kinds of energy in the form of worry, stress, sadness, despair, blame, or guilt. We'd then have plenty of energy to stay in the moment, be happy, be loving, be of service to others, or just relax. Besides, our lives generally, as the balance pendulum reflects, have a way of working out; what we thought were undesirable events eventually lead us to what we need.

Once upon a time, there was an adventurous and wise man who grew up in Chicago, where most residents live for their entire lives. One weekend after his divorce, he was almost killed by a bomb one day and a gun the next. Upon hearing the news, his neighbors came to visit.

"That's awful," they said sympathetically.

"Maybe," the man replied and then, acknowledging an unknown inner angst to move into the unknown, he added, "Maybe not."

The man quit his job, went on vacation to Key West, stayed there, and ultimately owned a houseboat restaurant.

His friends called him to say, "What good news!"

"Good news, bad news," he replied. He soon discovered it would be the most stressful job of his life. After several years, his floating restaurant sank one night.

His friends called to say, "How unlucky."

"Unlucky or not?" the man responded, partly relieved, knowing that he wanted to change his life once again. The man worked his way to San Diego, where he slowed down his lifestyle. After years of self-discovery, he became successful and owned a home.

His friends exclaimed, "How fortunate."

"Fortunate...or not," the adventurous man replied, knowing that life can change in an instant. One spring many years later, he was laid off and his mother died.

"How horrible," his friends recited.

"Horrible or not," the unemployed man responded. With plenty of time and receiving enough inheritance, he put his energy into writing a book that soon became an international bestseller.

People exclaimed, "How incredible!"

"Incredible...or not," he answered.

The man then wrote a second and, he thought, better book, but no publisher wanted it. Broke, he took any job he could and, over a ten-year period, accrued money again and even got married. Then, one year, he became unemployed, his marriage went on the rocks, and he lost his home.

Again his friends said, "What bad luck."

"Bad luck, good luck," the adventurous man countered.

The man then went within—again—and followed the UPs even more deeply, trusted that all would be okay, fell in love again, moved to New England, and wrote a third book that helped him on his journey and hopefully might help others...To be continued.

11

Energy Moves Towards Balance

These processes of balance occur within every cell of our body and aspect of our self, within the quietness of meditation, the cataclysmic aftermath of the Big Bang, and within all the varied forms of our relationships, businesses, and governments.

Balance intrinsically connects to our PIES and the UPs. The principle *Energy Moves Towards Balance* has to do with the driving force behind energy—that it's always moving towards a state of equilibrium. This state of balance is not static, but extremely dynamic. There is no exact degree, percentage, or placement for this state, but rather a desired frequency range. The balance we seek is not about having equal amounts of anything, but rather a healthy range of positive and loving frequencies. I'll discuss how balance manifests itself in different forms, look at examples of its working—or not working—in our lives, and list some of the roadblocks.

In an attempt to balance our minds and hearts, we use the pendulum process and several of its variations, which I call *the rubber-band process, the dualistic dance, the after-shock process,* and *stretching the bubble.* These processes of balance occur within every cell of our body and aspect of our self, within the quietness of meditation and the cataclysmic aftermath of the Big Bang, and within all the varied forms of our relationships, businesses, and governments.

Inherent in each atom, molecule, organism, and creature is an unconscious drive to attain stability within itself and its environ- ment. You can observe and feel the process of attaining balance when your body is sick and you're on the verge of getting better; when you've held on to a dysfunctional belief and are on the verge of letting it go; when you've held on to your anger for months and are on the verge of releasing it; or when you've always believed that this life is all that there is, have had an "ah-ha" moment, and realize there is a part of you that transcends this Physical plane.

> *"To talk about balance,*
> *it's easier to talk about what's out of balance.*
> *And I think anytime that you have any disease,*
> *and disease meaning lack of ease, lack of flow...dis-ease.*
> *So any time there's disease, you're out of balance,*
> *whether it's jealousy, anger, greed, anxiety, or fear."*
> Ricky Williams

Nature is in Balance

Many of our Western societies have surely lost their connection to nature. Institutions contributed to some of this disconnection. Centuries ago, Christianity squashed the connection people had with nature when it demonized paganism. Colonialism used religion to dominate indigenous cultures that were heavily tied to nature, and now capitalism abuses and sucks dry most of our natural resources. Nowadays, our societies idolize living with technology and comfort, and rebuke and eliminate people who live off the land. I truly believe one of the major reasons we, as a society and species, have lost our way is because of our lack of connection to nature. This systematic separation of humans and nature has unbalanced the human condition. Most of us live within cities, with asphalt rather than dirt beneath our feet. We eat, drink, work, and play indoors; we don't sleep under the stars, losing our wonder and awe of our connection to the Universe. We forget we're intrinsically connected to Mother Nature and need her not only for our survival, but also to keep us connected to our soul.

We come from nature, which is a by-product of the formation of the stars. Outside nature has an essential connection to our deeper, inner nature and is a perfect example of the dynamic process and state of balance. The UPs are perfectly embedded within nature: *Energy is Interconnected, Energy Just Is, Energy Must Flow, Energy Moves Towards Balance*, and *Energy Has A Vibrational Frequency*. I've had the privilege of experiencing the rainforests of Costa Rica, the Ecuadorian Amazon, and the world's oldest, the Daintree Rainforest in Australia. The overwhelming feeling is that of being surrounded by a palpable presence of life. Within the dense foliage, I felt the gentle, soothing buzz of its VF. Without working at it, meditating on it, analyzing it, or digesting it, I felt the pure essence of life in balance. You don't need to be in a rainforest to experience a sense of this balance; you can attain it in any form of nature.

One of the factors—or, more precisely, non-factors—that make nature so much in balance is the lack of mind. Nature has no ego, no beliefs that one aspect is better than another, no thinking about the future or past. When you are in nature, you have an easier time becoming connected, mindless, and present. The mind is a double-edged sword that, when balanced and conscious, can transcend us to heights that no other life form can experience and yet, when not in balance, can stop us from fully experiencing the moment.

Go out and get into nature as much as you can. Let your bare feet touch the dirt or let your toes wiggle in the sand. Allow your nose to smell the fragrance of a flower or the scent of a pine tree. Listen for the call of the hawk or the lapping of the waves. Allow your eyes to be captivated by a flock of birds or fascinated by the intricacies of a dragonfly. Go camping, hiking, walking around the block, or even just sit in your backyard or on your workplace lawn. People just feel better when they have some, any, connection to nature.

How many times have you experienced an angry or unhappy person while you've been camping, sailing, or hiking? When you immerse yourself in those activities, you'll find yourself and total strangers unconsciously making an effort to wave or say hi. Why would you or they do that? You rarely consciously think about it before it happens. You don't think *When I pass that boat, I'm going to wave* or *When I pass the next hiker, I'll be sure to say hi.* You just do it. The behavior just emanates from you. Does that happen in the streets of Manhattan or the Sears elevators in Chicago? So why do you do it when you are in nature? Because you are unconsciously living the UPs. Surrounding yourself with the balanced energies of nature influences you to behave in a balanced way. One of the most balanced things you can ever do is interconnect with your fellow humans.

"Balance is the perfect state of still water. Let that be our model. It remains quiet within and is not disturbed on the surface."
Confucius

Cycles Lead to Balance

Different types of cycles assist in bringing about balance in nature: seasonal, lunar, solar, celestial, and weather. There are also cycles of life: times we are alone and times life is hectic, times we have money and times we are broke, times we need comfort and times we give comfort, times we are happy and times we are mad...Well, The Byrds said it best (or, I should say, *The Book of Ecclesiastes*):

A time of love, a time of hate.
A time of war, a time of peace.
A time you may embrace.
A time to refrain from embracing.

To everything, turn, turn, turn.
There is a season, turn, turn, turn.
And a time to every purpose under heaven.

A time to gain, a time to lose.
A time to rend, a time to sew.
A time for love, a time for hate.
A time for peace, I swear it's not too late!

Amid the chaos of our lives, cycles give us a sense of order, a sense of familiarity, and a sense of perspective. With the rotation of the planet, our bodies move through a twenty-four-hour circadian rhythm returning us to a new day. After winter we revisit spring, a little bit changed, but on the same yearly cycle. As I write this paragraph, the Mayan cycle that occurs every 26,000 years is happening with the alignment of our planet, sun, and galactic center.

This cyclical, revolving, circular energy demonstrates that eventually everything returns back to where it once began—not so much like the closing of a circle as like a descending or ascending spiral. We all change somewhat during our journey, so we can never truly return to the exact spot. We are either a little bit closer to balance or a little further away.

There are cycles to our aging. Going to a class reunion will stir up old memories, beliefs, and feelings. Some aspects of our younger self we don't like and others we might love. This wake-up call gives us the opportunity to consciously change to a higher state of balance, to ask the question "Who am I?"

We can then measure how we stack up to where we are now. To help us through these cycles, we need to remember to step back and take a look at the whole picture. Our tendency is to think the present is permanent, rather than to see the present situation as only one part of a cycle. Have trust and patience, as you move along your journey, that things will change. Remember, cycles enable us to experience the fullness and breadth of life, in order to experience balance.

Breathe!
Realize, with each breath, that everything
is perfect in this moment.

Swinging Pendulum

The most predominant type of balance seen in nature, our lives, and institutions is the swinging of the pendulum. Nature provides many examples of this pendulum effect with the buildup of energy, the release, and the eventual buildup again. Rain and snow bring balance to the highly dense moisture in the atmosphere. Early-evening, onshore breezes occur to bring balance to the cooling temperature of the coastline. Volcanic eruptions occur to relieve the pressure of gas or water under the earth's surface. Our universe is in a constant state of moving away from and then towards equilibrium through contraction and expansion. Think of it as the universe's way of breathing—inhaling and exhaling.

On a personal level, this process reflects our two-dimensional, dualistic thinking: life is this or that, either/or, right or wrong. As we attempt to get in balance, we have the same back-and-forth tendency. The farther we move one way or the other, the more we'll feel the gravity of the pendulum, pulling on us to embrace both sides: life is going well and then challenging, we're happy then sad, we're in love and then alone.

We can sometimes see this in our socio-political systems; the electoral process swings back and forth between the Democrats and the Republicans, crime bills move from stringent to more lenient, social programs are initiated then dropped, and foreign policies are tough then lenient.

My golf game is another example of the pendulum effect. If my drives are slicing to the right, I'll use my knowledge of the game and my skill level to adjust with my next shot. My next shot will then usually go to the left; not my goal, but nonetheless a change in the direction of the pendulum. I will adjust again, and maybe this time it will go back to the right but not as far as before. If you continue to hit the ball left then right, you are said to be playing "military golf," as in marching—left-right-left-right. The process in golf is to keep adjusting your grip, stance, and swing until the ball goes straight. Be aware of the consequences of your actions in relation to your goal and then act accordingly in the next moment. This is a very healthy way to navigate through life.

Be Comfortable in the Swinging

There isn't a problem in moving to any position on the pendulum. More challenges occur, though, if you stay or become entrenched in one position. Why? Life is in a constant state of change. Being static is not a property of the universe. Life is rarely about the extremes; 99.9% of life falls between the edges, in the grey. Life is about all positions, thoughts, beliefs, and emotions. If you stay too long in an unhealthy, lower frequency position, you'll eventually find yourself unhappy. When that happens, realize your unhappiness, depression, or anger is providing you with an opportunity and the motivation to think, feel, and act differently.

Sailing a boat is the best example of how to navigate this process. First of all, you need to know your destination—your goals, your path. If you take your eye, your focus, off your goal, you'll soon be off course. The clearer you are about your goal, the easier it will be to know how to adjust. Lastly, you need to know the UPs. As you sail, the wind and water, like life, are always changing and flowing; therefore, you need to continually adjust. There's no wrong or right way; *Energy Just Is*. This process takes lots of practice, patience, and trusting that you can't make a mistake. You need to be connected to the boat, water, and wind. If your actions have not provided you with what you want, then just let out the main sheet, push the tiller, and try another tack. No big deal! Learn from it and continue to sail.

Rubber-band Process

A variation of the pendulum effect is what I call the rubber-band process. This occurs when a buildup of energy eventually needs to be released. As time goes by, the rubber band gets stretched further and further, creating more and more tension. Eventually it will break, or snap back. In that moment, there is a discharge of energy that tends to be dramatic.

When the whole universe was confined to a space no bigger than a pinhead, it expanded within a nanosecond, attempting to regain balance from its intense, highly condensed state. A similar situation, but on a smaller cosmological scale, occurs when a star goes supernova and then radiates a light that outshines a galaxy. Clouds, land, and rain can create a buildup of electrical imbalance. *Energy Needs to Flow,* so when a critical point is reached, energy is released as a lightning bolt, which brings electrical balance between air and land.

A more relevant and personal experience is when one eventually releases stored-up emotional energy. In my youth, I would hold on to my anger and frustration for months, until I'd eventually, briefly explode. I snapped from my dominant behavior of being "nice little Tommy" to a temporary angry Thomas. When you hold on to your emotions beyond a healthy period, lightning will occur and anyone who is close by unknowingly becomes a lightning rod, receiving the wrath of your emotions.

Another example might be if you, after forty years, were fed up with being a victim or always playing the rescuer. The rubber band might then eject you to the opposite side of the pendulum, where you would exhibit a behavior of take no prisoners, lash out immediately at people, or act selfishly. Even though it might not be the healthiest behavior, this reaction begins a natural progression of balance: withholding energy a long period of time, releasing that energy, and eventually learning how to allow the flow of emotions to occur at the time you feel them.

Take a look at any person you know who has an extremist or rigid viewpoint about how life should be. They are living on the far side of the pendulum and will have an energy buildup that creates dysfunction. Are they happy? Do they emit love? Or are they in fear, in a defensive mode, in an "I'm right" state of mind? The first clue to knowing if you are in balance or going with the flow of the Universe is asking yourself if you feel more love or less love in your present state of mind—your position on the pendulum. Your desire to stay on one side of the pendulum will eventually decrease if you continue to be conscious, open yourself to new perspectives, and integrate as many tools as possible into your personal growth. Eventually you'll find a range of healthy behaviors for your uniqueness.

After-shock Process

Another variation of creating balance occurs when no matter who we are in life, balanced or not, the floor drops out from underneath us. The best example of that is being in an earthquake. Moving to California, I left behind my encounters with tornadoes in Chicago and hurricanes in the Keys for the fires and earthquakes of Southern California. After experiencing a San Andreas tremor, I was literally and figuratively shaken. In the middle of the night, I stood naked between the door jambs of my fourth-floor apartment, while the walls swayed and the floor bounced and shook beneath my feet. I actually felt some minor vertigo after that event. Previously, I'd walked around this planet without ever thinking about how the earth had always provided me with a solid foundation. What I had thought was always stable and always present was suddenly not there. It took me a little while to trust that everything was going to be okay.

This after-shock process also occurs in our psyche when people, conditions, and things that we normally take for granted disappear or deteriorate. This process can take many forms: losing a job, receiving divorce papers, testing positive for cancer, being in an accident, losing your home, having an illness, or experiencing the death of a loved one. Having something or someone who has always been there suddenly disappear or taken away from you can leave you in a state of shock, as if you've been slammed to the ground or swallowed up by the earth. You'll search for something to hold on to as your psyche temporarily feels vertigo. You might go to your faith, or retreat into your cave, or turn to drugs and alcohol.

The after-shock process has the ability to get to your core. Realize that the tragedy you are experiencing can truly be a gift. It is providing you with an opportunity to observe your thoughts, feelings, and actions—a chance to test your courage, fortitude, and depth. Give yourself time to adjust, discover who you truly are, and identify what is really important in life. Hopefully you'll discover your true essence and realize that all that matters is thinking, feeling, and acting in love. By doing so, you'll not only survive this temporary setback but also learn to appreciate every present moment with gratitude, compassion, and forgiveness. Remember, all of these occurrences are just part of the human journey. If you follow the UPs, your foundation will return more quickly and easily.

The Dualistic Dance

Not as earth-shattering as the previous process is the attempt to find balance through the dualistic dance. Another variation of the pendulum swing, this adaption to navigating through life occurs dozens of times during your day. So you can understand how you perform this dance, I'll give you some examples of daily decisions: "Should I let go or act, follow my ego or my soul, go left or right, exercise or rest, eat that dessert or have a salad, protect myself or lay myself bare, plan for the future or just let it happen, yell or shut up, agree or disagree, confront or acquiesce, cry or suck it up, use intuition or logic, believe or doubt, trust in myself or believe this zany author?"

This process is not just about whether to take two steps to the right or one step to the left. These decisions usually need to balance out with some variation of left and right; maybe go one way now but in another situation or with another person, go the other way. Plan the best for your future now, but then let things happen and see how it unfolds. You might want to use your intuition in deciding whom to date but use your logic when deciding to buy additional clothes. Maybe you'll sit back now and take your time to weigh all the factors of buying a condo, but get off your butt and act on an important to-do item that you have been procrastinating. There are so many dualistic factors to consider in making those daily decisions. No wonder we stumble about and step on toes as we do this dance.

Again, being the sailor will help you make healthy daily decisions; be clear about who you are, know your goals, and how you want to be. If you're coming from your soul, your goals will be very different from if you identify with your ego. If you're unclear about your goals, your decisions and actions will be unconscious, and old patterns and behaviors will drive them. Your lack of clarity will probably capsize you. This dualistic dance can go much more smoothly if you follow the above advice and the UPs.

Breathe!

Stretching Your Bubble

Imagine you've created, with your mind, your own unique bubble of existence. Your perceived limitations determine the parameters of this bubble. If you were a spiritual being with no limitations, your bubble would be as big as the universe. Being in a human body severely limits that expansive state, and your bubble will be dramatically smaller. Add limiting conditioning placed on you by your parents, schools, religions, and institutions, and that bubble is even smaller. One of the characteristics of this bubble is that when it is repeatedly stretched, it will tend to stay in its new position.

> *"Argue for your limitations and they are yours."*
> Richard Bach

Children and adolescents constantly test their limits and try to stretch that bubble outwards. Most adults who accept their lives as "just the way it is" have stopped trying to stretch their bubbles and may end up leading stagnant lives. The same consequences happen when we limit the movement of our PIES. Have you seen or experienced people whose bubbles are so tight and confining that they are Physically constricted or hunched over, Emotionally stilted, Intellectually rigid, and seem Spiritually void?

To be in balance, you need to stretch every part of yourself. Imagine that each of your aspects of PIES have little hands that push, or not, the limits of your bubble. If you feel yourself tight and stiff, you're sensing your Physical limits. Literally stretch your body through exercise or yoga. In a conversation, when you feel you're *right* and the other person is *wrong*, you're experiencing the limits of your Intellectual openness. Mindfully expand to make room for others' perspectives. Next time you feel yourself holding back tears, you're feeling your limits of Emotional expression. Emotionally stretch and let the tears flow. When exploring new Spiritual concepts or a practice that seems to be too *out there*, you're feeling the limit of your soul's expansiveness. Allow yourself the Spiritual opportunity to have uncommon experiences.

Most people don't even know their limits, because their lives have been constrictive rather than expansive. They are fearful of the unknown, of being different, of not being in the status quo. Your intention should be to discover your perceived limits and then proceed a little further. If you go too far, then back off a little. When you stretch your bubble, there will usually be some discomfort or pain involved. Think of the process as being like a pilates or yoga workout. You need to discover your present Physical limitations and gently move a little beyond them. If you haven't done this in a while, your bubble might be a little brittle, but just because there's pain doesn't mean you should stop. Work within those boundaries and you'll develop more strength, a stronger foundation, and flexibility. After some time, and when you're ready, stretch a little further. Remember, there is a difference between soreness—the result of a healthy workout—and injurious pain.

Keeping within the framework of a workout, let's say you did go too far and became injured. Okay, you learned something about your body. Just stop exercising for a while. That doesn't mean you never go back to exercise, it just means that next time you'll do something different—go slower, don't go as far, or use a different technique. Your essence is much larger than you can imagine. Rarely will you ever feel unhappy or resentful for having a larger and more flexible bubble.

Knowing that this process of balance is natural, ongoing, and has different variations is beneficial. Hopefully, it lessens your self-judgment about not being perfect or not doing the right thing. Maybe you'll even enjoy tacking back and forth as you sail through life.

Main Points

- Balance is a dynamic state.
- Balance means being in a higher frequency range.
- The state of balance can be seen in nature and cycles.
- The process of balance can be seen in the pendulum effect, the rubber-band process, the after-shock process, the dualistic dance, and stretching the bubble.

Questions

- Where are you out of balance in your PIES?
- What different cycles do you have in your life? How have they brought balance to you?

- How has the pendulum effect played out in your life? What lessons can you learn from it?
- What rubber-band moments have you experienced? What could you have done to lessen the tension before the snap?
- How have you handled after-quake moments?

Challenges

- In each challenge, how have any of the processes of balance played out?
- Make a daily plan to achieve balance for each challenge.

Affirmation

- I am in perfect harmony with myself, others, and the planet.

***

Reflections and Corrections

There are many ways to achieve balance; some are obvious and others might seem unrelated. Stepping back and reflecting on various steps I have taken, I find there is one corrective action that, when done in a profound and heartfelt way, brought me to the core of my soul, which is the deepest form of authenticity. This process stems from love and is called forgiveness. I needed forgiveness in every way, whether I was dealing with my former relationships, bosses, banks, or family, but especially with myself.

Forgiveness

For most people, the mere thought of forgiving someone makes them cringe. Yet the act of forgiveness is one of the most powerful, positive, healing, and loving actions you can do for others—and, most importantly, for yourself. The angst between not forgiving or forgiving is really a battle between your ego-self and your soul-self. The ego rebels against the very idea of forgiveness. Our ego wants vindication, justice, but most of all to be *right*—all lower-consciousness levels. The image that comes to mind is of an ego as a hopeful, triumphant boxer. The ego's vision is that of standing over his battered and bloodied opponent, holding up a sign that says, "Now everyone knows that I was right." The feelings that accompany those wants, thoughts, and beliefs are always of the lowest VF: righteousness, anger, revenge, resentment, or rage. At minimum, the ego wants an apology and at worst, punishment or even death. A passage from the texts of the "old" spirituality encourages this negative ego state by supporting "an eye for an eye." I hardly believe that the Divine Source wants us to behave that way. Gandhi had a great retort; he said that, if we followed that advice, the world would eventually become blind.

"Always forgive your enemies – nothing annoys them so much."
Oscar Wilde

Lack of forgiveness appears in our deepest self-talk, our relationships, religions, governments, and international relations. "I can't forgive myself for not getting out of that relationship sooner." "I really screwed my life up." "I'll never forgive my spouse for not paying enough attention to me on my birthday." "I'll never forgive my daughter for getting pregnant." Most religions believe they are the "chosen ones" and are not forgiving of those who do not believe in their god. Throughout history, we've seen millions of people killed because of that particular lack of forgiveness. To various degrees, governments are not forgiving of those in their constituencies who are different, who are in the minority, or who voice dissent. For decades—and, in some cases, centuries—countries have not been forgiving of other countries for transgressions committed on both sides. The Jewish-Palestinian conflict could end in this moment if everyone were to forgive each other. In fact, that is the only way this conflict will ever truly end. Once each side forgives the other side, all the seemingly insurmountable details will be solvable. There is only one way to move through all that pain, hurt, and death. Forgiveness!

Your ego, or your country's ego, feels that through the act of forgiveness it will somehow diminish. Let me give it to you straight. To forgive does NOT mean condoning the actions of others, does NOT mean losing anything, does NOT mean you are weak, and does NOT mean someone is dominating you. To forgive means to accept that you might have had some role in a situation, that maybe you could have done something differently, that maybe there is another perspective that you have not perceived yet, that you possibly might not be 100% right, that you both did the best you could at the time, that maybe there could be something to learn from this situation.

"The weak can never forgive.
Forgiveness is the attribute of the strong."
Mahatma Gandhi

Forgiveness doesn't diminish you, but rather releases you; it releases your ego so you can be more soulful, releases anger so you can become more loving, and releases separation so you can be more connected. We all just want to be loved and understood. Forgiveness is a major step towards making that happen.

Remember, it's all about you and your reaction to the events in your life. You are the one who feels all your negative feelings, not necessarily the person you can't forgive. When you forgive another, you are actually forgiving yourself. When you forgive yourself, it is much easier to forgive another. Forgiveness allows you to have a fresh start—a clean slate—rather than to live with heavy baggage. No matter whom you forgive, you'll receive the benefits of a higher VF and automatically feel happier, more loving, and definitely less stressed.

Let's say you're still not going to back down, because you know that you're right and the other person is wrong. If that is the case, realize that you'll continue to feel those negative emotions that have a lower VF, because your rigid mind is not allowing energy to flow. Do you want to continue simmering in that negative, foul, unhappy, stressful-tasting soup? What is it that you truly want? Do you want your ego to rule your life or your soul? Do you want to be loving or angry? Do you want to be right or do you want to be happy? Your choice!

"He that cannot forgive others breaks the bridge over which he must pass himself; for every man has need to be forgiven."
Thomas Fuller

One of the most powerful techniques to accomplish forgiveness is an ancient Hawaiian healing system. An interesting read is *Zero Limits* by Dr. Joe Vitale and Dr. Ihaleakala Hew Len, describing their interpretation of a practice called *Ho'oponopono*. The following is a very simplistic takeaway from all the material I've read. I've experienced, and also heard about from friends and students, incredible healings that occur from reciting these words. This technique is so very simple, yet extremely powerful.

I'm Sorry

Your non-ego soul is sorry for any conscious or unconscious actions that might have resulted in negative outcomes.

Please Forgive Me

You are now asking forgiveness from the other person for the perceived transgressions. You are taking responsibility for anything that you might have consciously or unconsciously done.

Thank You

You are acknowledging an acceptance of your plea for forgiveness. Even though you might never get that from the ego of the other person, their soul most assuredly is saying, "I forgive you."

I Forgive You

You are now stating your intention to forgive the other person. We're all energetic transmitters and receivers. You're now bringing into balance both of your roles in this matter, whether or not the other party feels the need to be forgiven.

I Love You

Your soul is stating the ultimate heart communication. Translated, it means "I accept you for who you were, are, and will be. I accept your essence, your soul, not necessarily your behavior. I acknowledge the connection of our souls and know that we are all One. I love you and, since we are all interconnected, I love myself."

Don't worry about repeating the sequence exactly; that will come in time. Just say:

I'm sorry.
Please forgive me.
Thank you.
I forgive you.
I love you.

Say these words slowly and with intention. This might be difficult in the beginning and, as with your affirmations, it might feel as if you're lying. Know that feeling of dishonesty is coming from your bruised ego and not the essence of who you are—your authentic-self. Say it anyway!

You can do this technique with any energy form, whether it is a place, a structure, a person, or a soul at *The Celestial Bar*. Say it several times in one sitting, or use it as a mantra during meditation. The more you feel it—mean it—the more powerful and effective it becomes. This exercise truly manifests the invisible energy of thoughts, feelings, and intentions into palpable results. You'll be amazed. Take notice of how the recipient of your forgiving intentions, or sometimes someone else, responds to you from a higher VF. Try it. Your simple action comes at no cost, except the pain of a bruised ego letting go.

12

Energy Has A Vibrational Frequency

"If you want to find the secrets of the universe,
think in terms of energy, frequency and vibration."
Nikola Tesla

Through physics, we know that each form of energy has its own frequency. Even though we can't consciously experience most frequencies, there are many we can—such as seeing a color, feeling someone's touch, listening to the radio, watching TV, tasting our favorite foods, or smelling a flower.

In the spiritual field, the words "frequency" and "vibrations" are used interchangeably. I like to use the term "Vibrational Frequency" (VF) because it denotes a deeper sense of the Universe, representing that it is also vibrant, pulsating, alive, and constantly changing. Placing those two terms together may not create a true scientific term, but it is a way to characterize a blend of the unseen scientific and the metaphysical. I have used this term throughout the book, asking forgiveness from my "techie" friends and readers. In this chapter, we'll more clearly define VFs, discuss the advantages of seeing the Universe as VFs, and list what we need to do to raise the VFs of our energetic body.

Old Paradigm of the World's Being Solid

"String theory describes energy and matter as being composed of
tiny, wiggling strands of energy that look like strings. And the
pitch of a string's vibration determines the nature of its effect."
Roy H. Williams

The Greeks told us about the tiniest bits of solid matter in the universe, called atoms. The belief system that our world is made up of solid particles that can be broken into parts sets into motion all kinds of assumptions about our universe, our planet, and us. Some of those assumptions in science and technology have served us well, but not so much in the psycho-social arenas. When we adopt the belief that our universe is mainly solid and observable, we tend to carry that same type of thinking into other areas of life, such as in our relationships, our play, our work, and ourselves. Perceiving the world this way will nudge us towards undue focus on solid entities such as clothes, cars, pools, homes, our bodies, and electronic gadgets. After we accumulate those things, we usually find ourselves unhappy. Instead of changing our thinking, we'd rather believe that more of those things will make us happy. But as long as we believe that the important things in life are solid and not energetic, the harder it will be to be happy. We need to remember that the universe, most of which is invisible and unobservable, is made up of different forms of energy that resonate at different frequencies. In fact, we have created our reality with the invisible VFs of our thoughts and feelings.

Most VFs Can't Be Seen

> *"God is a frequency."*
> Alan Cohen

We tend to discount the unseen realities of life because it's difficult for our minds to grasp things we can't see. But if we open ourselves up to that invisible realm, we can experience our world in new and exciting ways. Associating different energy forms with each having its own unique frequency reminds us that ultimately nothing is solid, nothing is static, and nothing is permanent.

The easiest way for me to understand this idea of VFs is to think of the electromagnetic energy spectrum that measures frequencies as hertz (Hz). This scale comprises sound, radio, light, x-rays, and gamma rays. Soundwaves appear on the low end of the spectrum—such as middle G on the piano, which has a frequency of 392 Hz. On the highest end are gamma rays, topping over 3 billion billion Hz. Visible light ranges from red at 350 trillion Hz to purple at 750 trillion Hz.

None of these frequencies are solid, yet they have a huge effect on our reality. Our five senses can perceive only a small range of that spectrum. Radio waves from every station in your area are moving through you, but you can't detect it. When you blow a dog whistle and don't hear it, does the sound, the VF, exist? Just because we can't see gamma rays or x-rays doesn't mean they aren't there. In fact, our ignorance of them can be harmful. Just the right amount can help diagnose and cure diseases, but too much can kill us. As in life, everything is about balance.

Other than the electromagnetic spectrum, there are numerous other ranges of frequencies. Our brain state has frequencies that range from delta .5 Hz to alpha states 30 Hz. The planet has a frequency of 7.83 Hz. All of our foods have a frequency, with our fresher and healthier foods having a higher frequency than our cooked and canned; fresh produce ranges up to 15 Hz, and fresh herbs 20 to 27 Hz.

Just as a single note has its own unique VF, a complex chord that includes the combination of several notes has a unique VF. As we combine different energies into one form, such as our PIES, relationships, communities, cities, and institutions, it becomes increasingly difficult for science, at this time, to define those frequencies. Nonetheless, frequencies still exist. The important issue here is not necessarily the scientific identification of a frequency, but the concept that people, things, situations, institutions, stress, happiness, and love all have their own natural VF signature—that just because we can't sense those frequencies doesn't mean they don't impact our lives. Because of this, we need to pay more attention to the presence of them in our lives.

Transmitters and Receivers

Two qualities are present within all energy forms—that of being a transmitter and that of being a receptor. We aren't just walking around our world as a separate and isolated energy form. All energy emits a frequency, and all energy can affect or receive other frequencies. Our cells, organs, thoughts, emotions, and actions all transmit and receive VFs. We, in turn, are all affected by nature, music, light, cities, art, institutions, words, news, and other people's thoughts, feelings, and actions. Think of your aspects of PIES as each being a miniscule tuning fork. Each of these tuning forks emits its own unique VF and can also affect and resonate with other VFs.

Take Responsibility for Your VFs

"If words don't have vibration behind them,
and a real feeling behind them, then they're just words."
Charlotte Rampling

We need to take personal responsibility for our lives. In this context, that means to take responsibility for being the transmitters of our own VFs and for what VFs we choose to receive. I discussed this earlier, in the chapter on the Emotional aspect. No one can make you mad or sad. Disturbing and costly consequences occur with the present societal trend of not taking personal responsibility: living in a litigious society, blaming others, feeling hopeless, playing the victim, or being apathetic. We need to take responsibility not only for our actions but also for transmitting our thoughts and emotions, which are the precursors of our actions.

Distinguish Between Your VFs and Outside VFs

"Acceptance looks like a passive state.
But in reality it brings something entirely new into this world.
That peace, a subtle energy vibration, is consciousness."
Eckhart Tolle

In order to understand, adapt, and balance our PIES, we need to know that we are constantly receiving VFs from everywhere and everyone. Our task is to know our own VFs so that we can distinguish them from other VFs. This knowledge then allows us to align with the VFs that bring us to a greater state of balance. Meditation assists you in becoming familiar with your own balanced, energetic frequency, including your thoughts, feelings, and soul-self. As I mentioned before, nature is in balance and therefore transmits VFs of balance. Knowing that fact allows us the opportunity to choose to be in nature as a way of receiving and aligning with those positive energies. We are also affected by negative energies that others transmit. Several times while I've been at my favorite watering hole, out of nowhere I've picked up on anger or negative thoughts. Realizing that these thoughts and feelings are dissonant with my present state is a good clue that somehow I've picked up on someone else's, lower VF. After surveying my close proximity, I can usually identify the person. This process of discerning takes a lot of practice. Knowing the difference helps you protect yourself from the negative energies of others and gives you feedback about your own VF.

Breathe!
Feel the VF of your body before you breathe and then after.
Take four deep breaths.

VFs Can Be Magnetic

There are different ways our VFs can react within us or others: magnetize, repulse, dissonate, or harmonize. *Like Energy Attracts Likes Energy*—the Law of Attraction, as it is commonly known— reflects the invisible, magnetic quality of similar VFs being drawn to each other. Hold two magnets close to one another and you can actually feel this attraction. Striking a tuning fork, causing it to transmit, will cause another tuning fork of a similar frequency to resonate. You are a walking, talking, emoting, and vibrating human tuning fork that is affecting and being affected by other tuning forks. When you are loving to a particular person, you have more probability of receiving love back from them or receiving love from other sources. If you have (which means you are

211

transmitting) negative beliefs, similar negative VFs will be attracted to you. Self-fulfilling prophecies are created by this magnetic attraction: "No one likes me." "The world is a horrible place." "I can't find love anywhere." "Life is difficult." When you believe these statements, there is a high probability you will be attracted to and create the same reality based on those VFs.

VFs Can Repulse

Using the metaphors of magnets again, you can experience the power of repulsion, the opposing force of magnetism. If your VF is in a state of fear, you will magnetize those lower negative aspects of your world, repulsing any positivity and love from other energetic forms. The opposite is also true; if your VF state is that of bliss or happiness, you will magnetize the higher positive aspects of your world and repulse any negative VFs of fear and hate. This repulsion will happen without your even knowing it. It is a by-product of being at either a very high or very low VF. Listening to participants in my workshops, I heard that many of them had negative belief systems and complained about their friends, lovers, spouses, and family who were negative towards them. Months later, after they'd changed to positive and loving VFs, they noted the negative people and conditions in their lives had disappeared, were less, or had somehow changed in a more positive way. They had unknowingly repulsed negative VFs, merely by attracting positive VFs with their thoughts, feelings, and actions.

Dissonant VFs

In music, you cringe when you hear a discordant note being struck. That dissonant sound impacts your sense of, desire for, and need for balanced music. When dissonance happens in life, your accompanying feelings could range across uncomfortable, uneasy, stressed, or irritable. If you're the one creating the dissonance, you might remark to yourself, "I shouldn't have done…Why did I do...? I'm sorry. I didn't know what I was doing." When you create dissonant VFs, you are not in balance. Your actions or thoughts don't resonate with your authentic-self. Dissonant VFs may also come from others or outside conditions. I feel as if someone is scraping their fingers on a chalkboard when I experience people exhibiting loud, abusive, or egotistical behavior. I have choices about how to handle the dissonant frequency: I can stay and let it irritate me, I can be aggressive with the person and tell them to leave, I can remove myself from the situation, or I can energetically create a dampening energetic field that diminishes the offensive VF. If your goal in life is to have less stress, you'll need to eliminate the VF that is dissonant with your true-self.

Harmonizing VFs

If we again use a music metaphor, certain VFs can also harmonize, bringing you to a deeper state of being. These notes can be the same frequency as yours; some are similar but resonate at higher octaves, some are in synchronization, and some provide harmony to fill in for a rich and soothing chord. Feelings in this frequency might range across comfortable, content, happy, or even ecstatic. These complementing VFs act as healing vibes to nurture us back to balance. Pay attention to what lifts you up, brings you to lightness, fuels your passion, and fills your heart. The cause can take the form of a friend, a spouse, music, a lover, a book, vortexes, nature, water, or a movie. As in attending a live performance of your favorite music, surround yourself with these positive, harmonizing VFs.

Thoughts, Emotions, and Intuition

"I've had moments when I've thought about somebody,
picked up the phone to call them and they are on the line already,
and I think that maybe there's some vibration, some connection."
Clint Eastwood

213

Everyone's thoughts and feelings have VFs, which are always broadcasting yet not always consciously heard or felt. Even though we rarely consciously acknowledge the existence of unseen VFs, they are not foreign to us. Many of us have had the experience of receiving a call from someone soon after we've thought about them. That invisible energy, like neutrinos, moves through walls and can also travel great distances. We express this unconscious recognition through our language: "My heart felt your love." "I didn't resonate with that person." "I got bad vibes from that guy." When looking for a home or apartment, how many times have you said or thought "This feels great" or "Something about this place gives me the creeps"? When sitting next to a stranger on a bus or at a party, many of us have felt a positive or negative energy we couldn't explain. Heck, the Beach Boys sang about those "good vibrations."

Just as a radio receiver picks up transmitted yet unheard radio waves, our intuition can sense invisible magnetic, repulsive, dissonant, and harmonizing VFs. Our intuition, which goes beyond our five senses and conscious reasoning, needs our PIES to be in balance. This balance usually involves our turning down the volume of our thoughts and turning up, through silence, the volume of our authentic-self. Sometimes our volume is turned up by close energetic connections with friends, family, or loved ones. If you've ever been a parent, I'm sure you've felt the VF of a sick, sad, or happy child, even if they were in the next room, at school, or visiting their grandparents across the country. Being in a loving relationship with your significant other may enable you to be in tune with many of their different aspects, including unspoken mood changes. We tend to forget how strong and real these unseen Emotional VFs can be. For instance, be aware that taking an argument with your spouse into the bedroom, so that your children can't hear you, doesn't mean the children don't feel the effects of your thoughts and emotions. And staying married for the sole reason of protecting the children is probably doing quite the opposite. Your children will consciously and unconsciously be affected by the negative VFs of your relationship. We need to pay more attention and use our intuition to recognize and adapt to these invisible VFs.

Nature and VFs

Nature is constantly transmitting VFs, which we can easily feel. Two examples for me are water and the electromagnetic vortexes of Sedona. I'm not talking about the supernatural stuff; science has defined the frequencies of both. Being around energy that contains a high amount of negative ions—such as large bodies of water, waterfalls, or even a running shower—helps to provide a feeling of peace, enhance our mood, and even stimulate our alpha-brain waves. Feeling, or not, the energies of the vortexes is a good example of what it takes to be more in tune with VFs. The energies from the Sedona vortexes are created from natural rock formations, which have a distinct and geologically measurable electromagnetic frequency. The magnetic vortex at Cathedral Rock, like water, has more negative ions and a soothing effect. Bell Rock has more electric energy with an abundance of positive ions, which has an energetic effect.

I have friends who have gone there and told me the vortexes don't exist because they didn't feel anything. On further questioning, I discovered that, even though they might not have felt the energy frequency from a particular vortex, they at least admitted to feeling a sense of peace or calmness, or a sense of being more energetic even though they'd hiked all day. I reminded them that it also takes practice to feel those subtle energies. At any given moment, they are receiving VFs from many other sources, including the chatter of their own minds. Our ego VF plays very loudly and tends to drown out the fainter VF of Sedona's unique vortexes. There is no "fast food" approach to feeling these or other VFs. The more you can get into a state of quietness, the easier it is to recognize and feel those distinct, unseen VFs. You have to practice through meditation and build up your Spiritual muscles.

Having More Versus Raising Your VFs

"I select my players from a feeling that comes to me
when I am with them, a certain sympathy you might call it,
or a vibration that exists between us
that convinces me they are right."
Erich von Stroheim

We all want happiness in our lives. So what can we do to achieve it? Our typical response is usually to acquire more—more energy, in the form of money, men, women, sex, or things. Seriously, has *more* of anything ever brought true happiness? Science has told us that we can't create more energy; the first law of thermodynamics states that energy can be neither created nor destroyed. Your PIES, your energetic-self, only has a certain amount of energy; you can't add to or subtract from it.

So how can you change anything or feel more love or more happiness? It's not about having more of anything; it's just about raising your frequency. The energy spectrum demonstrates that the longer the wavelength, the lower the frequency, resulting in lower energy and the shorter the wavelength, the higher the frequency, resulting in higher energy. Changing a frequency is much easier than trying to change things that we perceive as solid. If you play guitar and want to change a low C to a high E, all you have to do is slide your finger downwards on a guitar string, creating a shorter wavelength and thus a higher note. If you would like to change sound to light, you can't add anything, but you can raise the frequency of a D note by a few hundred octaves and get a purple light. Boiling an ice cube, which is raising its VF, changes a solid to a liquid to steam. A mere focus of your thought while you're singing can change the frequency of your voice. None of these examples is about doing more or creating more; they're all about changing frequency.

A lower Physical VF occurs when you are sick or inactive, and a higher VF occurs when you eat nutritionally and exercise. A lower Intellectual VF occurs when you come from small, limiting ego-mindedness, and a higher VF occurs when you're open and whole-minded. A lower Emotional VF occurs when you feel fear, anger, and hate, and a higher VF occurs when you're filled with love, compassion, and bliss. If you want health over sickness, acceptance over judgment, and happiness over anger, don't try to add or subtract someone or something in your life; just raise your own frequency. I know you've read this a hundred times before, but remember: your focus is your reality.

For me, going through a divorce brought a myriad of negative thoughts, which all carried a lower frequency: "I've screwed up again. I'm a loser. What's wrong with me?" Accompanying those negative thoughts were lower-frequency feelings of sadness, guilt, and frustration. Maybe through a breakup or divorce, you've had similar thoughts to mine, or maybe you put your energy on the other person: "Look what he did to me. She never listened. He cheated on me." It's easy to get into "the blame game" with feelings of anger, revenge, or hate. If you come from the belief system that your world is mostly made up of things outside yourself, the answer to your problem might be to quickly replace that pain by finding another person, buying more clothes, or obtaining a new electronic gadget—the *more* philosophy. Many people get into this cycle, never really reaching the core issue and looking inwards—raising their VFs—for the answer.

Breathe!

Having been through that relationship cycle before, I knew better this time around. I didn't try to find more—that is, find someone new. I knew that I needed to work on myself. First, I had to allow myself to go through the grieving process. (No matter what side of the divorce one is on, there is always a sense of loss, a grieving process, that one needs to experience.) I used my Intellect to consciously and objectively look at my situation and accept responsibility for my part. I used my emotional intelligence to accurately assess my emotions and distinguish which were mine and which were my ex-wife's. I then needed to raise my VFs by changing my lower-frequency, negative thoughts to higher-frequency, positive thoughts: "I'll do what I need to do to be positive. I'll come out of this stronger than before. We're all just learning as we go through life." These more positive thoughts

217

changed my lower Emotional VFs of fear, hurt, and blame to higher VFs of compassion, forgiveness, and love. I can't change others, but I can change myself and my perceptions. Acting on this awareness is extremely empowering. I'm a work in progress!

Frequency of Pure Love

Remember, back in the chapter on the Emotional aspect, I discussed my premise that love is the one true emotion. If that is true, then why is it so hard to feel love? One of the reasons is that we're human and our frequencies are much lower than that of pure love. Our Intellect, with its beliefs, perceptions, and judgments, filters this constant pulsing frequency of love. The filtering process creates a lesser gradation of that primary energy, descending in frequency from love to joy, to anger, to sadness, and to fear. For argument's sake, let's say the frequency of pure love is 500 MHz, which happens to be beyond our human frequency of 1 to 100 MHz. As with a dog whistle, we can't experience it until the frequency is lowered. When we do experience it, therefore, it is only at a lower frequency. We could feel pure love's frequency of 500 MHz as ecstasy at 95 MHz, or euphoria at 90 MHz. Let's say your mind had some judgments and expectations. This would lower the frequency of love down to 45 MHz, which you might feel as frustration. If your mind contained critical thoughts, beliefs, and judgments, you might feel the frequency of love at 14 MHz, which you might describe as rage. All of our emotions stem from the pure energy of love but become diluted by our thoughts, beliefs, and expectations.

Let's use a simple example of driving at the speed limit in the fast lane of a freeway. Imagine you feel the frequency of joy at 85 MHz until you come upon someone in your lane doing 5mph less than the limit. You consciously or unconsciously believe they are preventing you from achieving your desire, which is to move at the speed limit. This feeling of joy has now been diminished by your thoughts, your state of mind, to 45 MHz and you feel the emotion of that lower frequency, which happens to be frustration. If the other driver continues not to move over, and you continue to focus on your needs not being met, you'll lower the frequency to 30

MHz, which would be anger. So if you want to continue feeling joy, change your thoughts and expectations of how other drivers are supposed to drive, or change your behavior, maybe by leaving earlier. The joy and love are always there; you just have to let go of your mind to experience them fully.

Main Points

- Experience the world as energetic and having VFs rather than as solid.
- All energy transmits and receives VFs.
- Recognize VFs as being magnetic, repulsive, dissonant, or harmonizing.
- Realize and act on the awareness that more is not better.
- Raise your VF.

Questions

- I play the piano and love to hear the music. But, more profoundly, I love to feel the sound as it moves through my body. My favorite note is the second-lowest C, which is 65.41 Hz. That particular note satisfies me like hearing thunder rolling through a valley, listening to a didgeridoo, or feeling the low trembling of a Tibetan Chant. Do you have a favorite note? If not a note, then what VF when you experience it is deeply satisfying—a word, a place, a smell, a song, a feeling? What can you do to experience that VF?
- When and where have you felt the invisible VFs of thoughts and feelings from others? Did you act on it? What were the consequences?

Challenges

- Can you feel the frequencies of your particular challenges?
- What can you do to raise the VFs of each of your challenges?

Affirmation

- I am raising my Vibrational Frequency in all that I think, feel, and act.

***

Reflections and Corrections

Reflecting on all my steps to attaining balance, I keep coming back to one point that I believe needs to be reiterated. So, at the risk of being repetitive: STOP! Stop your negative, habitual, unconscious thought loops. Stop focusing on lower VFs.

Every time you become aware of any negative thoughts, simply scream in your mind, *STOP!* When the thought returns, yell it again. If the thought comes back, yell even louder; if you're alone in the car or at home, yell "STOP!" out loud. Change the station that plays in your unconscious mind and tune in to a positive VF station. Use whatever word or action that gets you to stop that incessant negative, recurring, repetitive, recycled thought loop: "My life is too difficult." "She'd never like somebody like me." "I'll never get enough money to get out of debt." "My job is hard."

The first step is to become conscious of what VFs are playing in the background. Remember, you received and then unconsciously accepted many of those beliefs through parenting, peers, and then society. You must become mentally strong, take command of your Intellect, and break your habitual negative thought loop. Only when you're conscious can you have an opportunity to stop those thoughts. Upon examination, if those thoughts are not congruent with your being authentic, replace them immediately with any of the positive affirmations listed in this book—or, better yet, create your own.

The difficulty of this process is that your mind will want to replay the negative VFs over and over again as a phonographic needle becomes stuck in the same groove, repeating the same lyrical phrase. (Okay, that metaphor certainly shows my age.) Why is it so difficult to break this pattern? The answer is simple: because you've probably been thinking those thoughts a thousand, in fact thousands of times over years or even decades. That pattern becomes habit, using the same neural pathways.

How many times must you stop a negative thought and replace it with a positive one before it becomes a positive habit? Malcolm Gladwell did a study that states to become excellent in any sport, programming, or passion, one needs to spend about ten thousand hours repetitively practicing. I'm not expecting you to be the next Michael Jordan, Tiger Woods, or Bill Gates of taking control of your mind. But I am saying that you can become proficient if, instead of ten thousand hours, you create ten thousand moments of stopping negative thought loops.

Becoming aware of a negative thought, yelling *Stop!* in your mind, and then replacing the thought with an affirmation takes about twelve seconds; that's five moments to total a minute, three hundred moments in an hour, three thousand moments in ten hours. So, if you were to add all the moments together, you'd have to spend just a little over thirty hours to begin being skilled. I guarantee that just being proficient at taking control of your unconscious negative thought loops will change your life in ways you can't even fathom yet.

Better yet, don't worry about how many times it will take to change. Just know that every time you *Stop!*, change a negative thought, and replace it with a positive one, you'll move closer to creating a positive unconscious thought process. Eventually you'll discover, like I did, that your unconscious mind will effortlessly stop the negative loop and play only positive ones.

Let me give you a personal but different negative thought process. I was guilty of an unbalanced, negative, habitual thought process called catastrophizing. This means taking a situation and extrapolating all the possible negative outcomes that could occur from a particular situation, whether it is real or imagined. An "ah-ha" moment occurred in Chicago, when I was in my early twenties. As I drove in the fast lane of the Eisenhower Expressway, a car to my right swerved into my lane. I reacted and quickly veered into the emergency lane, narrowly missing the railing, while several other cars also had to quickly react. Within a couple of seconds, all cars were under control and back in their respective lanes. Of course my body had gone into an appropriate stress response. If I had given it a few minutes, I'd have calmed down, but, because I catastrophized, my mind took me to a different place.

Continuing to drive to work, safely and in no harm, I envisioned negative "what if"s. What if the car to my right had bumped my left bumper? I would have hit the guardrail; the car behind me would have then smashed me from behind, which would have sent me crashing into the car to my right. Of course, the mass of cars behind us would be fishtailing, zigzagging, and careening every which way, creating a massive pile-up. Oh, my mind didn't stop there. I envisioned that, as the pile-up ended, I'd untangle my battered body from my car as an oil tanker slammed into the carnage with the obligatory fireball explosion. Other versions of this scenario played over and over in my mind for the remaining ten minutes till I arrived at work, a mental wreck. I was so tuned in to the VF of drama.

As I sat at my desk and reflected on my last half hour, I realized I'd catastrophized many times in my life. In that moment, I made a strong commitment to become aware of any negative thoughts or processes and *Stop!* them from continuing. I soon recognized that my unconscious mind tended to override my efforts. Like a rabid dog searching for water, my mind was driven to catastrophize. I needed to stop my mind, to bump it, like hitting a record player to move the needle out of the groove.

So I began this *Stop!* method. I yelled *Stop!* in my mind, at home, at parties, while walking, playing sports, and driving. I used this method not only to end catastrophizing, but also for any negative thoughts that entered my mind. I yelled *Stop!* ten, twenty, forty times a day for weeks. There came a point when I didn't have to say *Stop!* as much and eventually only rarely. My mind had erased the negative unconscious habit and switched into a positive affirmation or into the present moment. The timing of that switch will be different for everyone. Just know that, whether it is your seven thousandth time or fifteen thousandth time, whether it occurs in two months or seven months, every time you *Stop!* you are one step closer to taking control of your unconscious mind.

I also understood that my self-induced catastrophizing was no different from the habits of people who worry, have negative self-talk, or are anxious about future events: "What if I get cancer tomorrow?" "What if I get killed tomorrow?" "I'm not *good* enough." "What if my son does not get accepted into college?" "What if I get laid off?" "What if I never have children?" Of course, it's okay to be aware of those thoughts and take action by setting up reasonable steps to address your concerns, but make sure you then let them go and replace them with positive thoughts. If you allow them to overpower you, you'll continue to be unbalanced.

13

Energy Must Flow

*Holding, restricting, confining any thing, person, or process
eventually causes harm.*

Having the eyes of an electron microscope, the knowledge of a
quantum physicist, or the common sense of a conscious human
being, one could easily realize that *Energy Must Flow*. This
principle is a major characteristic of energy. The universe is filled
with energy that is by its very nature active, dynamic, vibrant,
interconnecting, sharing, shifting, and changing. One of the major
reasons our individually and collectively created world is so
dysfunctional is that most of us act as if our world and life should
be solid, unmoving, static, inactive, or inert. This chapter will
define *Energy Must Flow*, show examples of where and when this
UP is operating, and explore the negative effects of when it is not.

Water = Energy

I like using water as a metaphor for *Energy Must Flow* because
it is constantly flowing—changing. Think of energy as a river
moving downhill; it has to flow according to the universal laws.
You can temporarily hold it back, but eventually that river/energy
will move under, over, around, or through that man-made or
mental/emotional dam. Wherever there is water, there is life. Look
around the planet and you'll see everything from flora to fauna,
villages to cities thriving on its shores. On the opposite side of the
spectrum is stagnant water. It doesn't flow, which provides an
environment of bacteria, parasites, and possible diseases, such as
malaria and dengue. Only through lack of movement does water—
and energy—become unhealthy.

Keeping within the water metaphor, H^2O flows between the varied states of solid, liquid, and vapor, and also within its own sub-atomic structure. Ice has movement, even though it is solid and in a state of low energy and frequency. Externally, the flow may occur as a slow-moving glacier, but internally, electrons and neutrons are spinning. Water as a liquid has a higher frequency and can flow under, over, and around with ease. It has much more movement and pliability in its higher-energy state as it travels around our planet. As water increases its VF, it changes into vapor; it can now move in the atmosphere, traveling around the world with ease. In the higher-energy state, it has much more life, resiliency, and flow than it does when solid.

PIES Needs to Flow

"Flow with whatever may happen and let your mind be free.
Stay centered by accepting whatever you are doing.
This is the ultimate."
Zhuang Zhou

So how do you want your energetic body, your PIES, to flow—like a solid, liquid, or vapor? Visualizing your PIES as flowing water/energy can help you to escape the perceived limits of your body, mind, Emotions, and Spirit. We think of our body as being solid, but in reality it is mostly composed of water and, in the perspective of quantum physics, space. Physically, our bodies are made to move. Ages ago, all the things we needed to survive— such as food, protection, and shelter—required a lot of physical movement. Today's world requires much less of the physical, as evidenced by many people being lazy, lethargic, tired, and sluggish. This lower physical energy state, like water in the state of ice, inhibits your movement and makes you feel as if you're brittle. The lack of flow within our muscles, arteries, bowels, and joints leads to pain and atrophy. What came to us naturally in earlier times is now something we have to consciously focus on. We need to provide flow by playing sports, running, working out, or performing other physical movements. Surprisingly, when we expend energy doing those activities, we become more energized. Ask yourself a simple question: do I feel better, happier, and more alive when my body is flowing—being physically active—or when my body is in stasis—being a couch potato?

Our emotions also need to flow in order to be healthy. That's why it is so important to use our EQ—our emotional intelligence. We need to become more aware of our feelings and heartfully express them. If we hold them back, the buildup of energy will wear on our body, mind, and Spirit. This blockage damages our organs, eats away at our mind, and disconnects us from ourselves and others.

One of the ways I didn't allow energy to flow was through unspoken frustrations that built into resentment. I'm a laidback kind of guy who rarely gets upset. I truly believe and live my life by the colloquial phrase, "Don't sweat the small stuff, and it's all small stuff." Yet, whether they are big or small, there are still many frustrating moments with loved ones and in life. Being a "pleaser" encouraged my behavior of not addressing those small or medium irritants when they occurred. After two or three years, I'd verbally explode, releasing all those festering, unconscious resentments.

The recipient of this outburst was usually shocked about what had happened to "nice little Tommy" and confused about what they'd done to deserve the full force of my wrath. My dysfunctional Emotional outburst made it difficult for me and the recipient to see the present situation objectively, because of my backed-up, undigested, unconscious emotions. This unhealthy pattern also shows how *Energy Moves in a Circular Fashion*. Because I didn't recognize and heal my blockage of emotions, they returned to me at a later time. The little bit of mental discomfort from expressing my emotions in the moment is much better than holding back the flow and feeling the negative consequences in my Physical and Emotional health.

"Life is a series of natural and spontaneous changes.
Don't resist them—that only creates sorrow.
Let the reality be reality.
Let things flow naturally forward in whatever way they like."
Lao Tse

We've already explored some of the many different facets of Intellectual energy needing to flow, as well as examples of when it doesn't. To reiterate some of those points: remember, when we restrict our minds, we become more exclusive and non-accepting. As we allow our perspective to widen and our mind to be open to all possibilities, we tend to become more inclusive and accepting. One way to accomplish this is to allow our mind to flow between the two sides of our brain. We don't want a hole in our brain, but rather a whole brain. Have you ever known someone who uses both sides? They tend to be less stressed and more interesting, stimulating, and happy. We've all met people who use just one side, usually the left. Most of our world is run by left-brained people—logical, reasonable, detail-oriented—and we can see the results, some incredible and many selective and divisive. If we had a world of mostly right-brained people—holistic, imaginative, creative—it would still be incomplete, with a different set of challenges. Balance is never about this way or that way, left or right, but rather about a flow of both/and.

Remember, whether you believe it or not, your unconscious mind makes most of your decisions. Yet most of us dare not look at that darkened place, therefore preventing any insightful examination to see if our beliefs align with our authentic-self. We need to forcefully use our conscious mind to slowly open that unknown aspect of ourselves. This examination of our unconscious thoughts, beliefs, and assumptions is necessary in order to sift out the ones that were created by our ego, parents, and institutions and keep the ones that align to our soul. This requires a conscious mental flow to free us from our chained and atrophied unconscious beliefs. I know this can be a painful and sometimes exhausting endeavor, but it is absolutely necessary to being authentic.

Spiritual flow involves experiencing the *knowingness* of love and connection to all things. Spirituality is all about allowing the flow of the Universe, allowing everything to unfold in its own way, including yourself. This is a challenge, because hundreds of layers of conditioned thoughts weigh down our soul. This heaviness occurs when our heart and mind hold back the flow of Spirit as we try to protect ourselves from Emotional or Intellectual/ego pain. The result is that we become jaded, sheltered, lonely, stagnated, shallow, and righteous.

Breathe!
Feel the flow of the inhale and the exhale,
Feel the flow of your thoughts as you read.
Breathe!

This lack of Spiritual movement seems prevalent in our society, as we witness the consequences of mass unconsciousness. But it is that very fact that can be a catalyst for us to think, feel, and act differently. Paul Hawken coined the phrase "Blessed Unrest," which suggests that these feelings of angst, anxiety, and uncomfortableness can be a catalyst for us to move out of our present state of affairs. Our "unrest" with a world of dirty politics, greed, vanity, war, and social inequalities can motivate us to Intellectually and Emotionally change—to do something, anything, different. The light of our conscious Spirit can quickly and easily cut through the darkness, exposing our blocked and stagnant mind and heart. This allowing process, this letting go of things, beliefs, and emotions is a "flowing" and is extremely valuable to the health of your PIES and humanity.

Change is Inevitable

"I really feel like life will dictate itself.
You should allow it to unfold as naturally as possible.
Just go with the flow.
When you're ready, you say a few prayers and hope for the best.
That's the way I've always lived my life."
Shania Twain

Energy Must Flow, therefore change is inevitable. Nothing is static; stars are dying and black holes are being born, forests are diminishing and water levels are rising, species are declining and humans are multiplying. As the Milky Way spirals through the universe, worlds change; as energy moves within you, your life changes. Your body, thoughts, emotions, and behaviors have changed to varying degrees throughout your life. You have changed from an infant to an adult, from a student to a worker, from happy to sad, from ignorant to knowledgeable, and maybe from single to married to single again. Change is a natural phenomenon throughout the Universe, yet most of us have been taught the exact opposite. Through unconscious, conditioned thoughts and actions, we've been taught to avoid change at all cost. No wonder most of us are in angst and pain most of our lives; we have been fighting the unstoppable and perpetual flow of the Universe.

Fight for Change

"Resistance is futile."
The Borg, *Star Trek*

I believe our institutions—on an unconscious and, many times, conscious or premeditated level—attempt to stop our mind and spirit expanding. They want to keep our behavior within the status quo. If we're all thinking, feeling, and acting in predictable, static, and unconscious ways, it's easier to manipulate us into their prescribed behavior. From saving our souls to saving our youthfulness, protecting our nation to protecting our homes, feeding our bodies to feeding our minds, these advertisers, corporations, media, and sometimes religions are trying to control us. Their need to control, for the purpose of power and money, requires us to be herded together by Physical, Intellectual, or Emotional fences. The easiest way to accomplish this task is to create fear. We need to be attentive, fluent, and active in our mind, heart, and spirit to ensure that doesn't happen.

Let Go

"If you love somebody, let them go, for if they return,
they were always yours.
If they don't, they never were."
Kahlil Gibran

Every thing, every person, every process needs to flow. Holding, restricting, confining any thing, person, or process eventually causes harm. Most people can easily understand that holding on to negative, lower VFs is not healthy. But the UPs are always operating, regardless of the type of energy that is involved, whether it is positive or negative. Now, here is the kicker that I get lots of resistance about: I'm even talking about love. I hear you saying, "Hold the bus, Tom!" Yes, I say, even love. Think about it. When you let go of the love you have in this moment, you allow yourself to receive more love in the next moment. Remember what happens to stagnant water; even love can turn sour if it is caged.

Whatever you resist doesn't go away; it actually sticks around and becomes stronger. Resisting someone, something, some idea, or some feeling that comes your way creates a dam that has destructive effects. When our bodies, minds, and emotions resist the flow of energy, there will be a plethora of negative side effects, from constipation to boils, anger to rage, prejudice to bigotry, and depression to suicide. Low self-esteem is like Velcro and will hold on to any negative energies that come its way. You can practice and act on this art of non-resistance with co-workers, family, or friends who deliver mental or verbal blows. To eliminate this resistance, you need to follow through with the over-used colloquial term "let go." What if you were like a judo expert—you didn't resist but rather moved *with* the blows, reducing the impact and returning to balance quicker? You want to be less like Velcro and more like Teflon, to which nothing sticks. Eventually, when you become more practiced, you will experience the words and emotions of others only momentarily. They will easily slide off you, allowing you to be open for the wonders of the next moment.

"What you resist, persists."
Carl Jung

Main Points

- Change is an essential part of life; allow it and accept it.
- Your thoughts, emotions, and actions must flow.
- Let go.

Questions

- What can you do to allow the flow within your PIES?
- How do you react to change? What can you do to embrace it?
- Do you block yourself from expressing emotions? If so, when?

Challenges

- Where in my challenges do I impede the flow of energy? What can I specifically do to release, let go, in those areas?

Affirmations

- I am letting go of my thoughts, feelings, and actions.
- I am flowing through the Universe.
- I am letting go of all resistance.

***

Reflections and Corrections

Again, and for the last time, I'm returning to the issue of stopping and changing a thought or belief. This is of paramount importance because, time and again, clients and students return to me after months or years with the same challenges. I ask if they stopped and changed their thought pattern in the moment it was happening. Their answer is almost always "No."

I want to give you a simple tool so that you can examine the seemingly complex relationship between your thoughts and emotions, and then change what is not in alignment with your authenticity. To get you started, let's look at my challenges, including being mad at losing my home, impatient from ankle surgery, defeated by not having a job, and sad about losing my marriage.

I began by stating the challenge in an objective way. As the old *Dragnet* series used to say, "Just the facts, Ma'am"—or, a little more recent reference if you're a Trekky, be like Data. Basically, put yourself in the place of a disinterested observer.

Example One

Step One: Express Objective State of Being

"I lost possession of my home."

Next, bring to light as much as possible your thoughts, expectations, and beliefs surrounding this challenge.

Step Two: List Accompanying Thoughts, Expectations, Beliefs

"I should've never sold my previous home."
"I should've played it safer."
"I should've planned better."
"I should've..." ad nauseam.
"The government and banks are to blame."

233

"I'm to blame."
"I have nothing left."
"I'm nobody."
"I'm a loser."

Dig deep, so that you can get to some of those unconscious beliefs. Depending on your expertise and level of consciousness, your discoveries will vary. (As with all of this material, please use professional assistance when you need to.) As your self-awareness and mastery of balance increase, you'll be able to more clearly identify those thoughts.

Then use your emotional intelligence to identify and list your accompanying emotions.

Step Three: List Emotions

"I'm sad, mad, nervous, and a little depressed at times."

Now go back and review those thoughts. Remember *Everything Just Is*. Stop the negative thoughts. Look at the situation from a different perspective. See if your beliefs disconnect you from others or yourself. If so, change them to be congruent with your authentic-self, which is aware of your deep connections to all things—*Energy is Interconnected*.
Formulate a belief, along with affirmations, that promote *Everything Moving Towards Balance*, including your PIES. Live in accordance with the UPs; *Energy Must Flow*.

Step Four: Create Balanced Beliefs and Affirmations

"I tend to live on the edge and push myself."
"Maybe I need to reevaluate if I do that in all aspects of my life."
"I need to take responsibility for my part in all of this and let go of blaming others and myself."
"The reality is that I could have made a safer decision and not bought such an expensive piece of real estate, but I didn't."
"I'll learn from my mistakes and live with my consequences in a positive way."

"I can survive renting or living with friends or family."
"I am not my home."
"I am much more…"

Step Five: Observe How Emotions Change

As you incorporate those beliefs, observe how your emotions change to positive ones. Be grateful to yourself for taking action and making a difference in your own life.

Example Two

Step One: Express Objective State of Being

"I lost my dexterity because of the ankle surgery and I'm in pain. I can't play sports for now."

Step Two: List Accompanying Thoughts, Expectations, Beliefs

"It's hard for me to just get a beer out of the fridge, let alone go shopping."
"I should have taken better care of my body."
"My mother always told me to stop playing sports."
"Am I ever going to play sports as well as I did before?"

Step Three: List Emotions

"I feel frustrated, annoyed, impatient, self-pitying."

Step Four: Create Balanced Beliefs and Affirmations

"The reality is that I'm in pain and housebound because of my surgery; that's all. I don't need to make a big deal about it. I don't need to be so tough on myself. I should allow myself time to heal, and do the things that will promote healing in my ankle, and deal with it."
"I am an athlete who at times, and because of my age, becomes injured."

"I am strong and resilient and I am bouncing back from this injury."

Step Five: Observe How Emotions Change

Example Three

Step One: Express Objective State of Being

"I lost my job and I'm having difficulty finding full-time employment."

Step Two: List Accompanying Thoughts, Expectations, Beliefs

"I'm a loser. I'm supposed to be the breadwinner."
"What's wrong with me that I couldn't hold on to my job?"
"I'm too old."
"Nobody wants me."
"I hate my present unfulfilling part-time jobs, which don't even come close to paying the bills."

Step Three: List Emotions

"I feel frustrated, angry, relieved, resentful, rejected, defeated, and hopeless."

Step Four: Create Balanced Beliefs and Affirmations

"I must identify what I need to do in order to survive, and then follow through."
"This is a tough economy."

I should reevaluate the question "Who am I?"
I should question my belief about having to be the breadwinner.
What part does my ego play in all of this?

"I don't need to be so tough on myself."
"I'm a survivor."

"I still have a healthy body and mind."
"I've always made it through before."
"I need to ensure that, no matter what, my authentic-self shines through in every moment."

Step Five: Observe How Emotions Change

Example Four

Step One: Express Objective State of Being

"My marriage dissolved."

Step Two: List Accompanying Thoughts, Expectations, Beliefs

"I'm a failure in relationships."
"What's wrong with me?"
"Why couldn't she have been different?"
"Why did I feel I had to be right all the time?"
"Why didn't I work harder at the relationship?"

Step Three: List Emotions

"I feel insecure, sad, guilty, relieved, weary."

Step Four: Create Balanced Beliefs and Affirmations

"I didn't run away from disagreements like I did before."
"I hung in there and tried to work it out."
"I did try the best that I knew how."
"I am lovable."
"I will learn what I can and take it with me."

Step Five: Observe How Emotions Change

Now substitute your own challenges. Be honest with yourself. Know that the more you *Master the Art of Balance*, the more your authentic-self will find deeper and deeper answers to the above questions. Remember, when you find yourself in a negative loop about any of your thoughts or self-talk, yell or think "Stop!" Immediately think a positive thought or affirmation. Repeat this move any and every time your mind wanders back to the negativity. Okay, I'll quit harping on at you about this process.

14

Energy Attracts Like Energy

Would you live your life differently
if you knew that your every thought, word, feeling, and action
would come back to you a hundredfold?

This UP directly relates to *Energy Is Interconnected*. The most appropriate colloquialism for this concept is "What goes around comes around." What drives this concept is the magnetizing effect of the VFs of energy, commonly known as the Law of Attraction. This energy loop is a natural process found throughout the Universe and nature, and also within the interaction of thoughts, emotions, and actions. I will address this circular energy as it is experienced in the laws of attraction, karma, and reflection.

Attraction

"I'm a true believer in karma. You get what you give."
Sandra Bullock

Most of us are unconscious of this attraction process. We're surprised when our outside life doesn't manifest our internal desires. We're unaware and unconscious of who we really are and that our thoughts, feelings, and actions directly relate to our perceived reality. We don't realize many things in life happen to us because the mindset behind our actions actually created those happenings. Let's start with the example of magnetic attraction. If all one thought, felt, and acted on was hate and nothing else, one's life would most likely attract and be consumed by various forms of hate. Hate can manifest in many different ways, such as through being self-destructive, mean-spirited, and hurtful to animals and others. The opposite is also true—that if all one felt was love and nothing else, one's life would most likely attract and be packed with various forms of love. Love can manifest in various ways, such as through helpfulness, acceptance, compassion, and forgiveness.

It would be easier to be conscious of this attraction process if everyone was either like the devil or Mother Teresa. We could then clearly see the direct correlation of thoughts, words, and feelings to people's realities. But life is rarely about living at these extremes of hate or love. We all have a myriad array of thoughts and feelings, and therefore send out and receive or attract a myriad array of VFs. We can love our brother but hate our sister, be fond of our friend but not tolerate a co-worker, be frustrated with our children but also die for them, be passionate with our lover but pull our hair out when they annoy us. We're complex beings and therefore this attraction process—a collage of positive and negative feelings and thoughts that we project and manifest—is harder to recognize.

> *"Change your thoughts and you change the world."*
> Norman Vincent Peale

We need to be conscious of our thoughts and feelings in order to change any part of this attraction process. We haven't been tending our mind garden—removing the negative, egotistical, self-centered beliefs and nurturing the positive, loving, and soulful beliefs. The harmful roots, if not dug up and thrown out, will continue to have a stranglehold on our actions.

Creating a momentary conscious thought doesn't mean it will override the more powerful, opposing, unconscious belief. If you consciously think you want more money but haven't rooted out your old beliefs about lack of money, then the more powerful, unconscious VF of lack of money will continue to manifest. Many of our comedic plays and films involve people who are so fearful of "screwing up" that they actually attract the consequences of their fears. If you want a new loving relationship but still badmouth your ex, that VF of lack of love will continue to be present in your life. Someone feeling constantly jealous believes that people are untrustworthy and possibly that they themselves are not lovable; both beliefs create a low self-concept and self-esteem. The person can scream at the top of their lungs about how much they want a committed relationship, but, until they examine the unconscious beliefs around their jealousy, they will continue to attract cheaters. (Or they will attract a positive person but still feel jealous, because they end up creating imaginary signs of cheating.)

The first time I became aware of the positive and negative sides of *Energy Attracts Like Energy* was after I got out of college. I worked as an occupational and recreational therapist at a Chicago psych hospital. The daily routine was for nurses to send up patients from their respective floors for their bi-weekly sessions. One day, I had a patient who was very agitated despite my efforts to find an activity that would calm her. Within her view, I sat myself down in a corner and started to knit in a tranquil manner. Consciously, I took several deep breaths as I watched her approach me. In a short time, she and two other patients were quietly and peacefully knitting next to me.

Later that day, the nurses sent more patients than were scheduled. (Once in a while, if space permitted, the nurses would send extra patients, so that they could have an easier time with fewer patients on their floors.) Because of the overflow, some of the patients became slightly agitated, as we didn't have enough personnel to take care of their needs. As time progressed, I noticed others picking up on the lower Emotional energies of their fellow patients. As this unbalanced energy continued to grow, the staff realized we should send them back down to their respective floors, before things got out of hand. We quickly lined them up outside the elevator. Now they were even more frustrated, because they didn't want to return to their rooms.

As the staff quickly lost control, they became more frustrated with the patients' lack of cooperation. The *Like* energy of frustration escalated as it bounced back and forth invisibly between patients and staff. I eventually exploded by shouting out orders in an angry voice to try to control the situation. Instantly, as if I'd thrown kerosene on a brush fire, the patients became unruly and extremely agitated and angry. Orderlies and nurses from all the floors had to quickly come to our rescue. (I had a vision of Jack Nicholson, from *One Flew Over the Cuckoo's Nest*, lashing out at me with a knitting needle, as if I were Nurse Ratched.) This was my first recognition of how quickly the Law of Attraction works both in a positive and negative way.

Karma

> *"Karma, when properly understood, is just the mechanics through which consciousness manifests."*
> Deepak Chopra

Karma, from the theosophical definition, states that when we live a *good* life, *good* things will happen to us and when we live a *bad* life, *bad* things will happen to us. The Hindu perspective is that the total effect of a person's actions and conduct determines that person's destiny. Karma basically states that whatever energy you put out will come back to you at some point in time.

Breathe!
Note through the day what is attracted to you
after deep conscious breaths.
Breathe six breaths.

The movie *Groundhog Day* shows a perfect example of karma. Bill Murray's character keeps living the same day over and over. He is conscious of his predicament, but no one else is aware of it. As he continues his old negative behaviors, he becomes stuck and never finds a way to move on to the next day. At first, he becomes hedonistic, attempting to get all the money, sex, and pleasure that he can. While he is somewhat amused by his selfish behavior, he's not really happy and still wakes up to the same situation. After behaving the same way countless times yet expecting a different result, he becomes frustrated with his lack of progress and tries to kill himself. As in our own lives, whether it be this one or the next, he finds himself right back in the same situation. Eventually, he turns inward and becomes loving and compassionate. In karmic fashion, the townspeople reflect his new ways back to him, thus giving him more motivation to continue his positive behavior. Eventually, he attracts the admiration and love of the community and Andie MacDowell's character. When he lives from integrity and compassion, changing his old negative VFs, he leaps out of the time loop and on to the next day—the next stage in his life.

Cause and Effect

"Things don't just happen in this world of arising and passing away. We don't live in some kind of crazy accidental universe. Things happen according to certain laws, laws of nature, and laws such as the law of karma, which teaches us that as a certain seed gets planted, so will that fruit be."
Sharon Salzberg

This circular karmic process is the same as that of cause and effect. Your action—cause—will create similar VFs of consequences—effect. This boomerang effect of energy helps those of us who tend to be unconscious. When the same situation happens enough times, the cause of our unhappiness will eventually seep into our conscious. And the cause is always about us—our thoughts, feelings, and actions. Once we are aware of our behavior, we have the opportunity to act accordingly—to change our thoughts and actions, and therefore change the consequences.

Relationships Show Us Our VFs

Let's look at several examples to see how our relationships attract similar frequencies. Imagine you're unconscious of transmitting low self-esteem VFs. Even though you say that you want an equal and loving relationship, your negative thoughts about yourself will unconsciously attract a partner who has the same VFs. I'm sure you know someone who has been in multiple relationships and continues to repeat comments like "My partner is mean and doesn't respect me." "She puts me down in front of my friends." "He treats me like I'm not even there." After the eventual breakup, they almost always place the blame on the other person. They always think the other person was the problem, so after they end that relationship they start another—the *more* philosophy. After they have several similar relationships that end up the same way, the person usually says, "This always happens to me," or "Why do I always end up with losers?" They haven't realized they've created this same energy loop with different people in different situations. Until they realize that they're the problem— they are the one creating and attracting those similar VFs, they are the cause, and they are manifesting the effect—they'll continue to create new relationships that will fail over the same issues.

Relationship manifestations of VFs can be simple, moderate, or complex. The simple ones are those with someone who shares your liberal or conservative views, shares your love for hiking, shares your tendency to be sad, shares your concerns for saving the environment, or shares your loving ways. The moderate examples are those with someone who shares your open-mindedness in politics but not in sex, shares your love of adventure in sailing but not in spelunking, and shares your focus on career but not on family life.

Let's look at a more complex example, of two people who have low self-concepts. In the classic dominant/passive relationship, they have similar VFs of low self-esteem. The passive manifests their low self-esteem by being a pleaser, while the dominant tries to feel self-worth by controlling others. Even though the opposing parties seem different, they are still both attracting the same VFs of a low self-concept.

Luckily for us, *Like* energy moves in this circular fashion, assisting us to eventually become conscious of our actions. The Universe, through our VFs, creatively continues to manifest new moments that offer us opportunities to deal with the real issues— so we can work on the inner-self, heal ourselves, and, like Bill Murray, move on to another day.

"Be very careful what you set your heart upon,
for you will surely have it."
Ralph Waldo Emerson

Rise Above Karma

Know that you are not always pre-determined to receive the karma from your past, whether in this life or the next. Many people have experienced a jump in consciousness, such as an epiphany, a near-death experience, or just an "aha" moment. That sudden elevation in VF can bring you to a point where you don't experience the full negative effects of your previous actions. In meteorology, there are lower and higher levels of winds that move in different speeds and directions. If you could raise yourself to the higher jet stream, you would not be affected by the winds at the surface. By making a significant VF jump in your life, you could jettison to the higher elevation and free yourself from the winds of your past. This action would most likely provide a welcome change in the direction of your life and the speed at which you move.

This elevation of VF can happen in many ways. I read a story about a person who was dying of a rare disease. Before being diagnosed, she had always tried to control everyone and everything in her business and personal life, making herself and others miserable. This belief system of needing to be in control was accompanied by a variety of low-frequency emotions, such as contempt, irritation, anxiety, fear, frustration, and anger. By transmitting those negative thoughts and emotions, she created situations that fostered those same negative frequencies. In the process of dying, she quickly let go of her thoughts about needing to control, and just allowed herself to accept her situation and friends. She soon gained an appreciation for her business, family, and friends just the way they were. In the later stages of her illness, the doctors discovered a treatment plan that eventually led to her full recovery.

She eventually went back to her business and daily routine, which were filled with the same people and situations from before her illness. Because she'd changed her thoughts to positive ones, her experience of life was very different. Her negative emotions were now transmuted to contentment, joy, happiness, appreciation, and gratitude. Her epiphany had changed her thoughts, which changed her emotions, which changed her karma. The lower-negative frequencies were not on her radar. The lower winds of her past were not affecting her as she flew with the eagles.

Your World is a Reflection of You

"Ask and it will be given to you; seek and you will find, knock and it will be open to you, for everyone who asks receives..."
The Bible

If you have integrated the concepts of "Your focus is your reality," *Energy Attracts Like Energy*, and karma, then your world must be, in some way, a reflection of you. If you hold on to the opposite belief, that this world is separate from you, this reflective concept will not sink into your consciousness.

Imagine a mirror that reflects your perception of your PIES, the people in your life, and the world. With this unique sight, your world becomes a reflection of you. This perspective allows you to use the mirror as a personal feedback system, to help you get a picture of who and where you are in the present moment. It would be great if you could obtain a mirror that never lies, like the mirror of the evil queen in *Snow White*. Otherwise, this reflection process will require an honest and sometimes painful self-appraisal.

If you are looking into the mirror with your ego eyes, you'll see a very different reflection from if you looked in a balanced, objective, and conscious way. When you look in the mirror, do you see blemishes and wrinkles? If you wanted to change those imperfections, would you spend time, energy, and money using potions and lotions to try to remove the unwanted aspects of your reflection from the mirror rather than yourself? Of course not! What if you saw envy, greed, or vanity in this self-reflective mirror? Would you try to change other people, situations, your external aspects? Think of all the wasted time and money you have expended on trying to change things outside of yourself, when all you needed to do was change your thoughts, feelings, and actions. You need to do inner work in order to change your reflection.

Direct Reflection

A helpful way of trying to interpret those reflections is to identify their subtle variations—direct, general, a reminder, or any combination. Thoughts, feelings, and actions intrinsically entwine with your reflection, which makes it difficult at times to tell the source of the VFs. Remember, though, that thoughts beget emotions, which beget actions, which beget your perceptions of reality. For the sake of this discussion, I will use Emotions as the reflective image.

A *direct reflection* is one that bounces back to you from the intended target of your Emotion. You see in this reflective mirror a co-worker who is angry at you, and you then realize you've actually been silently angry with them. If this direct reflection continues, this back and forth can easily escalate and break down communication so that no one is being understood. On the positive side, you could see the image of someone who is loving to you, and you will know that you have been loving towards them. This can escalate to a point of bliss for both of you.

A *general reflection* doesn't have to only reflect the target of your Emotion, but can also manifest from a broader source. This reflection of anger at your co-worker might also include your brother, sister, and friends who are mad at you or just mad in general. Your state of anger has now reflected a general view of your life. On the positive side, you could be very loving to your otherwise negative brother-in-law; he may not return or reflect that love back to you, but you do receive it back from strangers who reflect their positive sides to you.

A *reminder reflection* is a gentle wake-up call for you to fine-tune some aspect of yourself that is slightly out of balance. Imagine that someone displays anger towards you and you have a small charge in reaction to that emotion. Hopefully, you become objective, checking to see if this reaction is a direct reflection of your anger or a general reflection of your state of being. If your answer is no to both, then you know that you still have some layers to "let go" of regarding certain aspects of anger. Don't worry; there are very few humans on this planet who have mastered the art of not being affected by another person's anger. Your charge could be leading you to different areas of learning. Do you wish they weren't angry at you? Do you feel responsible for their anger? Do you need to change your expectation of that person or yourself? Do you need to give yourself and the other person more love, compassion, or forgiveness? It's just another layer of knowingness to unravel.

Be Careful of TV Reflections

> *"How people treat you is their karma;*
> *how you treat them is yours."*
> Wayne W. Dyer

A common way to see this concept in action is to observe people who watch certain types of news programs. Most people watch programs that support their beliefs. Some news stations are programmed to be negatively charged, preying on listeners who are attracted to that frequency. The ping-pong effect takes place as newscasters emanate outrage about a topic that increases the intensity of negative Emotional frequencies, which are usually the lower ones of frustration, anger, fear, and revenge. You stay tuned, giving the station higher ratings, which gives the stations more viewership and more money to continue their tactics and even notch it up a little.

Be careful of the frequency you are allowing into your living room and your mind. I watch a lot of TV, and I try to extricate myself from watching news programs. I know more and more people who are not turning on their TVs at all. Bless them; they are more actualized than me. They are eliminating that negative VF from their reality. So are you watching shows that reflect dysfunction, conflict, and controversy, or shows that reflect harmony, unity, and connection? Is it *Jerry Springer* or *Oprah Winfrey*, *Mixed Martial Arts* or *Dr. Oz*, *Big Brother* or the *Dog Whisperer*?

Energy Increases as It Circulates

*"The greatest revolution in our generation is that of human
beings, who by changing the inner attitudes of their minds,
can change the outer aspects of their lives."*
Marilyn Ferguson

Energy picks up momentum as it journeys through your world
and the Universe. The film *Pay It Forward* portrays this point. A
young boy creates a class project of doing three good deeds, with
the instruction that the recipients must repay those good deeds—
not to him, but to three new people who must then also pay it
forward. Even though the movie ends with him losing his life, it
shows how his three deeds circle back to his community, affecting
multitudes of people in a positive and loving way, including his
mother and teacher. We should all task ourselves with "random
acts of kindness." Hopefully, your intent is based on the natural
expression of your soul, though it doesn't hurt to know that your
efforts will circulate similar VFs back to you. Would you live your
life differently if you knew that your every thought, word, feeling,
and action would come back to you a hundredfold?

Main Points

- You are responsible for your own thoughts, feelings, and actions.
- You attract the energy you emanate.
- Energy returns to us, as does karma.
- Your friends, your family, and the world are reflections of you.
- Live your life as if every thought, feeling, and action will return to you a hundredfold...because it will.

Questions

- Give examples of your VFs returning to you through attraction, karma, or reflection.
- What have you done differently after you realized you were getting back similar VFs?

Challenges

- Identify your thoughts, emotions, and actions related to each of your challenges. Accept in your mind and heart that you allowed most of them. Know that you can change them. Act on changing your thoughts about your challenges and then notice what returns to you.

Affirmations

- I am conscious of my intention within my thoughts, feelings, and actions.
- I express love in all that I think, feel, and do.

***

Reflections and Corrections

As I have said throughout this book, being authentic requires you to be ever vigilant and conscious. Don't expect yourself to remember everything presented here about the UPs and PIES. To help you focus, I've condensed much of this information into the following reminder list and balance chart. Even if you forget portions of this material, trust that these ideas, facts, perspectives, and concepts will come to you at just the right moments.

Helpful Reminders

- Answer the question "Who am I?"
- Use your answer to help you make daily decisions.
- Balance your PIES.
- Create a strong self-concept.
- Remember that your focus is your reality.
- Experience yourself as an energetic being in an energetic universe.
- Stop seeing yourself and your world as separate.
- Observe how everything interconnects with everything else.
- Observe how your outer world reflects your inner being.
- Realize you create your meanings, so you can un-create them.
- Stop judging and be more accepting.
- Be patient with yourself and others.
- Allow your thoughts, feelings, and actions to flow.
- See change as a powerful and positive process.
- Change your VFs, rather than change others or outside events.
- Become aware of what you attract.
- Become aware of how the VFs of your thoughts, feelings, and actions return to you.
- Everything you think, feel, and do will return a hundredfold.
- Remember there are layers and layers of knowing and learning.
- Pain is a warning and tells us of our blockages.
- Allow your spirit to unfold in every moment.
- Be compassionate, grateful, forgiving, and loving in every moment.
- Enjoy your journey!

Balance of PIES

Blocks to Balance	Ways Towards Balance
Physical	**Physical**
Eating poorly. Too much or not enough rest or exercise. Identifying with false Physical.	Focus and act on proper diet, rest, and exercise. Identify with health, not physical things.
Intellectual	**Intellectual**
Over-active id or ego. Dualistic—this or that, right or wrong. Being unconscious. Not examining your beliefs. Being limited, rigid, extreme in your beliefs. Being judgmental.	Limit ego-self and come from higher-self. Be holistic—both/and. Be aware and conscious. Examine all your beliefs. Limitless thinking. Be accepting of others.
Emotional	**Emotional**
Not allowing flow of Emotions. Not feeling love in all moments. Feeling lower VFs.	Allow Emotions to flow in real time. Think positive thoughts. Feel love in all your thoughts, feelings, and actions.
Spiritual	**Spiritual**
Not recognizing your Spirit. Not feeling love and connection with everything.	Recognize, trust, and follow your Spirit. Know and act on the fact that you are connected to all things. Allow love in every moment. Trust your intuition.

15

Final Note

The caterpillar connects to this earthly world with its many legs. Grabbing, wriggling, and crawling over everything that it encounters, the unconscious organism consumes much more than its own weight. As time passes, doing the same old behavior, the caterpillar eventually questions the other gravity-stricken organisms: "Is this all there is? Is there anything I can do differently? Is there any way I can be something different? Is there any way I can stretch beyond this forest?" The creatures' responses are all the same: "This is where you and we are supposed to be — on the ground, in familiar settings, acting in familiar ways. This is the way of our world, this is the way of our ancestors, this is the old way, the way it has always been." Yet the caterpillar still feels angst about being the same, about being attached to the ground. Timidly it responds, "Something doesn't feel *right*. I believe I am something different. There has to be more." As it clambers on its way, the others heckle and mock the caterpillar for its strange musings.

As the caterpillar continues to ravage all the resources it encounters, it sheds its old skin several times, making room for the new. But after every change the caterpillar sadly notices it is still a caterpillar, only gaining weight, only getting bigger, only more of the same.

Somewhere along its journey, the caterpillar has an urge to stop consuming and stop its unconscious need to be busy. Trusting this instinctual and ancient urge, the insect goes within and creates a chrysalis to pupate within. This self-created void is an inward process unseen by the masses. Slowly and naturally, the metamorphosis transforms the caterpillar into its true, intended nature, a creature of beauty and flight.

As the fledgling butterfly — once known as a caterpillar — emerges, it flaps its wings; flaps its wings even though it doesn't go anywhere, flaps its wings even though it hurts, flaps its wings even though the gravity-stricken creatures belittled its effort. With every flap the butterfly becomes stronger and soon lifts off the leaf a little, then a little more. Every effort provides a feeling of being lighter and a *knowing* that its destiny is to be in flight. The butterfly soon flies; flies higher than it ever crawled in the highest tree, flies beyond the vision of those gravity-stricken creatures, and eventually, following the earthly breezes, flies beyond the confines of the forest.

This new stage in its life is only possible because of all the challenges it survived as a caterpillar. There was no right or wrong in any of its actions. It didn't matter what any of the other creatures said or believed. All that mattered was that it allowed itself to flow with the workings of the Universe.

"Who Am I?"

Being knocked off balance after losing my job, home, and marriage was the consequence of all my previous conscious and unconscious choices, along with the mere fact of just being in the game — living in today's world. How I perceived those situations, including my reactions, was all about me. Whether or not I got sucked into quicksand or bounced back was all about me. Whether or not I moved beyond, came out stronger than before, was all about *how* I bounced back. Did I bounce back because I got another job, received money from a friend, immediately fell into another relationship, or inherited a home from a long-lost relative? There is nothing wrong with any of these situations. In fact, I wished they would happen to me, but the truth is I came out stronger because they didn't happen.

I discovered a truer, deeper answer to the question "Who am I?" I built a stronger self-concept. I became more keenly aware of what it takes to be in PIES balance and flowed more easily with the Universal Principles. My consciousness, acceptance, and actions made my journey easier, happier, more meaningful, and more loving.

Living an authentic life, a life of flight, a soulful life, a life of "potentiality expressed" requires us to answer that question "Who am I?" This question has haunted me throughout my life — whenever I reminisce about the past or future, or even while I'm in the present and feel the delight of a touch or ache of a sore muscle, play golf or practice piano, write words or cheer for my favorite sports team, feel the pain of heartache or the throb of a broken ankle, see a morning sunset or wonder at a star-sprinkled night. My answer slightly changes as I continue to let go of layers, getting closer to my core. For now, my answer is this: I am an adventurous soul who, through compassion, forgiveness, gratefulness, and love, creates ways to make a positive difference in the world. I've broken down this answer into several components: soul, create, positive difference, the *how*, and adventurous.

Being a *soul* is at the foundation of my essence, providing me with a deeper connectivity to all things. I respect those who are atheists or religious but my personal belief is that, whether or not there is a God, I *know* that the essence of my soul transcends this Physical world. I've had many experiences, whether one would call them epiphanies or metaphysical "happenings," which have left me with a certainty about there being more beyond this earthly reality.

For me, the ultimate test or question is this: In retrospect, even if it turns out there is no Divine, no soul, no *Celestial Bar*, no existence beyond this world, would that change my answer, change my actions, change how I lived my life? Would I then have chosen a life of "winner takes all", a life of hedonism, a life of debauchery, a life of self-indulgence? My answer has always been a resounding "NO!" None of those styles of living resonate with me…Though a little bit now and then never hurt…That brings in a little balance…No?

One of the many reasons for that anguish-filled night of tearing open crackers was that for years I forgot to even ask that question, let alone adhere to its answer. The truth was that I'd drifted away from my soul and given a little too much focus to acquiring things and making money. Painful as it was, my journey provided me with another opportunity to align myself to what really matters.

I use the word *create* to mainly reflect my personal responsibility for choosing my reality. This knowledge repels the tendency to outwardly discharge negative energy by blaming others or being envious of their situations. Along with the accompanying pain of realizing I've created some negativity in my life is the hope of knowing that, if I created it, I can also un-create it. The term *create* also implies being creative, which denotes fun, passion, inspiration, imagination, and originality. I vote for that every day instead of living in *The Matrix*.

Creating this book was something I had to do. There was a neverending voice, words that had to sing, concepts that had to be released from the ether. What is that in me, or any other writer, that propels us to write, that motivates us to put pen to paper? What other profession could you endure where you go to work day after day, month after month for four years and not collect a paycheck, not have a boss motivating you to meet deadlines, not know if you'd ever receive a dime for all of your hard work, or not receive any feedback for months or years to know if your project is even viable? The joy of this style of creativity rises out of a solace, a struggle, an inner pain, and a deep search for truth. Yet others have done it, I do it, and maybe you've done it; if so, my gratitude and also sympathies go out to you.

Over the years, I've realized that *making a positive difference* in the world is my purpose. This aspect of my answer to the question took me down several paths of inquiry. First, I believe the desire to be of service to others is a natural state of our Spirit, our authentic-self; there is nothing I have to work on to make that happen. Years ago, I realized that, ultimately, I had to change myself before affecting the lives of others. My favorite quote from Richard Bach's *Illusions* states, "You teach best what you most need to learn." If I can't be what I'm teaching, my efforts will be futile. Remember, no one can change another, because each person creates their own reality. One, though, can certainly influence others by illustration, by *being* a shining example of whatever reality one has chosen. So maybe one of the unconscious ways I created my latest challenges was to become an example of a different way of *being* when life overwhelms you.

Specifically for me, there is a drive to make a difference on a larger scale, affecting large numbers of people. Realizing the scope of my purpose pushed me to internally explore its origin: was my desire from my ego or my soul? Did I want to feed my ego so that I could look important to others, or make a lot of money, or was my need altruistic? Because each of us has many selves, the truthful answer is almost always a combination of all perspectives. The trick is to be aware enough of your different selves in order to do an accurate reality check. So, in honesty, a small part of my ego-self would like to reach the masses for the attention and possible monetary benefits. But the overwhelming personal truth is that, after years of training and teaching, I have found that, beyond money or recognition, the greatest pleasure I obtain is when I see a student's lightbulb turn on or read an email about how a reader received insight from something I wrote. So, yes, I feel my purpose of wanting to affect change on a larger scale is in a healthy alignment with my higher-self.

Another realization involved my trying to be *okay* with whomever might be affected, whether I was teaching thousands of people, just one, just myself, or no one. I needed to remember *Energy Just Is*. I needed to feel peace in wherever I was and whatever I was doing, regardless of the results or responses of others.

The how relates to *how* I am going to *be* within all my moments on this earth. How am I going to *be* a parent, spouse, doctor, rapper, millionaire, teenager, or person? My answer is to *be* loving in the forms of compassion, gratefulness, and forgiveness. To fully embrace this process takes a lifetime of letting go of ego and coming from heart and Spirit. I spent decades attempting to *be* compassionate over apathetic, grateful over selfish, and forgiving over blaming. It took years of trusting that choosing all those facets of love over fear in my decision-making and actions would satisfy my soul — my authentic-self.

The last component of my answer is about being *adventurous*, which is the best adjective I could come up with to describe myself. Yet it is the linchpin that makes sense of what many would call a paradoxical life. Adventures can include having different escapades in different locales, but they can also be adventures of the Intellect, Emotion, and Spirit. The need for adventure is at my core and explains why I made choices that were different from other people's. I chose to leave Chicago, my friends, and family with no destination in mind. I chose to try many different careers and jobs rather than sticking to one or two. I chose to begin businesses in which I had no idea what I was doing, such as being a restaurateur, painter, publisher, and author. I chose to venture again into exploring marriage after a thirty-year hiatus. After my restaurant sank in Key West, I chose not to go back to the comfort of Chicago but instead took off to San Diego. Recently, I chose to take off with an incredible woman, leaving behind family, softball, friends, and a warm climate to face the frozen tundra of New England.

I chose adventure over security and money. Of course, with this choice, I wouldn't always have the luxury of a steady income. When I perceive myself lacking in finances, I constantly need to remember my essence of being adventurous. Not that adventure and money are mutually exclusive, but adventure involves risk, which in turn implies ups and downs, having and not having, valleys and peaks, right turns and U-turns. This truly has been the biggest angst of my life. I struggle with the anxiety of not having money for rent, money for vacations, money to retire, money for…When those lower, negative VFs of scarcity arise, I need to be aware of them, feel and let go of the negative Emotions that accompany them, and then replace them with positive beliefs and affirmations.

Being adventurous, I pushed my bubble and explored my unconscious. I chose to expand my beliefs about where I should live, who I should be, and what I should be doing. Several times I leapt with love, or the hope of a deeper love, while others and my rational mind screamed for me to stop. I moved beyond my pain and tried to be as Physically active as possible. My adventures have allowed me to visit places most have not seen. I've interacted with different cultures and been enriched. I've experienced dangerous situations and nearly been killed a half-dozen times yet have survived (okay, sometimes I might have pushed the envelope). I've experienced the full range of Emotions and eventually detached from them. I've discovered the metaphysical and traveled into realms beyond my knowing, beyond my teachings, beyond the status quo, beyond the rational. I've stepped into others' darkness and known it is also a part of me, and I've opened my heart and seen that it is the same as yours.

Balanced PIES Reinforces a Strong Self-concept

While working on that all-important question, I also had to succeed at strengthening and reinforcing my self-concept. The pressure of losing a home, job, and marriage put me to the test. Any of my false, negative, or non-soulful aspects would heighten. Any crack of vulnerability, doubt, or insecurity could start to erode my self-esteem. My divorce brought out old insecurities about my ability to make a relationship work. Not having a job and losing my home elevated all my negative financial beliefs.

Reinforcing a positive self-concept was something I had to do daily, just like eating and bathing. I couldn't let my perception of my situation bring me down. The truth is, the weaker the self-concept, the greater the challenge to regain balance; the stronger the self-concept, the easier it is to return to balance—just like a Weeble™.

I worked on my self-concept in a couple of ways. First, I needed to become quiet. Meditation, deep breathing, and yoga were tools I used to rid myself of the clutter and negativity in my mind. As I continued those practices, the subtle voice of my Spirit more easily rose to the surface, softly implying which direction to move in, slightly boosting my self-concept.

Second, I needed to reinforce all thoughts, feelings, and emotions that bolstered a sense of wellbeing. Surprisingly, most people have never thought about what enlivens them. If that's the case with you, begin by thinking about it in these terms: what floats your boat? What brings a smile to your face, what brings a sigh of contentment, what relaxes you, what brings peace to your mind, what brings joy to your heart, what brings a sense of connection to your spirit? It doesn't make a difference what it is — just do it.

I needed to do the following things as much as possible, even if I didn't feel like it: play sports, be Physically active, listen to soothing music, spend time with friends, play the piano, recite my affirmations, meditate, watch uplifting movies. I especially went to the ocean; being around water always nourishes my spirit. Throughout my life, even if I couldn't sail, fish, dive, ski, or kayak, I would just sit or walk along the water to revitalize my Spirit.

Physically, one of the major positive outcomes from *Mastering the Art of Balance* was my overall health. Given the major stressors in my life, any stress test would have overwhelmingly predicted the reduction of my immune system and the onslaught of sicknesses and possibly diseases. Yet the opposite happened. In the last six years, I have only been sick once with the flu. I know there are other factors that play into that outcome, but, as far as I'm concerned, balance was the key. No matter how Spiritual one thinks one is, if one isn't Physically healthy, life will be much more of a challenge.

My, and probably your, biggest obstacle to mastering balance is the Intellect, the mind—specifically, unconsciously accepting and repeating negative thoughts and beliefs. I needed to consciously, time and time again, *Stop!* those unbalanced thoughts and then change them to new, positive beliefs: "I am strong." "I am more than my predicament." "I am resilient." "I am a survivor." "I needed to do this." Change to these thousands of times, and say them with feeling, until the new positive thoughts are embedded into your self-concept.

Because of years of practice, it was easier for me to identify and release my Emotions. I'm not saying I did it perfectly or that it wasn't a challenge. There were moments of self-pity, but they rarely turned into feeling victimized, ashamed, or guilty; moments of fear that only sometimes changed into anxiety, worry, or feeling overwhelmed; moments of sadness that just briefly touched depression, despair, or hopelessness; and none of my frustrations ever built up into bitterness, hostility, or fury. A negative focus on my circumstances could have been devastating, but instead, because of my proactive practice of feeling, letting go, and replacing, I was able to keep my sanity, keep my positive outlook, and return to balance sooner.

My triple whammy highlighted that I hadn't been in touch with my soul as much as I used to be. As in any moment or predicament, there is always an opportunity to reconnect with the

Spirit. Using the perspectives, reflections, and corrections in this book, I allowed myself to live more authentically. I felt an immediate difference whenever I changed my focus from momentarily wallowing in negativity to feeling connected.

Universal Principles Ease the Journey

Mastering the Art of Balance included not only answering the question "Who am I?", building up my self-concept, and bringing about PIES balance, but also following the guidelines of how the Universe operates—the Universal Principles.

Seeing *Everything as Energy* provided a common denominator for the haphazard craziness of the events in my life. This perspective simplified the process of healing, getting back into balance. Perceiving the world as energy and frequency helped me change my focus; instead of looking for *more* of something or a *different* something, I knew *I* needed to adjust the frequency of my situation.

Knowing that all *Energy is Interconnected* reminded me that I needed to take responsibility for my thoughts, feelings, and actions. I had to admit that how I handled my predicaments not only affected me in the present but also shaped my future. I do have one gripe, though. I'm still baffled by saying positive affirmations about wealth and not feeling the benefits in my present situation. I'm doing all the *right* things; I'm aware of my negative false beliefs, I've changed them to positive beliefs and repeatedly said those as affirmations. Yet still nothing is different for me. I'm perplexed by my situation and it is the cause of almost all my consternation. Take away that issue and I'd have to say that my life would be great. So, then, what is going on?

Well, one factor is focus. The truth is that, instead of trying to make money, I've been headlong into finishing this book—which may or may not bring money into my life. If money had been my major focus, then I probably would have been doing other actions. So, as much as I say that money has been very important to me, I have been putting way more energy into my creativity, my writing this book, my efforts at making a positive difference.

Then there is this thing called Divine Timing. Sometimes the manifestations of one's affirmations have not materialized yet, but will when necessary and unknown ingredients come into alignment. I chastised myself for years for not following through with my plan to write my first book, *The Celestial Bar*, earlier. When I eventually did publish it, the timing was perfect because *The Celestine Prophecy* had just opened the doors for the public to be ready for my book. Many creative endeavors have not come to fruition until years or lifetimes later.

Another concept states that money is just energy and all energy has a VF. All my positive output of energy will return to me; yet it might not be in the Physical form of money, but rather other manifestations within a positive VF range. These materializations could be seen as my new love in New England, support from my friends, beautiful places I've lived in, and the opportunity to finish this book. I just have to trust that this *Interconnection*, this karmic loop, this Law of Attraction is always in place and be open to receive any of its manifestations.

When seemingly negative things occur in my life, I have to remember that *Energy Just Is*. When I examined my meanings behind losing my home, job, and marriage, some of them were of the negative slant: "What a horrible thing to lose your home, it is very sad to go through a divorce, losing your job is devastating." When eliminating any meaning to them, I could objectively look at the situation.

This perspective enabled me to be a little more detached and not take everything so personally. Some of my situations happened because that is how our economy works at different points in our history. I can't control the economy or the greed of institutions or the sometimes changing aspects within a marriage. But I do need to take a close look at what part I did play, learn from it, and use that knowledge to make better decisions in my future.

I needed to place a positive meaning on those events by seeing them as possible learning tools—seeing them as gifts, as opportunities to learn. Instead of "going to the dark side," how can I *be* within those circumstances? How can I be forgiving while losing my job? How can I be loving while going through a divorce? How can I be grateful while losing my home? How can I be compassionate towards others and myself while going through this difficult time in my life?

Any pain I endured I created when I protected myself Intellectually and Emotionally, so I tried my best to allow *Energy to Flow* during this period of my life. Letting myself feel, let go, and then replace negative Emotions with positive thoughts is "flowing." Being able to change my attitudes, beliefs, and expectations is all about allowing energy to flow. Leaving San Diego and moving to New England was about change and flow. Not allowing myself to hold on to negative beliefs about my situations and change them to positive ones is allowing energy to flow. Being open to what the Universe and life throw at me is flowing.

The ups and downs, left and right turns, forwards and backwards motions are at the core of *Energy Moving Towards Balance*. My life has certainly not been static. I've been on a rollercoaster ride, with the last several years feeling like a downward spiral. To go up requires coming from below; to get out means being within; to get on top requires being at the bottom. This is the pendulum of living, the natural cycle of life. *Mastering the Art of Balance* requires you to accept this process and allow love to flow during every step of your journey.

During the writing process, I did entertain thoughts of having some incredible success before finishing this book. What a great testament to provide my readers: "Struggling author, who writes about how to stay positive and be in balance through life's challenges, receives a huge advance and hits the bestseller status." (Is that a little ego creeping out?) The truth is that, whether or not those dreams happen, I'm still okay. I know that, whatever life throws at me, I'll be able to bounce back, as long as I use the UPs to achieve PIES balance. I know deeply that balance is a neverending process and I need to enjoy, as much as I can, the ride. That sense of balance has only appeared from discipline, hard work, practice, and being present wherever I am in that process.

From the PIES perspective: I feel Physically stronger and I'm eating better; my examinations of unconscious beliefs are deeper; my true-self has a stronger foundation; my range of Emotions is wider; I mostly feel the higher, positive, Emotional VFs; my belief and sense of Spirit is deeper; and there is a stronger connection in all my relationships.

From a day-to-day perspective: I've survived, I'm still breathing, I have food in the refrigerator, I'm still playing sports, I have a roof over my head, I have an incredible loving and supportive woman in my life, I have clean water to drink, I have wonderful and supportive friends, I have all my senses to experience the world, I have a sound mind, I'm healthy, I've been able to write, and I have the opportunity to express my unstoppable passion for presenting this material.

So here is a toast to my and your adventures. I know that it comes with a price—the pain of changing, the discomfort of standing on uncharted ground, the agony of shedding old beliefs, the fear of being shamed or ridiculed, the embarrassment of being different. But, through it all, our adventures are a vehicle for us to live authentically.

Energy Attracting Like Energy has brought us together on this journey. I trust that you've extracted a few pointers to help you along your way. Remember, you're not alone; we're all in this together.

Best wishes.
Enjoy your journey!

Tom

8/23/15

About the Author

Tom Youngholm grew up on the south side of Chicago and graduated with a B.A. in Communication and an M.A. in Human Development. His professional careers have included: family counselor and public educator for the Cook County Sheriff's Youth Services Department in Chicago; owner of a floating seafood restaurant in Key West; training specialist for General Dynamics in Professional Development; owner of a painting company; corporate consultant; facilitator for Awakening the Dreamer symposiums; and Quit Smoking in 60 Minutes Specialist. He loves playing the piano and enjoys playing all sports. He has been in Community Theater, as well as a few professional productions.

"As I was approaching forty and went to the Celestial Bar, I finally found out what I was supposed to be doing when I grew up—TEACHING."

Visit my website for additional info and services.
tomyoungholm.com

Tom Youngholm is available for Personal Coaching via phone.

The Celestial Bar:
A Spiritual Journey

Digger began to play... the music reminded him of the sadness he felt about his life. The humiliation of so many failures amid what he thought was a life brimming with promise... he was always going to be; but never was. Meet Jonathan "Digger" Taylor, a man who wanders from job to job, relationship to relationship, seeking–like so many of us–the intangible "something" that is missing from his life. When the restaurant he opens in Florida is wrecked in a hurricane, he moves to California, where he captians a softball team and pays the rent with an unfulfilling waiter's job; meanwhile all his relationships with women, including his wife, share the same fate as his restaurant.

Digger wants more from life, to feel connection and purpose. In the hardships that befall him Digger turns to his lifelong creative dream, composing music. But his spiritual quest is offset by a dark and increasingly menacing figure that haunts both his dream and waking worlds. Moments before a crucial make-or-break musical audition, Digger meditates to calm his jittery nerves and, in his meditation, is pursued by the ominous figure until he ducks into a door beneath a sign that reads The Celestial Bar. From that moment on, his life-and yours-will never be the same.

The Celestial Bar is a richly appointed way station for souls in transition, a place where wisdom is served with a smile and our most profound hunger is sated. There Digger meets his "old and forgotten" friends: Ahmay a pony tailed Shoshone chieftain: an interactive–and holographic-computer named Ramda, a mysterious bartender called Zorinthalian: and Paula, a beautiful waitress and soul mate. In the company of this unforgettable colorful and eccentric crew, Digger is "reminded" of the basic truths called the Universal Principles–the keys to all our most searching spiritual questions.

The Celestial Bar:
A Spiritual Journey

International Bestseller

24 Countries   17 Languages

"This is one exciting book to experience, and I love it! If you want a book that you can't put down—run, don't walk, and pick up a copy. You'll be glad you did."

Inner Self

"…energizing, riveting, enlightening and intellectually stimulating, filled with concepts and truths to be pondered, and then accepted!"
Metaphysical Reviews

"Read it once, then read it again and add it to your library. No doubt you will want to visit many times."
Pathways to Wellness

"Tom Youngholm strikes pay dirt...a dazzling array of well-conveyed, extremely visual experiences. It's not only a fun and very readable story; it's a good tool for explaining spirituality."
The Awareness Journal

"If you've read *The Celestine Prophecy*, you'll enjoy *The Celestial Bar*. If you haven't, try this one first."
NAPRA Trade Journal

"The dynamics here provide for a great read, and a wonderfully educational one at that! Grab it and read it. Meet the wise and whimsical characters…and learn about yourself in the process. You can if you hang out for a while at *The Celestial Bar*."

The New Times

In the Shadow of the Sphere:
A Journey of Heart and Spirit

Follow Digger's Journey

Costa Rica's unexplained granite monoliths—*The Stone Spheres*—serve as the jumping-off point for author Thomas Youngholm, who has skillfully woven together elements of Sci-Fi, Romance, Mystery, and Spirituality to create a new high standard for Visionary Fiction. This story of personal transformation will quickly find a place in your library—right next to books by Richard Bach, Dan Millman, James Redfield, and Youngholm's international bestseller, *The Celestial Bar*.

In this intriguing tale, musician/composer Jonathan (Digger) Taylor has embarked on a perilous rafting trip down a Central American river. He hopes the change of scene will wash away the last several weeks of his life. Instead, the journey is nothing at all like he'd planned. A beautiful, mysterious woman leads him deeper into the rainforest, where he meets a wise man, a black jaguar, shocking tragedy, and a host of individuals who change his trajectory forever. In a parallel story, Digger's girlfriend is propelled through her own journey into the unknown. After many startling twists and turns, neither of them emerges from the Costa Rican jungle as expected. Written for those who long for a good story along with their dose of Truth, Youngholm has provided the best yet in this new genre of Visionary Fiction.

In the Shadow of the Sphere:
A Journey of Heart and Spirit

"…original, compelling, intriguing, and fun!"
Arielle Ford, author of *Wabi Sabi Love*

"5-star review…skillfully written, highly recommended…a
riveting tale of personal transformation."
Midwest Book Review

"…an incredible book—wonderful, powerful, and brilliant!"
John Perkins, author of *Confessions of An Economic Hit Man*

"Youngholm is a gifted storyteller and brings a rare balance to his
characters—the women are intelligent and the men are sensitive.
This splendid novel is a joy to the mind, heart and spirit, with vivid
descriptions and genuine attention-grabbers that propel the reader
to set everything aside and keep reading. A total pleasure!"
The NAPRA Review

"What more can one ask for in a novel...that it entertain, that it
stimulate the imagination, that it expand your awareness of reality,
that it keeps you glued to the pages wanting to know more...This
book did all of that."
Inner Self

"…a finely crafted work…with an original and intriguing
plot…laced with provocative insights, fascinating ideas, exciting
action, and believable, in-depth characterizations. So, if you have
time for fiction and want spiritual content as well as enjoyable
divertissement, put this book on your list."
Tools and Rites of Transformation

Whispers of Wonder:
A Journey of Beauty & Balance

Release date Spring 2016

In collaboration with Kathy and Kamryn Clarke

This enchanting photographic coffee-table book offers a blend of
beauty, nature, rock-balancing & inspiration that will delight your
eyes as it stirs your heart and soul.

This book is a unique colloboration of three individuals.
Kathy Clarke shares her incredible rock balancing skills
and her photographic talents. Images are complemented with
inspirational words from Kamryn Clarke and thought-provoking
quotes from the works of international bestselling author Tom
Youngholm.

Visit the website clarkeandyoungholm.com